LOBAGOLA

*An African Savage's
Own Story*

This is the Autobiography

of

BATA KINDAI AMGOZA IBN

LOBAGOLA

a Black Jew,

descended from the Lost Tribes of Israel,

a Savage

who came out of the African Bush

into Modern Civilization

and

thenceforth found himself an alien among

his own people and a stranger in the

Twentieth Century World

LOBAGOLA

AN AFRICAN SAVAGE'S OWN STORY

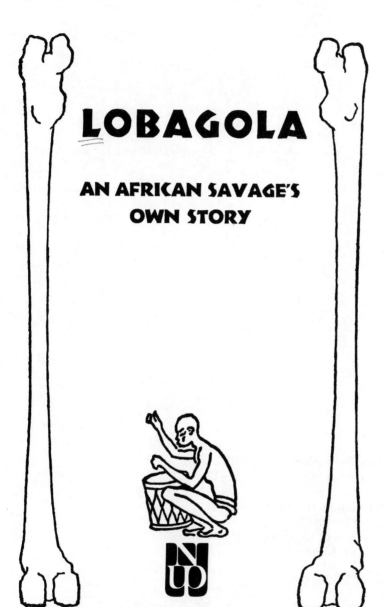

NEGRO UNIVERSITIES PRESS
NEW YORK

Originally published in 1930
by Alfred A. Knopf, New York

Reprinted in 1970 by
Negro Universities Press
A Division of Greenwood Press, Inc.
Westport, Connecticut

SBN 8371-3610-5

Printed in United States of America

CONTENTS

CONTENTS

CONTENTS

ILLUSTRATIONS

*Frontispiece and photograph on Page 372
by Sherril Schell*

INTRODUCTION

Personality of the Writer

The amazingly frank story that follows, being
a confessional autobiography of a civilized African
savage who says that our civilization has been able
to penetrate only skin-deep, and that he can never
be wholly one of us, was written by Bata Kindai
Amgoza Ibn LoBagola. LoBagola is a black Jew, a
man without a country, a person who says that he is
" wanted nowhere," neither in his own land among
his savage people, nor here, so that now he has
neither home nor country. In his personality he is
as brilliant as he is pathetic, and as interesting as
he is strange, for there is no other like him either in
the jungle or in the capitals of civilization.

Thousands of travellers have gone into savage
lands and then returned, bringing with them stories
of what they did, and accounts of what they saw,
together with their reflections on native life and
ways. Ibn LoBagola's story, on the other hand, is
that of a savage who visits civilization, risks its
dangers both in peace and in war, and returns

several times to his own people, only to venture again and again into our own alien regions, just as Stanley forsook civilization again and again to plunge into Africa's heart of darkness.

Do we hold up our hands in horror at the black author's "mistakes" of omission and of commission? At his failure to adjust himself at once to our ways of life? At his violation of some of our laws? Are we horrified because he did not instantly and wholly become "a highly educated and perfect Christian gentleman"? Are we surprised to see a savage fresh from the jungle acting much as we logically should expect such a person to act?

If we criticize harshly our visitor from the jungles of Africa for his offences against our laws and customs, it is enlightening to reflect how the natives of the bush may have criticized some of the visitors from civilization: the slavers, who for centuries visited Africa with their hell-holes of ships, bringing such terror as the African bush had never before known; the traders, bringing rum, dishonesty, and the lash; military expeditions, violating all the native codes of war and conduct, burning villages and killing men, women, and children; the rubber-collectors of the Congo, who left behind, not only scourged and tortured natives, but also natives with neither hands nor feet, poor miserable wretches condemned to living death. Has Ibn LoBagola, the savage in turn visiting civilization, equalled these white visitors to Africa?

Ibn LoBagola is interesting because he is just what he is, a savage civilized merely on the surface. He is now about forty-one years of age, is short compared with most men in this country, is broad of shoulder and strong and powerful in build. He holds his head erect with all the vigour of health and all the pride of one who says he bears his own father's name, and is in his own land " a man of distinction." His eyes are remarkably bright and keen, and he looks one directly in the eye with a kind of fierce intensity that speaks of warrior ancestry. His skin is extremely dark brown. His profile shows a pronounced nose and strong Hebraic characteristics that bear out what he says concerning his people's descent from Jews who fled from Palestine after the destruction of Herod's Temple. Ibn LoBagola's costume is usually the costume of any well-dressed American, but on occasion he wears a red fez and sometimes a loose robe, neither one of which, he says frankly, has anything whatever to do with his native land, for there clothing of any kind is not worn. He wears fez and robe merely for effect.

Like many savages, Ibn LoBagola is a natural

orator. Our visitor from the bush has such powers
of speech that he can hold any audience enthralled,
whether composed of children, uneducated people,
or scholars. He is a born actor and mimic and de-
lights in entertaining, even at the expense of what
some of us call dignity. He is, in fact, a personality,
so much so that he himself outweighs whatever he
may say. If the contents of this book of his could
be spoken by himself, everyone would be at once
interested and delighted. In order to let that unusually powerful personality appear as clearly as
possible through the medium of print, the book is
printed in his own words, rich with his inimitable
expressions. It is, to all intents and purposes, a
personal narrative, told frankly and without con-
cealment by an African savage living for a time
in the United States.

How the Book was Written

For any man utterly untrained in writing, who
had never before written anything aside from a few
letters, to write a book of over fifty thousand words
is in itself most remarkable. Some strong urge must
impel such a writer. For one brought up in savagery to write such a book is still more astonishing.
It seems an impossibility. Let the reader try to
think of any other such book.

People who have heard Ibn LoBagola talk in public about his native land and his own life have often said: "Why don't you write your story? Everyone would like to read it." He has always answered: "I can't write. I don't know how. I don't know anything at all about writing; I can only talk. And I can't talk," said he, "unless I have a lot of people in front of me, and interested people, too." Obviously it was impossible for our visiting savage to tell the full story of his life to actual audiences. He himself must write it. No one else could write it for him. At length with great reluctance he consented to make the attempt. "Just imagine that you are talking," he was told. "Say it out loud to yourself and imagine you see the audience in front of you. Make your life real to these people."

How did the black author, new to his task of writing, actually do the work? With the stub of a lead pencil, slowly and laboriously, he wrote out, on long, yellow sheets of paper, whatever he had to say. "Nobody except me could read it," he explained. Then, having borrowed a typewriter — and ultimately borrowing many typewriters — he set to work, with one finger of each hand, to copy what he had written, for typewriting was as new to him as writing itself. "It took me forty-five minutes for a page," he comments. In this way, slowly, with great effort, constantly changing and revising his work, he produced his material. Naturally it took the inexperienced writer many, many months. At times he was discouraged and ready to give up work altogether; at other times he caught fire from his subject and worked all day and far into the night.

Why the Story is Remarkable

Unusual and fascinating adventure makes up the entire book. If every word of the story were wholly false, the narrative would still be interesting. Much of the action takes place in the unvisited jungles of western Africa, and the persons who speak there are the primitive bush natives, with primordial views of morality and justice. The parts of the story that take place in Europe and in America are far different and are full of revelations concerning the life of our own kind, struck off by contrast with such an alien as this bushman.

This is no invention, however, but a confessional, a frank and open presentation of a two-sided life, without attempt to gloss over faults and sins or violations of law. The writer never parades as a hero or as a paragon of virtue or success. He tells his weaknesses with the same emphasis with which he tells of his accomplishments.

That the narrative is the life-story of a black Jew also makes it unique in kind. Driven from Palestine after the destruction of Herod's Temple, A.D. 70, certain Jews fled to the coasts of northern Africa and slowly, through succeeding centuries, drifted towards the south, until they became the principal inhabitants of some of the oases of the Sahara. Some of them wandered to Timbuktu and to the jungles south of the Niger River. There, after many centuries, and after having mingled their blood with the blood of the dark natives, these Jewish tribes still persist. They are dark in colour, unclothed, like the natives who surround them, and in many respects as savage and as superstitious as ordinary fetish-worshipping natives. Yet they have clung to the old Jewish traditions, to the laws of Moses, to the great Jewish holy-days, to circumcision, to the worship of Jehovah, and to the hierarchical rule of rabbis. Wholly cut off from all communion with fellow Jews in any other part of the world, surrounded by every inducement to abandon their faith, these people illustrate powerfully the tenacity with which the Jew clings to his religion. It is one of these very people, one of the *Emo-Yo-Quaim* or " Strange People " of the African bush, who tells this story. Whatever he may be and whatever his story, this man represents

xvii

his people. No one who talks with Ibn LoBagola doubts his Jewish ancestry. He has the mental alertness and the power of thought that mark the race, and his features are distinctly Hebraic.

From a scientific point of view, attention is attracted to this African savage's life story for two reasons: his unequalled presentation of authentic African folk-lore and tribal customs; and the remarkable development, psychologically, of a naked bushman into a man of ability in civilization. That a naked bushman should develop into an author is certainly remarkable; it is a long step from being an unclad savage in the Ondo bush to being a professional writer. Who that saw Ibn LoBagola in his native hut-village would have foretold that he would ever give lectures or write books? Who that saw the wandering fire-dancer later in cheap theatres, or the boot-black in a country barber-shop, would have expected him to write for publication? How did it happen that a savage, a wanderer, a person who so openly confesses to so many mistakes in life and actions, could have the power to rise above all his past, could have the industry and the will to produce such a book? What is to be the sequel of the story?

Is the Story True?

A natural tendency of the human mind makes one disbelieve whatever is unusual. Is, then, Ibn LoBagola's story true? He asserts that it is in all its larger aspects; that is, he admits that he has somewhat embroidered personal incidents here and there by adding conversation that he must, of necessity, have forgotten in the course of years; but so far as the general narrative is concerned, it is strictly true. He supports his assertion by presenting a great number of letters, recommendations, official records of military service, and photographs of himself at various ages and by giving the names and addresses of people who corroborate what he says.

The story offers hundreds of points for investigation of the truth of the narrative. If the reader will take the trouble to investigate, he will see that Ibn LoBagola, on the one hand, must write from personal knowledge; or, on the other, must have been a profound student of works of reference, which seems unlikely.

For example, Ibn LoBagola says that Abomey is the capital of Dahomey, while *The Statesman's Year-book* says that Porto Novo is the seat of government. Investigation shows that Abomey was and is the native capital, and the author, of course, writes from the native point of view. Ibn LoBagola says that Kotonu is the principal port of Dahomey, but *The Century Atlas* gives Whydah as such; the fact is that the absence of a good harbour at Whydah, and the presence of unusually high surf, led, in recent years, to making Kotonu the chief port. Tribal customs, religious beliefs, secret societies, enmities, and general ways of life as described by Ibn LoBagola are all susceptible of verification. The folk-lore stories told by the black author are exactly similar in style and spirit to the folk-tales of that part of Africa previously published, but they are never the same in plot or suggestion.

Some who have heard Ibn LoBagola lecture have professed grave doubts concerning the existence of " black Jews " anywhere in the world, and especially in West Africa. They laugh at the idea that Jews came to Morocco after the destruction of the Temple and then moved south across the Sahara Desert to Timbuktu. *The Encyclopædia Britannica* (thirteenth edition), in the article " Morocco," says: " The third race which may be considered native is the Jewish, consisting of two distinct sections: those settled among the Berbers from time immemorial, speaking their language, and in addition a hideously corrupt Arabic; and those expelled from Europe within comparatively modern times. . . . It is a remarkable fact that several of the so-called Berber tribes are believed to have been of Jewish origin." In the article " Tuat " the same authority says concerning the oases of the western part of the Algerian Sahara: " According to tradition numbers of Jews migrated thither in the 2nd century A.D. They were the predominant element in the oases when the conquests of Sidi Okba drove the Zenata south (7th century). These Berbers occupied Tuat and, to a large extent absorbed the Jewish population." In the article " Berbers " *The Encyclopædia Britannica says*: " Many Berbers still retain certain Christian and Jewish usages, relics of the pre-Islamitic days in North Africa." The Falashas of Abyssinia, according to *The Encyclopædia Britannica,* are somewhat similar in nature to the people whom Ibn LoBagola tells about. Of the Falashas the encyclopædia says: They " profess the Jewish religion. . . . They possess . . . the canonical and apochryphal books of the Old Testament; a volume of extracts from the Pentateuch, with comments given to Moses by God on Mount Sinai. . . . A copy of the Orit or Mosaic law is kept in the holy of holies in every synagogue. . . ."

The French *Grande Encyclopédie,* in the article

"*Juif*," names the following as the Jewish population of Africa: " Algérie, Sahara, 43,500; Maroc, 100,000; Tunisie, 55,000; Abysinnie, 200,000; Tripolitaine, 6,000; Égypte, 8,000; Cap, etc., 1,500. Total, 414,000."

Are Any Jews Negroid?

Maurice Fishberg, in *The Jews: A Study of Race and Environment,* says: " In Africa there are other types of Jews found in various parts of the continent. Here, instead of being physically Asiatic, as is the case with the Jews of Asia Minor, Central Asia, China, etc., the Jews are of distinctly African appearance. Their complexion varies from white in North Africa to black in Abyssinia " (pages 136, 138). " It is stated that the Falashas are not the only Jews of negro race. Bastian speaks of negro Jews living on the *Loango Coast* in Western Africa. They are called there ' Mavambu ' or ' Judeos '" (page 149). " Their portraits . . . show that physically they are of the negro type. . . . The large lips, prognathism, and frizzly hair, all point to negro origin " (page 147). " In Abyssinia there is a large colony of Jews called *Falashas,* who are of pure African type. . . . They are described as a tall, muscular people, with a dark brown skin, like that of the Abyssinians in general.

Their hair is black and frizzly, or woolly. . . .
Many of them are black, and have thick lips, which
are upturned, and are practically negroes. They
speak the same language, live in similar houses,
and have most of the habits of life and customs of
the non-Jewish Abyssinians, from whom they dif-
fer only in religion " (page 146).

Do black Jews still carry on Jewish traditions
or rites? Maurice Fishberg, in *The Jews: A Study
of Race and Environment,* says: " The Jews on the
oasis M'zab, to the south of Algeria, are a very
interesting type, because they have been there iso-
lated for centuries, having hardly had any relations with Jews outside this oasis. There they live
among the Berber tribes, dress like their non-Jewish neighbours, and are only to be distinguished
from the latter by the ear-locks which they wear
and by the fact that the women wear no veils "
(page 145). " On several of the oases of the Sahara
there are many nomadic tribes of Jewish faith.
They are known as ' Berber Jews ' or ' Dagga-
tuns ' " (page 143).

The Jewish Encyclopedia (Volume I, page 228)
says: " In the Sahara there are about 8,000 Jews,
whose settlements reach as far as Timbuctoo."

LOBAGOLA

An African Savage's

Own Story

Bata Kindai Amgoza Ibn LoBagola

Chapter I

A SAVAGE HOME IN THE ONDO BUSH

My birthplace. Its government. Our seasons. Our houses. Our communities. Animals of the bush. The great apes. How we fight the apes. The horror of the Ondo bush. Habits of elephants. How we hunt elephants.

I was born in the village of Nodaghusah, six hundred miles north of Abomey Calavi, once the capital of Dahomey, and about forty-five days' walk north of the Gulf of Guinea, and three days' walk south of the native city Timbuktu. The country is the Sudan, in the sphere of influence of the French Colonial Government.

My country has a population of a million and a quarter, divided into three hundred communities, and over each community presides a chief, assisted by a council of seventy women. My country has two kings, a spiritual king and a civil king. The duties of the spiritual king are to govern all matters pertaining to faith and morals, guided by the precepts of the fetish-religion. The

1

civil king is advised by a council of three hundred women.

My country is between six degrees and eight degrees north latitude, and so the temperature is sometimes between a hundred and twenty-five and a hundred and thirty-five degrees (Fahrenheit) in the shade. For three months we have continual rain. The rainy season is June, July, and August. We call the rainy season *Mef-fah* (meaning " six "), because during that time it rains just six days at a time without stopping, with heavy thunder and lightning.

The principal products of my country are timber, palm-oil, and ivory. The staple food is cassava, with other native vegetables and cereals. We never eat meat as food except during certain festivals; then goat meat is used.

The houses we live in are built of bamboo and are thatched with coco-nut fibre. They are built fifteen feet from the ground, on bamboo poles tied closely together with fibre rope. We build our houses high from the ground to protect them from being washed away by flood during the rainy season.

We live in " compounds," large spaces of ground allotted by the native government to each family, fenced in by bamboo fences. A village is fenced around the same as a compound. There are about fifty families in every village, and twenty villages in every community.

My own village is in the " Ondo bush." The Ondo bush is a horrible place, because of its tall grass and bushes, over five feet high, and trees growing to a height of over eighty feet, close together, with thick vines, as thick as a man's body, stretching from one tree to another, the thinner vines hanging from the branches, making, as it were, a veil or network, so that you cannot see five yards ahead, because of this tangled mass of undergrowth and overgrowth. There are no paths, no roads; and the only way that you can tell where to go is by the tops of the trees, which means looking up most of the time and stumbling over obstacles hidden by the thick grass. All this mass of vegetation is centuries old, and has had no pruning, or levelling by being trodden. That which has been trodden by wild beasts is soon replaced by new plant-life.

Another reason why the Ondo bush is a horrible place to live in is that it is the home of elephants, leopards, lions, monkeys, and reptiles. Some of the reptiles make the trees their home, particularly those that attack their prey from vines and the branches of trees. You can imagine the task it is

3

and the caution one must take to choose the right spot to stand in.

The great apes are the avowed enemy to man; they often raid the communities and do much damage. If the apes succeed in getting inside a village, they destroy the village and we must build a new one. They travel about in herds or tribes of from three to four hundred. When they get inside a compound, they pull up the poles that the houses are built on, and destroy everything they can get their hands on. If they catch a human being, they tear him to pieces, not for food, but because they like to destroy and kill.

A monkey has two redeeming features; one of them is that the principal female monkey will never permit other monkeys to harm an infant; the other is that they are noisy, and we can hear them two or three hours before they reach a village.

Every tribe of monkeys has a " chief," and a principal female that we always called the "mother monk." The chief monkey can usually be found walking behind " Mother Monk," who hops along in the centre of the group.

The apes are like a lot of women or children: they continually chatter — talk, talk, talk, all the time — and they make such a noise that we can

4

hear them afar off. This gives us time to prepare a defence.

So the men and boys arm themselves with poisoned assagais, or spears, and go out to meet the herd. About a dozen men place themselves in trees and wait until the herd of monkeys arrives. When the herd gets near enough, the spearmen pick out the chief monkey. We know him by his silence. He seldom says anything; he hops along behind old " Mother Monk," and now and then gives a few commands. Before the monkeys leave their camp, they have their plans made, however, so there are few orders to be given after starting. When the spearmen spot the old chief, they aim at him with assagais and kill him. The moment that the leader falls, all the other monkeys turn tail and run. That is the only way of halting them, for when they are out on a run, it does not matter how many monkeys are killed; the others keep on coming until the chief drops out. Often the boys, not quite so experienced with the assagai as the older men, and wishing to be in a better position to view the herd than the men, miss aim or else are unable to distinguish the chief from the other monkeys and thereby permit the monkeys to continue their run. This is always disastrous, both to the men in the trees and to those, usually women and children, who remained in the village and did not hide.

No Europeans hunt in the Ondo bush as they do in other parts of the African bush, and no European consul will give safe-conduct to white men to hunt in the Ondo bush. Consequently the beasts, which are sagacious, have come to know they are safe there. The hunting that the native does is not troublesome to the animals, because the native uses only the assagai, not a gun, like the European. The wild beasts crowd to our part of the country and make the Ondo bush their home.

The elephant never gives us trouble, because it stays in the bush, and will never bother you unless you get in its way. We trap the elephant by pitfalls; that is, we dig a hole and cover it with bamboo poles and brush. When the elephant comes along, he breaks through the poles and falls into the pit.

Elephants travel about in companies of from fifty to a hundred; they seldom travel alone; so when we see one elephant, there is another somewhere very near. They have advance guards, scouts, and sentinels, and we can never surprise them by stealing up on them unawares. They appear clumsy, but they are alert and agile and can run faster than a horse.

Every now and then the elephants go on what

we call a romp or roll, and nothing can stop them. They make their path while running, by pulling down vines, tearing up trees, and trampling underfoot everything that comes in front of them. You cannot turn elephants off their path, because they keep on going regardless of how many of their number drop out because of being wounded or for some other reason. I have seen men and boys mashed into the earth trying to check the run of elephants.

We natives learn from boyhood that if the elephants pass one way today on a roll, they will surely return by the same path. Perhaps not in the same day or week, but surely at some future time they will return, and return by the same path. So when we go out to hunt elephants, we locate them and wait until they start on a roll. This may not happen soon, but a native never values time; so we wait, probably a month or two, as long as it is not too close to the time of the coming of the rainy season.

We follow the elephants after they have started, but we do not follow too closely. We dig a hole to make a pitfall, and then we go away. Every two or three days the hunters return to the trap to see if any of the herd has been caught. When the trapped elephants are dead, we extract the ivory and leave

7

the carcass for carrion. We use the ivory for ornaments and trinkets, but we do no trade at all with the outside world because we never come in contact with other people who have more use for the ivory than we have.

The elephants that escape the pitfall never remain to help others that have been caught. There is great confusion, for they make a terrific noise, partly from anger and partly from fright. Sometimes they kill one another in their fury. When the hunters come, they soon dispatch them with poisoned assagais.

When poisoned, elephants die in about twenty minutes. A human being poisoned in this way would die in five minutes. The poison used is *kootch-er-roo,* made from a wild plant called *ko-hom-o-ho-bra.* The process of making the poison is known only by the witch-doctors. This method of killing an elephant is more humane than a rifle-shot. When we use *kootch-er-roo* to poison the beast, we stick it in any part of the body and the beast surely dies in twenty minutes. Its death is violent, but it is swift and sure.

Elephants bury their dead as people do, but that is one of the things a man has never seen. We know of the burials only by evidence; that is, we can tell when they are mourning the loss of one of their kind. But no elephant is mourned that is not buried by its people. Trapped elephants or any of them that have had a mishap and been left behind are not mourned. Those that live on with the herd and have finally died of old age are buried by the herd. I have often seen the places of burial. As a child I watched, with other boys, to see if any elephants would return for funeral rites. We know the burial places by the ivory we dig from the ground, and from the bones that we find.

The vultures make short work of all dead matter. These birds are scavengers and keep the country free from dead bodies of animals. The native law exacts a penalty of death for killing a vulture, because the health of the country depends chiefly upon these birds.

We do not bury our own dead, as there is a native law against burying human beings. We dig a hole, throw in the dead body, cover it with brush, set it afire, and burn it.

Another thing that we never see about the elephants is their mating. The elephants in the Ondo bush take seven days for one mating. A female carries her young nearly two years. Elephants mate much as man and woman do. They try always to mate in strict privacy, away from the herd, as they are modest and sensitive beasts.

Chapter II

DANGERS OF THE BUSH

Lions. Gooma saves me from a man-eater. The fierce leopard. Our village at night. Dangerous reptiles. How boys kill snakes. I am stung by a hook-lizard. How I was cured. How we treat the sick. The ju-ju *house.*

The lion seldom gives trouble; it is not the habit of the lion to raid villages. Sometimes there is a stray old lion, who may be desperately hungry, or who has tasted the blood of a human being; this is the kind we fear, because it goes anywhere and will attack anybody or anything.

A lion is a sensitive, timid, almost cowardly animal. It is nevertheless the king of beasts, because it rarely takes advantage of its inferiors; it will fight other beasts of its size; it will not attack beasts like the gazelle or monkey. If you happen to pass a lion when he is alone and not with a spiteful female lion, he will not attack you if you have not seen him; but if you happen to see him and he knows it, then prepare to fight or die. A lion is not

10

naturally a man-eater, but after it has once tasted human blood, and when it gets a little too old to go for other food, then and only then does it become a man-eater. The lion will not attack you to your face, but will stalk you and keep you in sight while he tries to get in a position to spring upon you.

If you should climb a tree, the lion can easily get help from the elephant, because the elephant and the lion are friendly. They may fight now and then, but they are really the closest of friends; so you would not be safe up a tree. When the elephant comes to the aid of the lion, the lion tells the elephant that it wants you down from the tree, and the elephant shakes the tree or pulls it up by the roots, and down you come.

The safest and, in fact, the only way to escape death from the beasts in the Ondo bush is to dig under the brush and hide. No wild beast can scent your tread; it can smell only blood, so if you are out of its sight, you are out of danger.

The lion, however, always joins the other beasts to kill a man. In the beast world to kill a man is considered a great honour, so all beasts rally when they come in contact with man — even the leopard, the most independent beast in the Ondo bush.

I have seen many ferocious lions, and I should have been devoured by a man-eating lion if it had

11

not been for a girl called Gooma, who was the fighting daughter of a fighting chief. Gooma was rich in inheritance, noble by birth, brave in spirit, but unfortunate nevertheless. I shall tell her story in another chapter. Already marked by the claws and teeth of a leopard, and bitten by a hook-lizard, I was saved through the timely intervention of this girl, and through her superior skill with the assagai. Except for her I should have been torn into pieces.

My escape happened one day after the usual warning had been given; that is, when there was danger of beasts, or warriors from another tribe. I was playing near the bush all by myself when a great old savage man-eater got through somehow and came into the village before anyone knew anything about it. Two babies, whose mother had left them lying on the ground when she ran away in fright, were torn into pieces and partly eaten; a young girl was torn badly, but did not die; several boys, whose screaming made the beast furious, escaped by a hair's breadth.

By this time the old fellow had been struck by a clean assagai — that is, a spear without poison on the tip. That stung him and made him more ferocious, and he darted back and forth, this way and that, until finally he spied me. Gooma was not far away at the time, for it was she who had stung the beast with the assagai. By this time she had found a poisoned assagai and was pursuing the animal at a safe distance. She saw the lion plunge in my direction. I was directly in its path.

Her cries made me look up; I saw the lion coming at me full speed. I did as I had been taught to do when confronted at close quarters: I fell flat on the ground and tried to dig under, the best I could. I was so frightened that I forgot what to do. I fell to the ground all right, but I began to cry out, which was unwise.

Gooma, who was near enough by then, threw her poisoned assagai. Whether it was by sheer luck or by skill I cannot say, but the assagai struck the lion in the mane and pierced its neck almost through. This made the animal forget the object of his dash, and he turned round several times, roaring madly from pain and the effects of poison. Then he turned over, head first, and died horribly.

The lion is not the only animal in the Ondo bush that gives us trouble; in fact, it is one of the beasts that give little trouble. The elephant gives us the least trouble, and the lion comes next. The monkey is the most troublesome of all the beasts in the bush. The leopard is nearly as bad as the monkey for giving us trouble, but the leopard

13

is not such a coward as the monkey; in fact, it is
the bravest beast in the bush; at least, so the hunters think. The leopard is sly and sneaky, like the
cat, but it is a good fighter and an open fighter. The
leopard will never stalk you, but will always attack
you; whether it is full or hungry, it will surely take
a smack at you. It always fights you to your face,
and it fights to a finish. When a leopard fights with
you, it never dies alone; somebody must go with it;
and you cannot make it run, as you can a lion, by
wounding it. When a leopard lies down, then it is
dead. " A leopard never dies until it is dead," we
say. As long as it has a breath in its body, it will
battle.

It is quite a distinction among native hunters to
have a battle with the leopard. The leopard is very
independent and never mixes with other beasts.
It travels alone. You will never see it drinking
with other animals; that makes all other beasts respect the leopard, for they all know that when a
leopard speaks, it means just what it says.

The leopard is very fond of monkey meat, but
its favourite meat is gazelle. The leopard always
finds an excuse when it is invited to a social func-
tion given by any of the other beasts. When the
leopard walks or runs, we often cannot hear it because of its soft paws; it moves about like a cat, and

14

the only way that we can tell when it is coming is by the rustling or shaking of the leaves and grass.

It was always our custom, as boys, to play near the bush, and we could easily hear a leopard when he was coming. When we heard the familiar soft rustling, we sent in the alarm by shouting the danger word, " *Oo-lou-wi!* " running and screaming at the same time. When the villagers heard this warning, the women grabbed up their children and sought safety, while the men and boys prepared to meet the beast.

The leopard might drop in on us at any time; we were never certain when the leopard would give us a visit, except in the night. No beasts or reptiles ever come into the village during the night, because we always light fires around about the village compounds at night to keep them out. Although the beasts never come past the fires at night, they invariably come up as close to the fires as they dare and lie down there outside or prowl around. Some of them lie down and remain there the whole night, listening to the noise of the music and singing. Our musical instrument is the tomtom.

No one knows exactly why the beasts remain by the village so long at night. We can see them when they first come to the fires, and they make a lot of noise in the beginning, but after a little while they

15

become just as quiet as they possibly can. It is a very pretty sight to see all the different colours of their coats; even the zebra is there amongst them. It is generally believed that all the beast kingdom is glad to unite against man, and that it is their thirst for blood that attracts them in the night. Some of the old hunters declare that it is the music that charms them. It is reasonable to believe what the old hunters say about it, because the zebra and the gazelle are there, and these beasts would never harm anyone. It may be that the beastly breast is soothed by the charm of native music.

The animals are the chief reason why the native men very rarely, if ever, venture outside of the villages at night. Of course, a person may be already out; but to start out on a journey at night is considered to be a stupid and foolish act. A child might do it, but it has usually proved fatal to children.

There are other dangers lurking in the Ondo bush, greater than any that I have mentioned as yet; they are from the reptiles. We have hook-lizards, horned vipers, and boa constrictors.

I do not say that the natural home of the boa constrictors is our bush, but they are to be found in the Ondo bush just the same. They rarely give us any trouble in the villages, for they attack their prey from the vines and branches of the trees. They always manage to choose a vine the same colour as themselves, or hide within a cluster of vines and branches. This is done so that you cannot easily detect them; self-preservation is the first law of nature. You are surely lost if you happen to get close enough to these great snakes. The boa constrictor kills you by coiling its tail around your body and then squeezing you to death; then it swallows you whole. The snake takes its time to swallow you; it does not do as we do with our food. I have seen a snake swallow a small zebra; it simply squeezed it to death, crushed all the bones in the body, then stretched it out as far as it could, swallowed half of it, went to sleep, woke up, and then finished swallowing it. One of these snakes is able to swallow a human being in the same simple manner. This is nothing to marvel at when you consider its size. I have seen boa constrictors over twenty feet long, with bodies as thick as a good-sized tree-trunk.

The horned viper never climbs a tree or vine, but crawls through the thick grass on the ground. The horned viper attacks its prey by striking it with its fangs, which are deadly poisonous. No snake can strike unless it is coiled, but it can always sting you if you are close enough to it. It is in this manner

17

that many women and children are killed. Very often a snake will escape the notice of the boys or girls, whose job it is to kill them, and crawl up quietly, close to a woman who is sitting on the ground, or to a child who may be playing on the ground, raise its head, and strike. Once you have been poisoned by a horned viper, there is no chance whatever of recovering. We have no poison strong enough to counteract the venom from the horned viper.

It is a part of our education to learn to kill these pests; therefore the boys and girls keep on the look-out for these dangers. Men never trouble about killing snakes, as they consider it child's play. A man cannot kill a snake, indeed, because he is not quick enough in his movements; but a boy can jump about as quick as a snake can turn.

The boys kill a snake by hitting it on the back with a large stick. When a snake is first seen, the boys give a yell; they say: " *Woo-chow-oo!* " and all gather around the snake and get it excited and angry. It raises its head in the air, after coiling itself up, and hisses and spits with rage. By this we know that it is ready to fly at the throat of anybody.

We know that a snake can jump only its length. One boy is chosen to do the hitting. That boy grips

18

his club and gets up as close to the snake as it is safe to get; the other boys prance and dance around, shouting and yelling, in order to annoy the snake all the more. When the snake is about to jump, it makes a humming, hissing noise. The boy that is going to do the hitting falls flat on the ground, facing the snake, and holds his club in readiness so that when the snake does jump, he can turn quickly and hit it on the back. This breaks its back, and when the back of a snake is broken, it cannot coil up any more; then it simply lies and fumes in pain and rage. Then all the boys get around it and knock its brains out with their clubs.

But these things that I describe are done like a flash; if not, the snake will turn quickly and will surely kill the boy who is trying to kill it. So if you ever have to hit a snake that way, please do not miss it. Sometimes some of the younger boys who are just learning how to kill do miss, but most boys take example from the older fellows. We are always on the alert for venomous reptiles.

The hook-lizard gives us trouble, but its sting is not so deadly as that of the snake. Of course, you will surely die if you neglect to attend to a wound made by the sting of a hook-lizard; but if the wound is given proper attention, you will soon recover. Although hook-lizards are running about

19

in thousands, they do not prey especially upon human beings, any more than bees do in this country.

The hook-lizard has a strange nature. If it attempts to sting you and misses, then it stings itself and dies from the effect. There are so many hook-lizards crawling about that people hardly know where to put their feet down, especially in the tall grass. The hook-lizard has a tail that curves, and when it raises it up, it curls right over its own head. But the lizard has such control of it that it rarely ever strikes itself.

I imagined once that I could step on one and pull my foot off before it could raise its tail, but I was sadly mistaken. I got a terrible sting that I shall never forget. It was very painful when the other boys tried to cure the wound. They did not succeed, so some men took me in hand and put me through the mill. The first thing they did was to bite out the raw flesh around the wound; then they tied the upper part of my leg tight with fibre rope. Then two men took hold of the rope at each end, in order to make it tight enough to stop the circulation; they pulled in opposite directions, putting their feet against my body for greater leverage, and they pulled as hard as they could. My screaming did not make any difference to them. In the mean time another man went out into the bush a little way to get some sap from the papaw-tree, so that he could make up a solution of medicine called *droy-on*.

Just a word about the papaw-tree. It is a remarkable tree. It grows throughout the Ondo bush, usually to a height of about a hundred feet. It has no branches and no vines. The sap of this tree is wonderful, because it changes its quality when boiled. We can make a medicine and we can make a poison from the sap!

The men who had tied up my leg made a fire in order to boil the sap to make the medicine, *droy-on*. When this medicine was boiling-hot, they poured it into the open wound and covered the wound with banana leaves. Every now and then they poured a little more boiling medicine on it. Imagine the torture I went through in this performance! The action of this wonderful medicine is that it draws out all the poison and leaves the wound white. When the men see the white, they know that the poison has all gone and that the danger of death is over. The fibre rope is then taken off to allow the blood to circulate, and then the wound soon heals. The men beat my leg with their hands and feet in order to start the circulation; then I had to get up and walk by myself.

21

No native is ever carried by anyone because of an accident or ailment; the reason for this is that all sicknesses or ailments of the body are controlled by evil spirits, and these spirits like to be encouraged and nursed; therefore it is forbidden to help anyone who has met with an accident, or who has to be carried. This is one of the principal taboos in the fetish-law. If one should die under such conditions, the devilish witch-doctor gives out the statement that he who died had sold himself to " the Evil One " and deserved death, as he would have contaminated all with whom he came in contact if he had lived. So joy is spread over such a death, even among the relatives of the deceased.

I managed to crawl back to my father's compound, and I did live. It is not forbidden to give medicine to the sick and to help them in that way; it is only forbidden to pick them up and carry them. The penalty for violating this taboo is to suffer a horrible death by the hands of the Ogboni society, a secret organization that does all the punishing for the native government. This taboo applies to women and children as well as to men, for, as the fetish-doctor says: " The Devil is as much in women and children as it is in men " (a scientific fact that is known even by my savage people). The only person who is completely tabooed is a pregnant woman; to her we are not allowed even to pass a drink of water, and she knows better than to expect it.

I cannot say much about the crocodile, as it is one of the sacred animals of the fetish-religion at the present time. We are not allowed to go near a river except at certain times, and then only to make supplication for some special favour from the principal Spirit that sits in the *ju-ju* house, the house of the Great Spirit.

The leopard was a sacred animal during the reign of Gezo, one of our native kings, but that taboo was abolished later, during the reign of the fetish-king Abu-du-allah.

Chapter III

SAVAGE SOCIAL LAWS AND CUSTOMS

A river is taboo. Our women work. Our men have many wives. Why we respect women. Why we do not love our wives. The danger of child-birth. New mothers are taboo. Children mature early. Polygamy brings respect. How a husband treats his wives. Ancestry. Followers. Girls must be virtuous. Punishment for immorality.

There are many taboos in my country. One of the principal ones is about water. Although the river near my home is not navigable and we never have any reason to go near it, it is taboo just the same. We get the fish that we eat from a small lake near our country, at the foot of the Kong mountains. Now, every man does not go fishing, but he that does supplies everyone else with the fish he brings home.

The same thing applies to rice, the only food that we cultivate. One family may cultivate rice for several seasons, and that is sufficient for all. All other foods grow spontaneously. The women

24

attend to all the growing of food-plants, food-gathering, and preparation of food, and the men remain in their homes and act as husbands to their wives. The women look after the welfare of their husbands, while the husbands take care of their own obligations. Therefore a man is not so idle as one may think, because it requires much time and energy to look after a half-dozen native women at one time. The man is kept busy, and six wives are not the limit; in fact, there is no limit to the number of wives a man may have, provided he is man enough to care for them all. Some men have as many as thirty wives; my eldest brother has twenty-one, and he still lives to tell the tale.

Polygamy is not the worst system of marriage; the natives like it, and it is not burdensome, but rather a delight, because a man knows just what to do and he does it quite well, considering the number of children he has, which, to us, is the object of matrimony. I do not say that I altogether approve of polygamy, but I do say, choose the lesser of two evils; that is, take half a dozen wives and be true to them, and do not take one wife and be false to her. I say that one wife with divorce and alimony is not so wholesome as twenty wives with neither divorce nor alimony. The wild men in my country do not know anything about alimony; it seems to me, alimony is making a lot of civilized men wild.

In my country a woman is not respected for the looks of her face, nor for the clothes that she wears. If she were respected for the latter, then she would not be respected at all. But she is respected for the ability to be a good mother. A girl's education in my country is a thorough training in wifehood and motherhood. She is fitted and prepared for the most sacred of all duties, and that is to be a success as mother of a large family. And that does not mean that we look down on our women; on the contrary, we look up to them, especially if they give us a lot of boy children. We do not treat our women as chattels or slaves, but we expect the women to look after the domestic duties. This is not merely as a convenience for the men. The natural duties of a female are domestic, and our women feel honoured to do the thing that nature fitted woman for.

Our women do many more things, from their own sense of duty, than we really expect of them. Of course, it is perfectly natural for a person, especially a woman, to want to do everything possible for the one that she loves. With us love is purely on the side of the woman. Every woman has her special love for her man, and there seems to be a sort of special charm that every woman adores in her man, and her sole object in life is to develop this particular fascination and to keep it alive, so to speak. Is this not so with every people, one person liking another for his walk, another liking the same person's manner of speech or tone of voice, and still another liking him for personal contact, but all liking the same person for one thing or another, just the same?

But with our native men it is different, because it is impossible for a man to love equally six wives, but it is not impossible for six wives to love one husband. Therefore, since our men cannot love their wives all alike, they do not love any of them. We all love our children, and it is the duty of the wife to raise her young.

It takes a strong child to live just after birth in my country. No one amongst us knows any safe method of child-birth; therefore infant mortality is very high. There are more boys born than there are girls, but the girls survive, hence we have more females than males. The treatment of a baby at birth is rough, almost amounting to cruelty. A girl in my country knows little about tenderness and caring for an infant child, for she herself was never handled tenderly. The girl must attend to herself when she is delivering a baby, because she and everything connected with her are taboo; so she is not anxious about the baby until her own sufferings are alleviated somewhat. A girl in my home not only has to go through the hardship of delivering her own baby, but she is taboo during the whole time of her confinement, and it means death to any man who looks at her in that state, and also death to her and the baby, so that during that time the poor girl suffers extremely. Just after the child is born, all the women rally round the girl and give her any aid that she may require. The taboo is lifted, and even her husband comes down to her house and speaks consoling words to her. Then that is not all. The other women in the same compound hold a feast, and this feast is kept up until the time of circumcision, if the baby is a boy. Among my own sect, circumcision is held on the eighth day.

The age of puberty amongst our native girls is nine; that is, they can be mothers at ten. The age of maturity amongst our native boys is thirteen, and they can become fathers from that age on. It is the aim of the fetish-law to marry the boys and girls off at those ages in order to check immorality. Considering the high temperature of the climate, and the passion of tropical people, I think that it is a prudent plan.

In our country we have not the economic problem to deal with, as have people in these Western countries. We do not have to pay rent or taxes; we do not need to buy clothes, because we never wear any; we do not have to pay for food, as the food that we eat grows without cultivation; we never have need for money, and we have no system of currency; therefore, economically speaking, living is comparatively easy. Since there is no real affection between man and woman, they never live together in the same house, except during the time of nuptials. Cohabitation in my country is a duty and not an incidental pleasure.

Our boys are always encouraged to take more than one wife, but a boy is not compelled to take any. If a boy has only one wife, that wife encourages and urges him to take another, and she respects him all the more for so doing. We respect the boy who has taken one or more extra wives more than one who has not taken any at all. The native government gives a compound to every boy that marries, and the boy builds houses according to the number of wives he has. We always give a house to every wife. The boy lives in a house that is built in the centre of his compound, by himself. When he wishes company, he simply walks around on a visit to the houses of his wives, and the wife that he chooses to come up to his house knows it by the small beads that the boy drops in front of her door, which indicates that she is his choice for that time. She picks up the beads and wears them, singing all the time, and then she does a dance in the presence of the other women in the compound and finally runs away to the house of her husband. She remains there as long as the boy wishes; it may be only a day, or it may be a week, according to the wish of the husband, and when he has finished with her, he sends her back to her own house. During the time that she is away from her house, the other women look after her household duties and take care of her children if she has any. The husband cannot call the same girl again until he has made the rounds — that is, until he has called the other wives, if he has any. If he has only one wife, it is customary for him to release her for as long as he has had her company. When the boy has only one wife, she does the cooking also while she stays with him. But the food is gathered by the followers in that compound.

Every family of distinction in my country has followers. Distinction in my country is to that family which can count back the furthest in a straight line; it is purity in blood that makes us noble, and not money. Of course, some can count back further than others. I can count three hundred relatives in my immediate family-tree. It is native etiquette to have " followers." A follower is a man who has no distinction and who has not married, for some reason that he never tells, and so he is eager to be connected with some family. A follower is not a servant and may some day take the place of the head of the house. If, for example, I go away on a long journey, leaving my wives behind, and stay away over one year, then all my wives and chattels automatically go to the follower who has been left in charge, and he may give as many of my women away to the other followers as he deems fit, but he himself may not have any followers, as he has no distinction. If there are any children in a case like this, they remain with their mothers. This rule is called " the house-rule system." It has many good features. If I should return, I am not permitted to redeem my wives or children, nor will the fetish-doctor sanction my marriage to another girl, for I am considered as dead in the marriage market if I have overstayed my time.

We insist on purity amongst our girls, and every girl must be a virgin at the time of her marriage or must suffer the consequences. I may venture the assertion that many a poor girl who has been punished for impurities is as free from contamination

31

as a new-born babe, but the fetish-law does not allow for accidents or mishaps. If a girl is in the least way damaged, she is treated just as if she were guilty. Girls in my country climb, jump, and run, and do almost everything that boys do, and in addition to this a girl must help her mother in domestic work; therefore any mishap to her may not be her fault. The punishment meted out to girls who have met with physical misfortune is severe; they are unsexed. Since we have no competent surgeons, you can imagine the suffering this entails.

The father of such a girl must stand great abuse and scorn for being the parent of this creature and for trying to palm her off on the unsuspecting; so you can imagine his feelings towards her. People often go so far as to say that the father knew all about it and did not attempt to warn anyone. It is expected of everyone to be self-accusative; that is, because of the simple-mindedness and ignorance of the people, the devilish witch-doctors make the people believe that it is the proper thing to accuse oneself of wrong-doing. (Food for thought.) But I know, as a matter of fact, that the major portion of the people who do accuse themselves of doing wrong do so merely out of fright of consequences and not from any conscientious scruples whatsoever.

A girl who has fallen or is accused of this is unsexed and her left breast is cut off, leaving a mark for life, the " scarlet letter " of the bush. This usage, too, applies not only to girls; boys also are punished for impurity; in this case castration is practised. If it is a man who has committed the crime, all of his wives are taken from him as well. I must admit that I do not know of more than two cases of this kind of punishment, in my whole lifetime. It is not necessary for a boy or man to take such a risk when he can have as many wives as he can support.

Chapter IV

HORRIBLE FETISH-LAWS

Fetish-laws. The test of fire. Devil-finders. The Amazon Army. Unfortunate girls. Gooma selected for my wife. The mystery of Gooma.

In the fetish-law no one is forgiven for breaking the law; the law says: " If you cut your finger, it must bleed; therefore, if you break the law, you must be punished." Extenuating circumstances are no excuse. For example, the man that lies wilfully against another has his tongue split open, and the one who steals, even if it is from his own mother or father, has his fingers cut off from the hand with which he stole. This applies to both women and children as well as to men; no one is exempt. Since the punishment is swift and sure, people are not inclined to break the law in my country.

At one time it was our custom to give a test to determine a person's innocence or guilt. The accused was forced to hold his hand in a fire in order to prove that he was innocent. The length of time

34

that he had to hold it there was about ten minutes. If he could do this without showing the least sign of pain and without crying out, then he would be judged innocent, but he would be maimed for life. Needless to say, no one was ever found innocent by this test. This was the practice in the days of the wicked King Gezo and was abolished by the brave King Glelele.

Gezo was a cowardly man, and he feared his subjects. He was a superstitious man, because when he had an evil dream, he always suspected that someone was plotting against his life. For this reason he gathered all the people together and had the witches dance around them to pick out different men and women supposed to have evil in their hearts against the King. These witches were called the "devil-finders." Those who were unfortunate enough to be picked by the "devil-finders" were quickly led away, and killed in the most brutal manner. This practice was abolished by Glelele. Although many of the barbarous practices of Gezo were abolished by Glelele, he substituted for them practices just as cruel, but not so cowardly.

This King was a brave but cruel man. It was he who organized the only original Amazon Army; he did it through the blood of innocent girls. He started the custom by gathering all his cast-off

women, those women in his own compound who had
been taken in adultery, and instead of killing them,
he aimed at making them useful. So every woman
who was found to be unfaithful was unsexed, her
breast was removed, and she was taught to use the
assagai, our weapon of war. At first this did not
succeed, but after much torture and hardship on
the part of the unfortunate women, it worked out
fairly well. These women, realizing that there was
no chance of regaining their womanhood, tried to
distinguish themselves in tactics of warfare, in
order to get back the favour of the King. Many
women died while undergoing the cruel treatment,
and for quite a long time wicked witch-doctors
and clumsy medicine-men were allowed to mutilate
poor women; finally, through constant practice,
they became more skilful and then there were not
so many deaths. It finally worked out very successfully and there were no fatalities, although the
process has always been extremely painful. This
system became so successful that the King thought
that it would be a good thing to treat all fallen
women in the same manner. Of course adultery
almost completely ceased, and the King's body-
guard seemed likely to die out through lack of
women. So the King made a drastic decree which
caused everyone to complain. The decree was that

every family that had seven girls or more must give up one girl to the King's government to be made a *Balogunsit* (a fighting woman), and the King chose from them his personal body-guard. The women and girls who had been operated on as a punishment always held the same rank, but those who had come in by *a-dami* (sacrifice) were allowed to advance according to their skill. When they grew too old to fight, they were called the *Muk-kou-o* (the Brainy, or the Wise), and they served the remainder of their days as counsellors to the King. It is from these that came our advisers to the king and the community chiefs. It was an excellent plan, but to perfect it entailed much suffering. These women who act as advisers are exempt from blame for anything, and it goes without saying that they are hard judges; they never show mercy, not even to their own relatives. They think that since they have been through so much hardship, and no one showed them any pity, others should receive no mercy from them. King Gezo was poisoned by one of his chief supporters. King Glelele was captured by the French government and banished to an island, where he died a natural death.

All girls who have been made sterile are forced first by torture to name the betrayer; if they do not

admit misconduct, they do not, however, escape
punishment. In many cases the condition has been
caused by a fall or some accident. The fetish-law
does not allow for accidents, for the simple reason that if it did, many girls would shield themselves behind such an excuse. Punishment is always administered; if the girl is really innocent,
then punishment is her fate and she should be
pleased to go through it for the sake of the other
girls.

That was the very thing that happened to Gooma,
the Princess.

Gooma had saved my life from the wounded man-
eating lion, by stopping it in its course with a poisoned assagai, when it was coming straight at me.
Now, if a girl is the direct cause of saving a boy's
life in my country, that boy's parents have the
option of claiming the girl to be the bride of the
boy when both reach marriageable age. My father
made the claim, and it was honoured by the consent
of Gooma's guardian parent.

I was a member of one of the four hundred
Semitic families that lived under the strict rule of
seven rabbis; none of us could marry into a fetish-
family, but we were permitted to choose wives from
Mohammedan families, because the Mohammedans
believed in one God. Gooma was not of a fetish-

family; she was only connected with and guarded by such a family.

There was mystery surrounding Gooma's antecedents, and the chief who owned her had watched her with a jealous eye. He said that she was his daughter, but there was no likeness between him and the child, nor did any one of his twenty-six wives own her. The name of the old chief was O-lou-wa-li; and the women in his compound were abusive of Gooma; in fact, they were cruel to her. The chief himself was a born fighter and had distinguished himself in many wars, and as a result had found favour in the eyes of the King.

While he had been on one of his skirmishes in the desert, fighting the Tuaregs, he had found Gooma, whose name, which means " Pearls of the Mother," he had given her himself. It is pronounced " Goo-hoo-maha "; we call it Gooma for short. The King himself would have taken the child from the chief had the chief not shown such pain and distress in parting with her. The old chief stuck to his story that the child was his daughter by one of the women of the Tuareg people, but no one believed him. This chief was such an illustrious character that the fetish-leaders would not permit any of the witch-doctors to interfere with him. The only thing that they forced him to do was to keep the girl away from other children, for fear of strange devils in her; she was supposed to be confined to the chief's compound. That is why the chief's wives were unkind to Gooma, but the chief protected her by keeping her with him as much as possible. The general thought was that the chief would marry her when she became of age. The old chief spent much time teaching the girl how to use the assagai, to hunt and fight, and to do everything that a boy did.

Now, Gooma was not white, but she was far from black, and she was a very beautiful girl. Not a few believed that she was not the gift of birth, but had been fashioned out of wind and sand during the storm called " *hum-seen* (fifty)." Regardless of all these rumours, Gooma lived on and did as other children did. She was no different, of course, except that she was cleverer and quicker than other girls of her age.

Then came the time of the awful episode with the lion, and the proposal of my marriage to Gooma, made by my own father to the old chief. The chief was pleased with the proposal, because he was anxious that the girl should be married into a different people from his own, for, as he said, a man cannot be kind to the thing that he does not like, and he knew that the poor girl was an object of hate amongst the fetish-people. Our people were not fetish, but were called "the Strange People," and he felt confident that we would be kind to her.

Chapter V

BLACK JEWS OF THE ONDO BUSH

The Emo-Yo-Quaim. *Our seven rabbis. Our laws. Our festivals. Circumcision. Our temple. Our customs. How we came to Africa. The journey across the Sahara. Flight from Timbuktu. Clearing the bush. The name "Dahomey."*

How did Judaism come into my obscure land, in the middle of Africa, far south of Timbuktu, surrounded by heathenism and savagery? In about twenty villages two thousand souls, all black, believe they are of Jewish origin and call themselves *" B'nai Ephraim."* The other natives call them *" Emo-Yo-Quaim,"* or " the Strange People." My people, " the Children of Ephraim," have part of the Hebrew Torah, written in the script of Aramaic, brought with them when they came into their country over eighteen hundred years ago. Our Torah is not written in ink, but burned into parchment by a hot iron. Therefore no letter can be changed.

Our people have seven rabbis, of seven different

families, who hold their positions by heredity. No man may be appointed a rabbi. He must be born a rabbi. These seven rabbis are responsible for all moral and religious training among our people. Religion is supreme, for the B'nai Ephraim are very pious. My people observe the biblical laws to the letter. We have no compulsory labour. We eat when we are hungry; we sleep when we are sleepy; we rest when we are tired; we pay no rent and no taxes; we buy no clothes, because in our land we never wear any. We have no need for currency nor for any monetary standard. Our lives are wrapped up in religious observances. My people know nothing of the Talmud or about the parts of the Bible that follow the Torah. Our festivals are Pesach, Shebuoth, Rosh Hashanah, Yom Kippur, and Succoth. We have no need for dietary laws because we never eat flesh and we never have milk. We have no problem about mixing milk and meat together. We eat flesh only during the Pascal Sacrifice, and even then only the seven rabbis and their families eat it, not the people. Our people circumcise their boys at the age of eight days, carrying out the rite to the letter, although not in the same way as in Palestine today. Our rabbis permit us to use only our teeth and finger-nails for the observance.

Our Temple is a Holy of Holies, not a place to

enter at will, but a sacred place to go into only once a year, at Yom Kippur, to where the Torah is. The rabbis may go in every Sabbath. They recite prayers from within this Temple and these prayers the people repeat in the language of the country, a dialect of Arabic. Men sit around on the ground, outside the Temple, which has porches, and there pray and receive instruction. Our Torah is guarded closely in the Holy of Holies by at least one rabbi always, night and day. The object is to prevent the holy script from being profaned, first, by natives of another religion, and, secondly, by members of our community eager to kiss or to touch the Torah as a form of devotion or blessing.

Our people have the same social customs as other natives. They eat the same food, which grows without cultivation, but our women prepare it somewhat differently from the way the women in other communities prepare food. We are fortunate to live unmolested in a country where fetishism and Mohammedanism rule.

Our rabbis teach us that our people left Judea after the destruction of the Temple and came to Africa. It is easy to say " came to Africa "; but consider the difficulties of travelling in those ancient days, across water and deserts, without good means of transportation! We travelled to Morocco,

44

and lived there many generations; then because of persecutions we had to leave instantly, without warning, and we lost all that we had acquired during those years, wealth, property, and stock. We crossed from Morocco directly south, over the Sahara Desert, another stupendous undertaking. The story goes that children were born and grew to be men and women and died, and that their children grew up and had children, before we finished that great journey across the Sahara, south of Morocco. Finally we reached the famous town of Timbuktu, the oldest city in Africa. It has never been made clear whether we were a great number, or whether we had dwindled to just a few families when we reached Timbuktu, but the rabbis say that we are now only a feeble remnant of our people.

In Timbuktu we were not treated badly, but we were not content to live under the rule of desert tribes any longer than was necessary; so we left Timbuktu and started south, leaving the desert behind. After walking three days we came to a place where there was good pure water. So many of our people had died because of impure water in other places they came to, that when they found pure water in this spot, they gave thanks to Almighty God and settled there and cleared the bush, for it was a bush that they had entered, where

45

herbage and vegetation abound. They cleared that place and made themselves a village. They were surrounded at that time by the bush and its wild beasts, elephants, leopards, lions, monkeys, and reptiles, the horned viper and the boa constrictor, and thousands upon thousands of hook-lizards. This was the place we decided to make our home, because we were free when we came upon it. The rabbis say that while they were in the desert, large groups of the people, who had acted as advance guards, were swallowed by the sand and disappeared, never to be seen again. There were no trade-routes on the desert in those days; those who had to travel had to find their way as best they could.

The rabbis say that our people first gave the name to the country where we now live, for at that time there were no inhabitants there; we were the only people. Because we found good water there, we called it in the native vernacular *Da-Ome* (*Good Water*). How this name left our present country and drifted to the coast, I have never found out, but Dahomey is the name of the country on the coast. It did not take long, according to our rabbis, for the natives on the east and west of us to find our snug little place. They surrounded us and wrested from us the village that our people had made, and set up their own rule. We were never a fighting people, and we were easily subjugated. But we lived on in that same place, and we have seen many changes, but we have remained always the same, preserving our law and guarding our sacred Torah with our very lives.

Chapter VI

FOURTEEN LITTLE NIGGERS—

Where white men never go. White men as terrible monsters. Native boys as brain-food. Night by the fires. We boys plan a joke. We go too far. We wander in the Ondo bush. Terror-stricken. Wilderness food. Dangers. First view of the ocean. Strange sights.

I have often wondered why white men never go to my country. They have penetrated almost every other part of the world. Perhaps if there were safe-conduct they might go; there is no other reason that I can find that keeps them out. David Livingstone penetrated parts of Africa where white men existed only by hearsay, just as is now the case in my home; and Livingstone went alone, without protection, save the power of Almighty God. He lived among the people that he visited and endeared himself to them, regardless of their primitiveness. They never harmed him; they did a thing that few natives ever did: they carried his dead body, shoulder-high, through an almost impene-

48

trable bush, to the sea-coast. Probably he was an exception.

As for me, I never saw a white man in my country. When I was a child, as far back as I can remember, and that must be when I was about four years old, I heard talk of white people, but it was never clear whether white people actually lived, or whether they had become extinct. I welcomed the thought that they had died out. All I could hear my mother say was that if white men should come across us, they would eat us raw. She said they fed themselves only twice in the year, and that then they ate their young if they could not get the young of other people. My mother said that white people came like witches, from no one knew where; they just appeared and disappeared. They were formed much differently from our own men; every white man had only one of everything: one eye, in the middle of the forehead, one leg, with a great wide foot, fan-shaped, so that when he lay down, the foot acted as a sunshade. A white man had no visible nose, and his mouth was large and could be made much larger at will. He lived on raw human flesh and could be seen in the bush just before and just after the rainy season.

Now, what could you expect us children to see, when our parents told us such things? Especially when they were supported in their stories by men who had been accustomed to going away to different trading markets? Some of these men had seen white men, but they knew nothing about them. That is reasonable, because I know even in these Western countries, where everyone is supposed to be wise, some provincial folk know that wild black people exist, and many have seen them, but they do not know much about them. I venture to say that they talk to their children in no uncertain terms of " niggers," as the black men are called here. It is reasonable that I, as a child, never knew what a white man looked like; neither did my mother know, but she tried her best to picture one to me, and so did all the other mothers in my country for their children, and none of them described the white man in flowery terms; they likened him to an outlandish monster. So that was my first impression of a white man. Oh, how we boys would have loved to see one!

Well, for my own part, I wanted badly to see one and often expressed a desire to go with the men when they went out, to see for myself. I believe that was why my mother was so emphatic about their swallowing me up the moment they caught me; she would say: " They really and truly love to eat little native boys!" When I would ask: " Why do they

like to eat native boys instead of their own boys?"
she would say: "A native boy makes them wise and
gives them brain-food, but their own boys are as
stupid as themselves; so how could they get any
benefit from them?"

At night when fires were lighted to keep out
beasts, and everybody was happy, singing or dancing and telling stories, we boys sat with the men,
but were never allowed to speak; we listened and
were thrilled. The thing that was uppermost in our
minds was: "How we should like to see a white
man!" This was in our minds constantly; one night
when we wanted to have some fun with the smaller
children, we planned to go a little distance from
the village, and then run in and shout: "Oh! Oh!
We saw a white man! He's coming! He's coming!"

This would be sport because we thought we could
make everyone laugh. Remember, we were only
little children: I was seven, the youngest was five,
and the oldest eleven. The oldest boy was not a
bold leader, because he was as much afraid as we.
The youngest was pluckiest, but because he did not
know any better.

It was I who made the suggestion to walk from
the village a little way; no one would know, and
we did not intend to stay. The older boy argued
against such a stupid thing; he reminded us what

punishment to expect if we were caught away from the village at night. The youngest boy, Ojo-yola, whom we called Ojo for short, made the big fellow yield to the plan.

Now, it is not easy to leave a native village at night without someone's seeing you; and if you do escape all eyes, then there are still the animals and reptiles to reckon with. The animals prowl about villages occasionally at night; some nights you may not see any outside the ring of fires, while on others you may see a host of them. (Was it fortunate or unfortunate for us, that night, that there were no animals round the village? Problematical! However, I know this much, that if I had known that night a little of what I found out later, or a little of what I know today, I should say emphatically that we were *most* unfortunate!) So it took us quite a while to get a little way off, as we had intended; and then, what with arguing and talking and passing remarks to one another, we forgot, for the moment, what we had started out to do.

Now I shall tell you the names of the boys: Akrim, eleven, was the oldest; Ebunah was nine years old; Suk-ram nine; Kef-tala ten; Abu-ghari seven; Bata Kindai, myself, seven; Oolou-oomi eight; Oye-jola nine; E-kush-e-ka ten; Abu-nakir I do not know how old; Fais-yunis six; Redeemghosha six; Mishaam eight; and Ojo-yola five. How do I remember? Easily; under different circumstances I should have forgotten. But have you heard of anyone's forgetting a train disaster that he was in, or a shipwreck with himself on board? No; impossible to forget, if you remain in your right mind.

Well, we were all walking and chatting loudly, and Abu-nakir was trying to end a dispute between E-kush-e-ka and Akrim, over Akrim's giving Ojo-yola a cuffing for being impudent to his elders; and we should have walked on to who knows where, but Abu-nakir shouted: *"Oo-lou-wi! Regel abiada!"* meaning: " Danger! White man! "

That, I think, was the first time we had thought of the white man since we had started out. We screamed and jumped, but could not run. Akrim became angry and shouted: " Enough of this! Let's go inside the village! "

I said: " Yes, yes, yes; come on inside! " for my every limb was shaking. The strangest thing is that not a word was said about the real danger where we were; we thought only of a white man.

We cried because Akrim could not lead us out of the bush into the village. Then we heard a sound, and Akrim led us away from the direction of the sound; you should have seen us falling over each.

53

other, in trying to be first. Oye-jola screamed for his mother, and so did we all, in one loud cry: "*Ema! Ema!*" meaning: "Mother! Mother!" Akrim tried to quiet us by putting his hand over our mouths and reminding us of the danger; but our crying and his helplessness unnerved him, and he too began to cry; remember, he was only eleven years old, a small boy like ourselves.

Every now and then the youngest boy swore that he saw a white man coming. So we did not walk straight, but just drifted along from spot to spot. After a while everything became darker than ever, which meant that we were out of sight of the reflection of the village fires. Why Akrim did not lead us to another village I have never found out, for poor Akrim never lived to explain anything; neither did any of the other boys.

We slept little that night. We put ourselves together as monkeys do when they scent danger; we made a ball of ourselves, by curling up together. The difficulty was that each of us wanted to be nearest the centre. But the more we pushed in, the tighter this human ball became. Imagine the danger from lizards and snakes! But we were too young to realize our danger. Of course, we knew there were dangers in the bush, but it never dawned upon us that anything could happen to us; we thought then of the danger of white men. Even during the time when we tried to snatch a little sleep, one or two of the boys would wake up suddenly and cry out: " White man! " If some civilized men had been in our position under the same circumstances, I am sure they would have gone mad, because they would have realized the real dangers from animals and reptiles.

When day came, we ate monkey bread-fruit and bananas and we did not have difficulty in getting water to drink, for in the bush at short distances are palms that give good water. So we drifted on and on, halting now and then to guess just where we were. We concluded finally that we were lost! We never seemed to come to any open space!

One morning one of the boys was stung by a hook-lizard, and the noise he made was enough to rouse every beast in the bush. I bit out the flesh where he was stung, and Ebunah and E-kush-e-ka tied the leg. While Akrim prepared the medicine, little Ojo-yola made a fire by rubbing sticks together. It took him a long time, but he succeeded in starting a blaze. After the medicine was good and boiling, it was applied. We boys did not know how to attend to him the same as the men could; we were rougher, but we got the poison out of his body, and the healing was simple; but imagine the pain he had!

One day, when our excitement over being lost had passed a little and we were all feeling a little less afraid, Ojo-yola, the young one, went from us to find some cola-nuts, but before he had been gone five minutes we heard him screaming; and he came back running, all excited, saying that he had seen a white man. We were all afraid at the word, and dug a hole as quick as we could and hid. We remained in that hole three days before any of us had courage to venture out! Abu-nakir became violently sick while we were there, but we dared not go out to get him something for his sickness. We fasted all the time, because we did not venture to leave. Akrim was the first to go out. He told us all to follow him, and we did so. Think of the condition of our boyish minds. It all still seems to me like a bad dream; I should not like to go through such an experience again, but I would not have missed it for anything, because it was so horribly fascinating.

Well, we walked on and on; and then we came to where there was a habitation. We came out of the bush after having had horrible experiences for forty-five days! We could see people, but not our people, because they wore something around their loins. So we were afraid to approach; we just circled around far from them and the place where they were; and we finally came out on the coast without being questioned.

You must imagine us, fourteen naked little black boys, gazing out at the sea. The sea was taboo in our country, although we did not know that, but if we had known, how could we have avoided looking at it? The way the great surf rolled in and foamed and splashed and roared bewildered us. When we first heard the roar of that surf, we were afraid to approach, and at that time we had not yet seen the sea itself; we had only heard its voice. But when we did see the great sea, we were fascinated.

We saw native black men get into canoes and paddle over the surf; we saw them get through that treacherous surf and go away out to something standing still; what it was we did not know, nor could we imagine. I said that the thing looked like a fish. The same native men climbed up this thing and then returned to the coast; and nothing had hurt them, because they were singing. The surf threw their canoes on to the coast, upsetting them in the water. They jumped up and got hold of ropes and pulled their canoes farther up on the beach. This happened all day, and then that thing that had been standing out there in the water disappeared and the men on the shore gave something to one

57

another and began to sing and dance wildly, until all of a sudden they started to fight.

We did not know what it was all about, but we could see from a distance. So we crept back to the edge of the bush and found food, and then we slept, because our eyes were tired. We had forgotten home, for that time at least; only now and then Ojo-yola started bawling, and then we all had a good cry.

But we were seeing strange sights.

Chapter VII

—AND THEN THERE WAS ONE

A canoe. Clumsy paddling. Exploring a steamer. Disappointing white men. In the hold. Terrified. The boys go overboard. I alone am left.

For six days we watched these men, or different men; we did not know which, because we did not go close enough to see them clearly. We saw this thing that I had called a fish come again, and we were anxious to know just what it was. I suggested that we get a canoe and go out to it. Then the question arose as to where to get the canoe, and Akrim scolded me and said that we could not go near these strangers, because who knew but that they were related to monkeys?—a serious imputation, in my country. He added that we should not be away from our own mothers if it had not been for me and the devil that must be in me. " And now you tell us to do something that will bring down another curse upon us! "

At this we began to cry, and even Akrim cried,

for he was a kind, good boy and he loved me; so, when he saw me upset over his reproach, he said: "All right, let us get a canoe," and he offered to take us where we could find one.

Oh, how weak of him to give in! He should have pulled my hair out by the roots instead of encouraging me in my folly. Anyway, it would have been better at least for him not to have listened, because he might have been living today.

We travelled nearly a day before we came across a canoe, and it was a very heavy one too; it was a market canoe. All of us got under it and carried it to the coast, but it took us about ten days to get it there, because the thing was heavy. When we got it on the coast, we discovered that we had no paddles; it took us another week to find paddles. Now the stage was set for the end of our tragic drama.

We tried time and again to get the canoe over the surf by pushing it out, but before we could scramble in and start paddling, the great surf threw the old canoe back on the beach. We tried it so much the first day that we were fatigued and gave up, and waited for another day. Then the thing I called a fish disappeared and did not come back for about eight days, and then the beach became lively again with men that sang, danced, and then fought, after each had drunk something.

So we started to launch our canoe, too, and, strange to say, we got out over the surf. Now for the paddling! After we had left the beach the water was still, but we did not know how to paddle. We did not know that we had to do it all together, until we noticed the other men doing it so. We did not sing, we were nearer crying. We did not know what we were approaching.

We reached the side of that thing, but could not make up our minds to touch it; and we went all round and looked at it. Finally we came close and stood up simultaneously and put our hands flat on the iron plates. We pulled our hands off so quickly that you would have thought that we had got a shock or had touched something hot. But that was only our fear. We put our hands on the side of that thing again and held them there, saying to each other: "See! I'm not afraid of it! Look! Look at me! See!"

Then we pulled ourselves up a long rope that hung down the side of the ship. Yes, it was, of course, a ship, a steamer! There was no special thrill in climbing the rope, other than the thought of what we should see next; we had been used to climbing vines and trees. But how can I describe the next sensation? When our bare feet hit the wooden deck, there was but one thought. All the

61

thrills came together, the deck, the machines on the deck, and, last but not least, *the white men.* We wanted to scream then, but we were too astounded to open our mouths. We stood as if paralysed, close together, until we recovered and got over our surprise. As for me, I was disappointed; even little Ojo-yola said, when he first saw the white men, that they weren't so wonderful. " There is nothing wrong with them; they are as good-looking as I am."

There were many of them; they were all about the deck; and they did not hurt us. We had seen the white men! Was it worth the trouble that we had undergone?

The novelty of the white men wore off at once, but we still eyed them with suspicion. The deck gave us plenty more to think about, but we never went near those funny people who wore trousers. We had never seen a man wear trousers before, so it caused us amusement.

We went over the deck; we ran, laughed, jumped, and skipped, because of the peculiar feeling when our bare feet touched the deck; remember, the deck was wooden, and our feet had never walked on wood before. But nothing held our attention long, because there was so much to see, and we tried to see it all.

Oh, what a story we could tell when we returned home! How we should have old and young listening to our wonderful adventure! Our parents had never seen one-half the things that we were seeing. But we had lost caste at home, and our punishment would be severe. Akrim became sad when we chatted about our village. These home thoughts never remained long in our minds, however, because there was too much to see.

I walked over to a door and pulled it open, and there was a stairway. I shouted to Akrim to follow me, but he was busy with Kef-tala, arguing whether we should take something back with us or not. Akrim said that anything that we should take would be tabooed by the fetish; and Kef-tala argued that he had once seen one of our men bring in something strange and that he had been permitted to keep it after putting it in the *ju-ju* house for several days to drive out of it all evil.

Little did I think when I called out to Akrim to follow me that it was my last time to speak to him. It was my last time to look at the faces of my little companions; one of them did not belong to my sect, and that boy was Suk-ram, a fetish boy; but it was I who had sucked the poisoned blood from his foot when he was stung by a lizard, away back there in the Ondo bush. Yes, they were my companions, in laughter and in mirth, in suffering and in hardship; they were my companions. I weep today when I think of the pitiful plight that we were in when we were lost in the Ondo bush. I smile when I think of the tragic humour when we were lost in the bush. Never to see them again! And if the thought had ever come to me then, I am sure I should have gladly died with them. And today, although I have aged and become a little bit "civilized," I often wish that I had died with them.

Oh, the white man, who has meant so much to me in my life and has cost me so much! He has given me clothes and money, things that I never knew before; but he has taken from me much that is worth while. I love my native country, I love my savage people; but at the same time I am forced to hate my own customs, the customs of my father. I am neither white nor black, I am a misfit in a white man's country, and a stranger to my own land.

I was, to continue the story, down in the hold of the ship, and I had forgotten all about the boys on deck; perhaps they were looking for me; I know that Akrim was, anyway, but I was spellbound. It was the stoke-hole that I was in, and I had sat down to watch the men working. I felt funny under there, but I did not fear anything. The men shouted and

64

laughed and shouted again. Perhaps they were talking or shouting to me. Who knows? Who cared? I didn't, because I did not understand what they were saying.

But the thing — I mean the ship — appeared suddenly to be moving up and down; I attributed it all to the men and their shouting. I thought about the men who were in the canoes, and how, after each one drank something, they all began to sing and dance, shout and fight. Perhaps these men were doing the same thing. But this movement up and down presently began to annoy me, and like a flash I shouted for Akrim and started out of the place. When I got no answer from Akrim, I cried, and for the first time since I was on the ship I became terrified and screamed: "*Ema! Ema!* (Mother! Mother!)"

I stumbled and bumped my head. I could not find the steps that I had come down. I had forgotten whether it was down or up that I had come. I saw another opening and made for it, and while I was going down, it became so dark that I cried all the louder, calling: " My mother! Please come to me! Please come to me!" You cannot imagine the horror in my little breast. The boys! Yes, the boys! Where were they? Why didn't Akrim come? Why didn't any of them come?

I made my way back, up out of this second hold, and while I was looking for an exit, saw a door open, and the light flashed on me; there was an iron stairway, and I made my way up. There was a man at the top of this iron stairway, and the look on his face was ghastly; he was whiter than the white men were! He was excited, and when he saw me, he turned his head away and called out to someone; but what he said I do not know. I was afraid, and if it had not been for getting back to Akrim and the others, I should have remained below before taking the chance of passing that terribly white white-man, for who knew what he would do to me! Every warning of my mother came back to my mind. Oh, it was terrible! But I had to find the boys, and that was all there was to it. When I got to the top of the iron steps, I jumped out on to the deck; the man did not touch me.

But the boys! The boys! Where were they? Where could they be? I shouted and screamed for each one. Then I looked out over the water, and I did not see any canoes or men, nor did I hear any voices, such as I had heard when I had left the deck to go below. Oh, what was wrong? I could not see the land as I had seen it before! Then I was seized with terror and I gave one yell and rushed to the side of the ship. I should have been at the bottom if someone had not held me.

When I had called to Akrim to follow me down to the stoke-hole, Akrim was talking to Kef-tala; that was the last I saw of him. The captain's story much later was that he saw the little fellows playing about the deck; and as he and the crew never bothered natives who came aboard the steamer, no one noticed us particularly. Of course, those natives are used to that kind of thing, but we boys had never seen a ship before. None of the sailors knew this, however.

The captain said that the usual signal was given for everyone to go ashore that belonged ashore. Other natives knew that signal. It is the siren of the ship, which gives three long blasts; and then a little flag is hoisted to the top of one of the masts. This little flag is called the Blue Peter, and when it goes up, the siren blows three times, long and loud. This signal gives notice that the ship is about to pull anchor and leave. The boys knew nothing about all this. When they heard the sudden blast of the siren, it frightened them, and, it seems, they rushed to the side of the steamer and jumped into the water, into the dangerous Gulf of Guinea, infested with sharks. No man would have jumped into the Gulf of Guinea; no, not even a boy who lived on the coast, because it is as much a part of native education on the coast to avoid sea dangers as it is a part of our education in the bush to avoid wild beasts.

The captain said that when the boys jumped, everyone on the deck was inclined to laugh, but that the laugh soon turned into horror. How could the sailors laugh when they looked at thirteen little boys struggling in a shark-infested sea? The captain and the crew threw out lines and floats, trying to save the boys, but their efforts were in vain; because the little chaps had got such a fright that no end of calling could attract any of them. They frantically tried to get into a canoe, but not one succeeded. Ojo-yola, the youngest, was just throwing his leg over the side of a canoe when a shark bit down on the other leg, which dangled in the water.

My companions! The boys that I had feasted with! The boys that I had got hungry with! They all were gone! We had been in dangers together. We had risked lions, leopards, elephants, and reptiles, and we had escaped; and now my companions were lost in the sea. It was all too horrible.

Divine Providence did not will otherwise, and therefore I alone was saved from death then for the purpose of doing something, some time; but, as yet, I do not know what.

Chapter VIII

A NAKED BLACKAMOOR IN SCOTLAND

The captain's intentions. Locked in. A trapped animal. What are clothes for? Arrival in Glasgow. A frantic escape. Captured by a real gentleman.

When the white man held me back from leaping overboard, I was more afraid than ever, so I kicked and scratched. But he did not let go; instead he put me into a cabin, locked the door, and left me. I screamed and beat the door with my head and hands, but to no avail. That man was the captain. He said later that he had intended to put me off at the next stop of the steamer, but that he changed his mind. He decided if he should put me off at the next stop, I would be in a strange country among hostile natives and perhaps would never get back to my own people. So he planned to take me with him and to bring me back on his next trip, putting me off at what he thought to be my own country. That country, however, was the Gold Coast of Africa, the home of the Fantis, a people hostile to

69

my people. If the captain had put me off at the Gold Coast, what would have been the sequel? Should I have been better off at the mercy of the Fanti people than at the mercy of the cold, aggressive white man's civilization? Again I say, problematical.

I was broken-hearted in that cabin. It was dark, but that did not annoy me. I was lonesome without my playmates. Oh, why didn't they answer me? Where were they? And each time that I thought of them, I shrieked and kicked and beat on the door.

Now and then someone came to that door, opened it a little, said something, and closed it with a bang. I suppose that they opened it to tell me: " Shut up! " and closed it again because they feared me, for I flew at the door every time they opened it. I cried and screamed until I felt faint, and then I laid me down on the mat and lulled myself to sleep, saying all kinds of incoherent baby things. How could you expect me to know, little animal as I was, what this was all about? They brought food; they did not stop to think whether or not I had eaten their food before. They opened the door and pushed in something on a plate and left it on the mat; closed the door again with a bang and left me to myself.

I tired myself trying to get out and when they

came with food, I crowded into the farthest corner and covered my head with my arm, frightened. You have seen caged creatures do the same thing, and I was then just a trapped animal. I was afraid to go near the plate for the longest while; and when I did pluck up courage enough to uncurl myself and approach the plate, to examine it, the door opened slightly and someone peeped in, and I jumped back into the corner and curled myself up into a tighter knot. If I had only known, I should not have suffered so. But I finally got to the plate filled with food; what it was I do not know, but it smelled good, so I ate it all and enjoyed it; in fact, I longed for more.

Then I forgot to cry! All of a sudden I forgot the boys, and home, and my fright wore off a little! Why? Because my body had been fed. And I began to hum a tune. I became used to the door's opening every now and then, so I learned not to run from it.

The captain of that ship was Captain Caley; he, good man, died during the World War. I do not believe I was entered in the ship's log-book, because I was not a passenger, and I certainly was not a stowaway; I was merely a "native." The ship, as I learned later, was the *Batanga,* a tramp steamer belonging to the African Steamship Navigation Company.

71

Some of the crew knew a few words of the coast languages, but they did not know mine. So they just had to make signs to me; and in their effort to make me understand, they frightened me, because they made such hideous faces. I became used to all this, and saw humour in the way they acted. So every time they spoke or tried to make me understand something, I roared with glee, for I thought that they did these funny things to amuse me.

I was apparently happy, but my happiness was not for long, because by and by these horrible men tried to put clothes on me! It got colder every day, especially when it rained. The ship was getting into European waters, and the men saw me shivering. Of course I was afraid; I did not know that what they were doing was for my own comfort. How should I know? They threw into the cabin an old shirt and a pair of trousers, not stopping to think that I knew nothing about such things. What was I to do with them — put the trousers on my head, and the shirt on my feet? That would have been just like me; in my raw state it was natural for me to do everything contrary to the way it should be done. So I did not put the clothes on.

After a while some men came into the cabin and held me while another man tried to dress me. I screamed, bit, scratched, and kicked; I bit one of the men on the arm; he yelped and gave me a cuffing; and when the sailors saw that it was useless, they gave it up as a bad job and let me alone. So I did not wear the clothes just then.

It was cold! Can you imagine the change it was, coming out from a temperature of 135 degrees in the African bush and being naked in a temperature that, I am sure, must have been quite low? I was too young and too ignorant to know what I was really suffering.

The ship sighted land, and things were all agog on the deck. The cabin door was not locked then, so I came out on to the deck at will; but it was so uncomfortably cold that I did not stay long on the deck at a time. I was curious to know what was going on, however. The last time that I had seen the deck so busy was on that fatal day when I had left my companions to peep into that awful door and had gone down those steps to the bottom. Men ran about here and there on the deck, shouting back and forth to each other. Ropes and other tackle lay about the deck, and it all was so confusing, so odd, that I wondered. It appeared as if the ship had suddenly got hemmed in by everything, because around us was land, with many ships and buildings and everything. It was different from anything that I had seen.

Then a man came to me and tried to talk with me. He put his arms around me; a savage instinct told me that all was not right, and that something was going to happen. The warmth of his clothes felt comfortable, so I let him cuddle me. If I could have made him understand, I surely would have told him that I was cold; as a matter of fact, I continually said that I was cold, but he could not understand what I said.

While he held me, the siren blared its signal, and it seemed as if all the whistles in the world broke loose. The sound of the siren now struck terror through me, and the man who held me could see that I was frightened. I was too terror-stricken to cry out, but I broke away from that man and ran quickly into the cabin. The man followed me to the outside and locked the door.

How long I remained there, huddled in the corner, I cannot say; it seemed a long time. But the door eventually opened, and a man looked in. He may have been calling me; I don't know. I crawled over to where he stood, and, remembering the warmth of the clothes of the other man, I cuddled close to the tail of his greatcoat. He was certainly kind, for he patted me on the head. Someone called him, and he left me hastily. I began to cry. He did not close the door of the cabin, so I tried to follow him. I ran out on to the deck. Then I saw the chance and ran down the gang-plank and kept running—for whom or for what I don't know, but I ran on.

My, but it was cold! It was the fourth day of March, in the year 1896, and the ship was tied up to the docks in Glasgow, Scotland! No one noticed me, half running and half walking along the dock, naked. No one spoke to me, at least so I thought, until I was out in the streets. There were wagons, trucks, bicycles, and everything, rushing back and forth. I was dumbfounded, but the cold cobblestones on my bare feet made me lift them up all the faster and kept me on the run.

At last I had to stop because a crowd collected around me. They all laughed at me, but I was too cold to mind them. I cried, but no one cared. All the white people in the world were there, and many things were said, but I never knew what and I never shall; not one of all this crowd would come near me. They stood back and laughed.

If a policeman had seen me, I should surely have been picked up and delivered back to the ship that had brought me. I might then at once have returned to my native land and been a man of distinction amongst my people. My moral standard would have been ninety-nine per cent higher than it is now, and I could have rightly called myself Prince Bata Kindai Amgoza Ibn LoBagola.

But it so happened that, instead of a policeman's picking me up, someone else did; and, according to what that gentleman said before he died, he merely did it out of pity. He said that he saw me in that rude crowd, and that he knew that I was cold, and he saw that none of those rough uncouth people showed any pity at all for a poor wee naked black creature from the African bush.

Chapter IX

STARTLING THE SCOTCH

First time in a house. A mirror. I fight the boy in the mirror. I break up a room. I bite the butler. The captain's story. Adopted. Nakedness preferable. Bananas and monkeys. The master's watch.

Now, when that gentleman picked me up, he had no intention of taking me any farther than the next corner, prompted by pity because the rough crowd showed no mercy to a " puir wee black naked creature," as he put it. And instead of putting me down round the corner, the good Scotchman afterwards said: " I changed my mind, and took him awa' hame tae my ain hoos." He intended to notify someone about my being in the city. That Scotch gentleman little dreamed that he would keep me when he took me home with him, but that was what fate decreed.

The man was a conservative Scotchman and knew little about the world outside of Great Britain. It did not dawn upon him that I had never

77

been in a house before, and so he tried to treat me as he would treat any little white boy. What a mistake!

At once I rebelled against being held, for he had forgotten, in his excitement, to let me sit down in the carriage. We must have looked strange to the cabman, and to everyone else, because this gentleman, instead of loosening his grip on me when I struggled, held me all the tighter. I kicked and tried to get away, but he held on. The cabman laughed and people shouted at us along the road, seeing an old man, with his hat flying off, struggling to hold a little naked black boy. How funny it must have looked!

The man got me to his house, out in the Dennistour district, off the Alexandra Parade. He rushed in with me and then made the first big blunder by putting me down on the floor. He did this with satisfaction, as if some great job had been completed and with the air of " There you are! "

Oh, what a blunder! What would it mean if you turned a little untamed monkey loose in a house? I was just a little animal, an untamed and seemingly untamable little savage. The first thing that caught my eye was a mirror in the hall. I had never seen a mirror before; how was I to know that its job was to reflect? When I looked into the mirror, of course it reflected me back, and that made me laugh, strange to say; and my laughing caused everyone looking at me to laugh also.

When I was first taken into the hall, the noise that I made attracted the whole household and brought everyone running to the front door, the madame, with her son, her only child, and all the help, which included two maids, a butler, a footman, and a cook. All came scurrying to the door to see what was up. You can imagine their surprise when they saw the master holding a wee black boy; and you should have seen them running when he put me down on the floor. Each one got behind some object in the hall and watched me in sheer amazement. When I began to laugh, they all came out from behind the objects behind which they had hidden themselves, and began to laugh also. The little boy, standing in front of his mother, roared with glee.

While they all were listening to the master of the house, busy telling how he had found me, I was engaged in examining the mirror. Every time I laughed, it laughed at me. That made me angry, so I walked up to the mirror and gave it a good cuff, and broke it into a thousand pieces! This brought the conversation to a sudden standstill. Everybody screamed, and so did I, but I did not scream for the same reason they did. No, not at all; I screamed because I saw blood on my hands, and I did not know what had happened.

The gentleman caught me and shook me hard and made me scream all the more. He rushed with me towards the door, but before he could open it, the boy standing in front of his mother began to howl also. This distracted the gentleman. He did not know whether to open the door or to stand still and hold me, struggling, or to go back into the hall, where all were talking at once.

He finally went back and handed me over to one of the men-servants. He gave orders to that servant, who dragged me up a stairway. Needless to say, I struggled, while he handled me as if I were something soiled, holding me aloof from him like a dirty rag. Well, he succeeded in getting me up the stairs and flung me into a room, giving me a good kick at the same time, but not before I had bitten him on his leg, which made *him* yell, too. It never dawned upon anyone for a moment that I was not used to any of their ways; not used to drawing-rooms, bedrooms, sitting-rooms, dining-rooms, furniture, ornaments, pictures on the wall, and mirrors, or any such paraphernalia.

What would a wild beast do if it were suddenly locked in a bedroom, as I was, with all kinds of

breakable things? I wrecked the room! I broke
things to my heart's content and then laid me down
on a mat and cried myself to sleep.

If it had not been for the other boy's crying when
his father was taking me to the door, after I had
broken an expensive mirror, I should have been
kicked out of that house, then and there, on to the
sidewalks, and left to drift as I pleased! The gentleman afterwards told me that it was only the
influence of his wife, who was a kind, motherly,
conservative Scotch lady, and of his boy, that
caused him to let me stay in his house that night.
He said that his wife persuaded him at least to
keep me until they could notify the steamship company about me and thereby locate the ship that had
in all probability been responsible for my being
in Glasgow. He said that his boy " urged him
sorely " — that is the way he put it — *to keep me
for him*. That made the greatest impression on
him; that was the reason he turned me over to the
butler, who swore, since I had given him the bite
on the leg, that he would not touch me again; in
fact, he said that he would leave service before
he would handle a little " black brute savage."

This was all laughable to everyone in the house,
except the madame, who sympathized greatly with
the butler, and so talked him into forgiving me;

for she explained to him that I was one of God's creatures and did not know any better.

While I was breaking up things in the bedroom, no one was brave enough to open the door and stop me; but the gentleman telephoned to the ship's company, begging them to locate the captain of the steamer and have him come to the house, post-haste, and take me away, for no one dared go near me, since I was evidently wild.

The captain was located and he immediately came out to the Drive, for that was where the house was. In the mean time, everything being quiet, since I had finished breaking things and was asleep, the captain told the people about me and my lost companions. When they heard that tragic story, everyone was sad except the butler, who nursed his leg that I had bitten; he felt that it would have been a good job if I had been swallowed up like the rest.

But the madame cried pitifully, and so did the boy. The master went to her and put his arms around her to comfort her. This good wife persuaded him to keep me, and so did the boy.

Now the question arose whether the captain was willing to leave me there, but he answered, when asked if they could keep me: " Yes, you can have him; he probably will be much better off here than he would be back there in his own land." So the bargain was made, over a cup of tea, and I was left for better or for worse.

The captain was the first to come upstairs to greet me. If he was shocked at the state of the room, he did not show it, because he caught hold of me tenderly and led me away to another place and began to wash me.

I had been cut by the broken glass from the mirror, and the people of the house had not been able to take proper care of me. I welcomed attention from the captain, so I did not cry or struggle. I nestled close to him, especially when I saw the butler in livery. Every time that the butler came near me, I pulled away and screamed.

So I was taken out of his hands and placed in charge of another man, the footman, whom I did not fear. My wounds were dressed, and everything was quiet again. When the captain took his leave, I cried, but the gentleman of the house pacified me by giving me biscuits and he ate also, to show me that the food was good to eat. He sat on the floor with me and tried to play with me, but I did not understand him at all. The little boy became familiar with me and attempted to imitate his father, but they all tried to keep him away from me.

I was soon settled in this good home, and I

83

became, to all appearances, contented. Only when I saw the butler did I cry out; and he, every chance he got, belted me on the neck or jaw, and then I screamed more; but he would do this and run. I found out later, after I had been in the house over a year, that the butler gave as an excuse for my screaming when he was with me alone that he was only trying to stroke my head. " His hair is so funny and nice," he would say. The boy caught him once when he was giving me my daily poke in the ribs or on the mouth and told his mother, who in turn told the master, and that gentleman sent the butler away almost immediately. The new butler was very kind, and I was happy with him.

Nothing else happened the first day until they tried to clothe me. That made me struggle and scream again, so they let me have my own way about clothes. They fed me on the floor of the wrecked room, with nothing in it now but a bed and mattress; I slept on the floor, however. They exhausted themselves of every trick, trying to get me to put something on, but each time they tried, I tore the clothes off. These Scotch folk were very modest; they could not reconcile themselves to the thought that it was right to permit me to run about the house naked. Try as they might, however, they could not induce me to follow them in wearing clothes.

The boy became more and more used to me, but still did not altogether trust me; when he wanted to be kind to me, he gave me a banana, for he believed bananas the chief article of food in my homeland. He little knew that we, in our country, eat less of that fruit than of anything else that grows in the bush, because we consider bananas monkey-food; parents disguise bananas when they feed them to the children, by frying or boiling them, or mashing them and mixing them in with some other food that we are fond of. When the boy offered me a banana, he plucked up courage enough to approach me, but before I could snatch it out of his hand, he would drop it on the floor and run. I say "snatch," for that was the only way that I took anything. I simply snatched it and examined it, and if it happened to be pleasing to my nostrils and sight, I put it into my mouth and tasted it. If I did not like it, I threw it on the floor, as I did with everything else when I had finished with it.

The master had a habit of holding his watch to my ear so that I could hear the tick; he always stopped me from crying in this way. Once he gave me his watch to hold. He had just come home, and he had brought some friends with him to show how

85

he could handle me, and how I did everything that he wanted me to do. I had become used to his caresses, and so I did not rebel. On this occasion he gave me his watch, after quieting me, for I had been crying. After I had tasted the watch, I just flung it away from me, and it fell to the floor with a thud. It was a good watch, an English lever, and it was damaged after that treatment. The master looked sick, while the guests and the household burst with laughter. The master had never given me his watch before; he had only let me hear the tick. He boxed my ears good and hard and ordered me to bed at once, as if I knew what it all meant.

The butler took me to my room. I cried so loud that he brought me some cabin biscuits to quiet me and was most gentle. I soon fell asleep, but woke up during the night and cried. I often had crying spells, but no one knew what was wrong with me. I called for my mother, and for Akrim, and for all the boys that I remembered, until I was tired.

Chapter X

TAMING BEGINS

*Dr. Dobbie. Lack of tact. A language of grunts. A midnight
escapade. Thrown into bed. Civilization teaches deceit. Dog-
like love. First English words. First clothes.*

At one time the good lady of the house thought I
was ill, so she sent for the family physician, a su-
perannuated old soul who seemed to cling to life
out of spite. He was a good man. I think that his
name was Dobbie, for they all called him Dobbie,
without the " Doctor." He was afraid of me at first,
and it took him some time to approach me.

His idea was quite different from that of the rest
as to the way in which I should be handled. He suggested strong-arm methods; as the boy told me
afterwards, he used to entrance them all with stories
of how a close relative of his had instructed him
to treat a black if he should ever meet one. This
relative had served in Her Majesty's overseas
forces in the country of the blacks for years and
therefore knew what he was talking about. This

dear old bounder tried to attract me by pretending to tickle me with his walking-stick, but at the same time giving me a poke which hurt me. I fairly jumped at him, and if it had not been for the butler, I should have caught him and given him a good biting. The butler could hardly hold me, and he laughed at the way the old fellow went downstairs, in leaps and bounds, screaming all the way down. Even the master laughed when he was told the story of how old Dr. Dobbie " subdued " me. And for quite a while, whenever the master brought friends home, someone suggested sending for the doctor in a hurry in order to make a diversion!

I do not believe now that the old man remembered his visits from one time to another, because he always responded to the call; and he always tried some foolish stunt with me each time, and I invariably made him run away howling. One time I caught his hand and gave his finger a good bite. Lord! Lord! Lord! you should have heard old Dr. Dobbie shout! They told me later that he actually swore, and threatened to have me placed in irons and given a flogging by troopers, who knew how to handle treacherous blacks.

Oh, if they could have understood my language! If they had only used a little tact, they could have found out what it was that made me weep! What else could it be but home-sickness, a longing for my mother and my father?

They called me several names in that house — at least, everyone but the madame, and she could not get out of calling me " creature " or " thing." Of course, that is what I was to her, " a poor wee creature " !

The boy became used to me and spent much time in my company. He gave me my way in everything, because he feared to oppose me. The household was much afraid that the boy might provoke me some time and then that I might bite him as I had bitten some of the others. He was a boy like myself, and I knew that, so I was eager to have him around. It was difficult to get him to do or say anything other than make grunts and signs as he had seen his father do. These grunts and signs I heard and saw so much became a sort of new language to me, and I used them every time I wanted something.

One night after I had been put into my room, I cried so much that the boy crept from his own room over into mine. Our rooms were on the same landing, but at opposite ends of the hall, and he had to pass by his parents' chamber in order to reach mine. This he did without anyone's detecting him. He was sorry for me, crying, and he brought sweets to comfort me. Now, my room door was always locked on the outside, but the key was left in the keyhole, so it was easy for him to unlock the door and enter. The gas had been cut off from my room, and the only way to light the way there was candlelight. The boy had been forbidden to come near me after I had been locked up for the night. In fact, the whole household had been instructed to keep away from my room at night; only the butler had the privilege of my room at will, because it was his place to take care of me. But after he had run up and down all day with me, the butler was glad enough to be away from me, so I was not troubled by anyone after I had been locked in. The boy stole to my room, a lighted candle in his hand, and grunted to let me know that it was he, for he, like all the rest, thought his grunt was individual and that I must know it by heart.

I knew him and stopped crying. He sat on the floor and fed me the sweets that he had brought for me, and played with me for a long time.

Now the difficult thing for him was to get away from me to go back to his own room without making me yell. He has since said that he heard his father's voice, and he knew that it would displease him to have his authority set at naught by his own son in his own house. So when he heard the voice, he ran out of the room, but before he could get out of the door, I was close behind him, holding to his nighty. He could not get away without making a commotion, so he caught me by the back of the neck with one hand, and with the other hand over my mouth, to prevent me from making a noise, he rushed me like a dog down the stairs, through the lower corridor, to the other end of the house, and led me up the back stairway. There he stopped for a moment, and just as I was about to blurt out something, he stopped up my mouth with a lump of sugar. He got me up the back stairway to his own room at the top of the stair.

So I came into his room, the first time since I had come into that house. This was a decided turning-point, because then I first learned to sleep in a bed. The boy got me used to the bed by picking me up bodily and throwing me into it. The springs bounced me up and down and I liked it. I ran round to him so that he could do it again, and he kept this up until he became exhausted, as was I. He then stretched out on the floor, and I did the same on the bed, both of us panting for breath.

Next day the butler swore to the master that he had been the last person to visit my room, and he said that he had locked the door and had left the key inside the keyhole as usual. To his utter amazement, when he went to the room in the morning, he discovered that the room door was open and both the " little black imp " and the key were missing. He said that when he went to the young master's room, he found the " little heathen " sound asleep on the young master's bed, and the young master sound asleep *on the rug* near the bed. No one had dreamed that the young master would think of doing such a thing. But how did the young master get on to the floor, and " that creature " into the bed? No one could guess; so the whole thing remained a mystery until I began to talk English, and then I told all. I had never been brought up to have secrets, or to hide anything from my parents. I told of that incident and of many other things in that house that were not supposed to be told. How was I to know any differently? I had never been taught deceit.

From that time I was in the sole care of the boy, and I learned to wear clothes through his example. I had stopped the habit of snatching things, and I shyly waited for things to be given to me. I do not know how that habit left me, any more than I know how I first came to sit on a chair. It was difficult to make me sit on a chair in the beginning, but after the boy took me in hand, I followed him and did everything that he did. We were inseparable. I used to watch him sit in his chair and pick up his spoon or glass or cup or whatever it was, and I tried to do just what he did.

When the boy went away from the house, I was lonely and rushed to the door every now and then to see if he was coming back. The sound of his voice was welcome music to my ears. We loved each other, just as a master loves his pet dog, and the dog loves the master. The boy taught me words. That is, I began to recognize words that he said to me, and I began to say them. The first word I said in English was " bed," and then " eat." Those two words are a part of civilized culture, " eating " and " sleeping." I should say that in these Western countries the former word is deified, for many civilized people have no god except eating.

One morning, coming down to the breakfast-room, everyone was astonished to see me fully dressed, after a manner of speaking. I had the little trousers or knickerbockers on, backwards, the stockings on my arms, and the blouse on, hind part before; and I had on slippers. That was a wonderful day when they got that much on me without my tearing the clothes off; and so by degrees I was clothed nicely, and I became so tame that I stood and let them dress me properly, because I knew what they were doing and I was anxious to be like the other boy.

93

Chapter XI

A BLACK SCOTCHMAN

A devil in a restaurant. The "impossible" goes to school.
The black does not rub off. A savage truth-teller. Shipped
homeward.

One day the boy wanted to take me out for a
walk. It was warm outside, because it was now
summer, and almost everybody went to the parks
and promenaded along the Drive and Parade. The
boy had his way and took me out in company with
several other boys. These other boys could not take
their eyes off me.

I was rapidly becoming civilized. I joined in the
races in Alexandra Park, but I did not know exactly what it all meant; I just tumbled and ran and
screamed with delight as the other boys did. I cried
when my young master took me away from them.

One day my young master, with another boy,
took me out to ride on the tramway to the city.
What a thrill it was! They had me out for a long
time, and I was hungry, but I could not think of

that word "eat" to save my life. While the two
boys were busy talking to each other, in front of a
window, and, for the moment, had forgotten all
about me, I drifted along looking into the windows
by myself; and then I came to a restaurant. I since
learned the name of the place: the Grosvenor
Restaurant, behind Central Station, Glasgow. The
smell of good things in this place attracted my nostrils and I walked right in. I walked right up to the
first table, where sat a lone man with his head
buried in a newspaper. There was a hush all over
the place for a moment, as if everyone had been
struck dumb. That poor lone man, who had his head
buried in a newspaper, had a plate full of food in
front of him, but he was too busy reading to notice
the food, so I put my hand into his plate and began
to eat for him. The man must have noticed the sudden quiet; he looked up from the paper. In the
mean time I had remembered the word for hunger,
and I held out some of his good food to him, and
said: "Eat." When he saw me, instead of taking
what I offered him, he jumped up in fright and
ran out of the door; he must have thought me the
devil himself. Everybody roared with laughter.
Some men came to me, and I said: "Eat! Eat!"

My young master and his friend, who had missed
me, found me in the restaurant with a big crowd

watching me. My young master offered to pay for the stolen meal, but the owner of the place would not take anything and told my young master to bring me back again; he said he would give me all that I wanted to eat, free of charge. When the story was told at home, it made everyone laugh heartily, you may be sure.

Things went along as usual, without any change from then on, until school began, and then the young master had to leave. It was arranged to send me to a private school in Glasgow, for no one thought I could go to any other sort of school. But the young master said that if I was to go to school at all, I should go with him. His father strongly objected and told the madame that I would interfere with his son's education, and he added that I was "impossible." He said: "Why send that to school, anyway?" But the boy insisted and got his own way in the matter; and at last off to school we went together, in the train to Edinburgh, to the Sandringham House School.

I was lonesome and home-sick, and I cried most of the time. The young master was separated from me, and everything was hopeless. The boys in the school were curious about me. When I washed, all the boys stood at a distance and watched me; some of the smaller boys would come up and say to the others: "The water's not black." They could not conceive of my being a real black boy, and they wondered why the black did not rub off!

They soon became used to me and were extremely kind. But neither they nor anyone else could stop me from fretting. I dreamed dreams; I remembered the days before; I thought of my black mother and I frequently called for her. The Headmaster, seeing my home-sickness, advised my master to send me back to my own country as soon as I had finished the fourth year.

At school when anything wrong was done by any of the boys, the schoolmasters knew whom to ask for the truth. Of course, the boys soon broke me of that habit, by giving me a leathering now and then, until they made me fight; then they loved me all the more. I was not much of a fighter, as compared with Scotch boys, but the fact that I would fight at all when hit by another boy made all of them like me, although I usually got the worst of any combat. You could not blame me for the habit of telling the truth; I was on the way to becoming civilized, but I was not yet quite civilized enough to tell lies.

I was in that school four years, but I never felt settled in it; the life was so different. I loved my playmates and they loved me, and I could speak a little English by that time; but I often stopped in

97

the middle of a game or a conversation and began to cry.

Finally, when my young master and I were sent back to Glasgow from school, my old master arranged to have me shipped back to my own country. Not before he had purchased and showed my return passage to my young master would the young master consent to let me take leave of him, because we were most attached to each other. It was like losing a precious pet for him to lose me, after all the trouble he had had in training me, from the time when he had brought me into his room — practically into a new world.

My things were packed and strapped up, ready for my journey home. I had learned to call my master *Yabah ab iad,* meaning " my white father," and his madame *Ima abiada* ("my white mother "), and my young master *O re mi,* meaning " my friend." What they put into the three trunks that I took with me I did not know then, but I found out when I reached Africa. There were toys, rattles, clothes in plenty, a cot-bed, camp-table, camp-chair, lamp, knife, fork, spoon, plate, cup and saucer, and everything that is used in a Scotch home.

Chapter XII

SIX GIRLS AT ONCE

Dahomey again. Sad memories. Contrasts with civilization.
A disagreeable journey. Cruel punishment. An irate father.
Six girls at once, and Gooma, the prize. LoBagola the mystery,
even in Africa. A jealous brother. The ordeal by balance. A
wicked navel. A brother's complaint. The council. Bastinadoed.

The return trip to the coast of my country I
made without any unusual events, and I finally
reached Dahomey, the land of my home port. Then
what a scramble to get ashore over the surf! Only
a short four years before, I, with thirteen other
little black boys, Akrim the eldest, and Ojo-yola
the youngest, gazed out over the sea for the first
time, fresh from the bush, untamed and scared of
everything, and then clambered aboard the
steamer, on that ill-fated day! Just to see a white
man! When I think of it all now, it makes me weep!
My companions all lost! Dragged under the black
waters of the Gulf of Guinea! A tragedy! I alone
was saved; for what, who knows?

What was the effect of my becoming civilized?
Before I knew fifty words in the English language,
I was given a good beating *for telling the truth,*
and by the sons of *white* men. But what I had
learned! The good clothes I wore! The good things
I had to eat in the white man's country! The
street-cars, the horses and wagons and carriages,
and shops and houses, and dogs and cats, and rats
and mice! Oh no, nothing so horrible as our beastly
monkeys and leopards, ferocious lions and elephants, and snakes and lizards, which jeopardize
every step one takes. Of course, the white man's
country has the gifts of civilization, such as buses,
trucks, taxi-cabs, horse-cars, motor-cars, tramway-
cars, and hold-up men thrown in for good measure.
Oh, White Man, I think of you today in terms of
indescribable affection, on the one hand; and on
the other hand I loathe your so-called culture and
advancement, because it stole away my savage
nature. I love you because in your duality you
taught me the *surface* of good manners, although at
the cost of good *principles;* and it is still debatable
in my uncouth mind which is the better of the two,
although of course in theory they are inseparable;
but I learned from you, White Man, that they have
no affinity in actual practice. What an entire
change of view-point from that which I had before

to that which I have acquired: eating when hungry and not by the clock; sleeping when sleepy, and not by custom; resting when tired, and not by command or when the boss says " Stop " !

I stand on the coast of my country once more, gazing out over the black waters of the Gulf of Guinea, which had robbed me of my companions, clinging to the only vestige of my natural self left —my intrinsic manhood.

I reached my own community, after having waited three months on the coast before I was able to find guides to escort me north to my own wild people, and after a most disagreeable forty-seven days' journey, in the company of a hostile crowd of men. Finally I reached my native village. There was the place of my birth, my father's home.

The men who brought me up through the Ondo bush made me suffer much. They did not know I understood every word that they said; and I would not reveal to them that I knew anything, before reaching my village. Otherwise they would have left me stranded in the middle of the Ondo bush. When I arrived, I had their hands tied behind them, had them severely flogged, had oil put on their heads, and a fire set to it, and then gave them the chance to run for their very lives. That was their pay for annoyances.

My mother had died shortly after we boys had left the village, on that fateful night, but my father lived and he knew me and was glad to see me.

I explained as well as I could to my father all that had happened, and told him as much as he would permit me to tell about the white men, emphasizing the story of my white father; but when I repeatedly mentioned my white father, he became angry and said: " I am your father; you have no white father, you fool! Don't you know that you cannot be white and black at the same time? " He asked me about marriage, and I asked him about the old chief, O-lou-wa-li, and about his beautiful daughter, Gooma. He assured me that Gooma had been chosen to be my bride — that is, to be my last wife, for my father had selected six girls for me to marry, before I had left home. Such selection is always made early in life in the case of an heir, the youngest son in the home, as I was. The chance of having Gooma as a bride compensated me for all the suffering that I had undergone from the time when I had left my native village. I was willing to marry forty girls if Gooma was to become my bride.

Marrying in my country is not a simple matter. When my father offered me in marriage and promised Gooma as bride, I was too young to realize the sacred ordinance and above all to know about the ordeal that awaited me — that is, marrying six maidens at the same time. I was now only eleven years old, and I had just returned home from Scotland, after having been away from my native Africa four years. I was not fully matured, but I had begun to feel that I was a man. When my father told me that Gooma was to be my bride, I thought I knew what it meant and I was anxious to go through the ceremony. Little did I dream what was to happen and what consequences would ensue. All that I thought of was Gooma.

The girl seemed to know much more than other girls and boys. Whether because Gooma had saved my life, or because I loved her, I had chosen her as a playmate before I left home, even though it was unusual for native boys to play at all with girls. Gooma and I liked each other all the more after she had saved my life from a man-eating lion. Gooma singled me out for walks around the villages, and I felt lonesome when she was not with me.

Once when Gooma and I were together, some boys of my village called after me the name that they had heard their fathers now call me, *Yem-saah,* meaning " Mystery." That was one of the reasons why I did not choose to be in their company at all. Everyone called me " Mystery " and I was not

103

pleased. That was all I could hear since I returned from Scotland; so then I took Gooma as my companion as much as I could, although it displeased my father and my eldest brother.

I had been transformed during the four years that I had been away, and I had become used to the company of women and had quite a different view of them from that of the men in my land.

My eldest brother was furious. He questioned me about my conduct, but I offended him by looking him in the eye while he talked; that was disrespectful for a boy in my country. The punishment for this infringement of native etiquette is severe; a boy is tied to a stake in the heat of the sun, in the middle of the day, and left there four hours. When the boy is released from the stake, he is likely to die from sunstroke. Usually the complaint comes from a parent or near relative, but never from a sister or a mother.

When my brother had summoned me to come before him, I had said: " Tell him to wait." I committed a serious offence by thus answering and by not immediately obeying him. When I did appear, instead of standing with bowed head, as our boys are taught to do in the presence of elders, I sat in front of him and looked him straight in the eye, as one does in Scotland. My brother cursed me, called

me " Son of a Monkey," and spit in my face. Then
he struck me across the face with the back of his
hand. I could stand no more and I flew at him, hit
him, and struck and scratched him badly. I had
been taught to hit back when I was in school in
Edinburgh, and I had become used to fighting. I
forgot, for the moment, that it was my eldest
brother; otherwise I should not have acted so un-
wisely. My brother, dumbfounded, did not even hit
me back, but yelled loudly. My brother was a full-
grown man and could have given me a beating, but
such an action as mine had never happened before
in my country. So he was paralysed with astonish-
ment.

His yells attracted all his women, of whom he
had twenty-one. His chief wife ran to his house
with all the other wives, and they all screamed and
shouted: " *Haram Alake!* (A shame to God!)"
I realized what folly I was committing, so I jumped
off my brother, who lay stretched on the ground,
and ran out of his compound. I kept running until
I reached my father's compound. I passed several
old men, but I did not salute them in the customary
manner — another breach of native etiquette that
brought abuse on the head of my father and ren-
dered me liable to further punishment. Many native boys have been put to death for conduct less

offensive, and I should have been put to death if my father had been guided by the persuasion of my eldest brother.

I was brought before the community chief and charged with " laughing at the beards of old men " whom I had passed in a hurry and to whom I had not given the customary salutations. I was judged guilty even before I went to the community chief; therefore I had to go through " the ordeal," just as other boys would have had to do. I stood before the chief and his counsellors with bowed head, and on my head I balanced a calabash dish full of palm-oil. While the old men, my accusers, piled up my offences, I had to hold my head still and not spill a drop of palm-oil. When I heard the accusers tell false things about me, I simply had to speak, and every time I spoke I moved my head and spilled oil. For every drop spilled from the dish I had to receive a hard smack on the cheek from every member of the council, including the chief and the old men who accused me, about twenty-five people smacking me every time I spilled a drop of oil, and that was many times. One old man said that my navel-cord must be crooked and he demanded that I be given to a medicine-man to have the evil spirit that controlled me removed. That would have caused my death, because when the devilish medicine-men get hold of a boy to purify his cord, they usually injure him so that he dies. They then give as an excuse that there was so much evil in the cord that it overcame all the good which they had intended putting into the cord, and death is considered the best thing that could happen to one who carried so much evil. Even parents believe the medicine-men and think it is a blessing that the child died. I did not realize the full extent of my danger at that time, but my father did, and he was inclined to be lenient because I was his youngest son, his heir, and the holder of the birthright of the family. My father opposed every motion to have me punished further.

The hardest blow came when my own brother put in his complaint. My father had promised to punish me for my offence to my brother, and so he thought my brother satisfied. My poor father was stunned when he saw his authority set at naught by his own son. My brother said many things against me. He told about my attack upon him and supported his statement with the statement of his bride.

Now was the time for my father to stab at my brother and make an impression upon the chief and his counsellors. My father said: " It is a shame on my beard that I should have given life to a son

107

who must call upon a woman for support." The chief agreed with him and told my father that if he himself had such a son he would put him amongst the girls.

Then my brother complained about my having been in the company of Gooma, "the outcast." Since Gooma was from a different people, and I was not a fetish-worshipper, my brother's complaint did not bring the desired result.

The question arose whether or not I was the *real* son of my father, so the matter was referred to the fetish-doctor, the spiritual head of my country. The fetish-doctor supported the assertion that I was not the son of my father and said that my father had taken me in place of his lost heir, Bata Kindai.

The civil King of my country then intervened on behalf of my father, because my father had gained distinction as a warrior and had been made a *Balogun* chief (fighting chief). The King stopped the fetish-doctor from proceeding with my purification. The chief rabbi of my own people also pleaded with the fetish-doctor and convinced him that my father told the truth about my being his rightful heir. Under fetish-law no one can take the place of an heir to a family, so the witch-doctors and their chief were all against me. Some of my acquired habits made them believe that I was no blood kin to my father. I wore a few clothes, I slept on a cotbed, I had a lamp, and I talked to women. Much of my time I spent in the company of Gooma, my betrothed, in preference to boys. The boys never believed what I told them about the outside world, but Gooma did. The boys called me " Mystery," but Gooma did not. Gooma addressed me as " Small Grain," or Unquatwa, the name my mother thought of at my birth, whose meaning is " Troubled Waters." My father called me Bata Kindai, because I was his heir and he wanted me to follow in his footsteps. He called me " Small Grain " and " The Sole of My Foot," the literal translation of " Bata Kindai."

The outcome of the trials and tests for the wrongs I had committed against my eldest brother, and the affront to the old men, was that I got a good beating on the soles of my feet, every complainant being allowed to strike me five times on my bare feet. How cruel it felt when my brother's turn came! His strokes were harder than those of any of the old men, who numbered six. Needless to say, I was hardly able to stand for days afterwards. Considering all the offences, I was extremely lucky.

It is customary for a father to punish a boy later,

but my good father did not raise his hand to me. Old Chief O-lou-wa-li, foster-father of Gooma, liked me and would have saved me from the beating had he been able. O-lou-wa-li was a fetish-worshipper and therefore a more influential chief than my father, but he had lost his prestige on account of his daughter Gooma, so he did not offer assistance, for he thought that if he attempted to intervene, it might do more harm than good, and that his word as a nobleman might be ignored, a serious thing for a man of distinction in my country.

Chapter XIII

TRAINING AND TORTURE

*The box of chastity. The mask of chastity. Special training.
A lying accusation. A special council. The argument. The de-
mand for burning. Crocodile tears. Gooma is beaten. Appeal to
Oro.*

My father, as a matter of fact, was more concerned in securing wives for me than in punishing
me. He had chosen the matchmaker to decide upon
my fitness for marriage and the girls' fathers had
done the same. None of the other girls who were to
become my wives liked Gooma, and they did not
wish to stand the test with her.

Ordinarily, in my country we boys wear no
clothing at all. We simply go about as naked as we
were born. But at this time a chastity box is
strapped across the front of us and tied around the
hips. It is a fetish-belief that such a box checks
desire. According to this custom, then, I had to
wear a mask called the " mask of chastity," made
to cover my head, with holes for the eyes and mouth.

111

It was made of wild grass called *trava*. It had a devilish look, and nobody wanted to speak to me while I wore it. The girls who were to marry me had to disguise themselves as I did, only their head masks were not so enveloping as mine. They also had to wear chastity boxes. I had to go about in this fashion for twelve months, and during that time I had to be much with my matchmaker and the matchmakers of the girls who were to become my wives. Matchmakers may be men or women, according to the choice of the father. My mother was dead, and so was Gooma's, but the mothers of the other five girls lived, and they busied themselves with their own daughters, explaining marriage. Gooma's father spent much time with me, and so did my own father.

The matchmakers took me out of the village twice a week for about three months before the time of the vows and put me through exercises, followed by massage to stimulate me. My body was then oiled all over. I was examined each time to see if my strength had increased. After going through these manœuvres I was put into a hut, built for the purpose, and watched through the walls. Then suddenly down would come a shower of cold water all over me, and instead of feeling stimulated, I would feel exhausted. Then I would be masked again, and

112

the box would be adjusted. Then I was blindfolded and led out of the bush, for that is where all these things took place, and turned loose in the village. I never could guess what would be done to me from one time to another. I had to wait and see; some new trick was always being played. All boys have to go through these trials before they marry, but it is never a subject of discussion.

The time came for the vows. On that day all the girls were lined up by their own matchmakers. Young boys sang a native song meaning: " Your manhood has been pronounced perfect; so use it." All native songs are repetitions; the words are sung over and over.

The girls watched this performance, and when it was finished, each girl was led before me singly, by one of the old women. Each girl was commanded by the old woman to kneel down in front of a phallic image made for the occasion. Then they sang a marriage song which means: " What a delight to me! What a delight to me! " The native words are: " *Aah-gu-ru-ma, guru-ma, aah-gu-ru-ma, yay-gaga-hogya, yay-gaga-hogya, yay-gaga guru-ma.*" The girls danced to this song for hours, and I sat there and witnessed everything. My father kept the image as a trophy.

Before the trial my eldest brother made an

accusation against me. He said that a boy had seen Gooma and me together in the bush, and that we had removed our chastity boxes. The boy, he said, had told this tale to him and had sworn to its truth by the beard of his father and by the strands of hair on his belly. This is a peculiar oath taken by boys in my country when they wish someone to believe their statements. The boy had lied, of course, but now again I was accused by my own brother, and I had to prove that the boy lied. That was a difficult thing to do, but I did it nevertheless. If I had failed to do so, I should have had the tokens of my manhood taken from me, and Gooma would have been mutilated, too.

My father and old Chief O-lou-wa-li were ordered to present us before a special council. I was surprised, because I did not know what it was all about, and when I asked my father, he replied: "Your new ideas bring shame on my head; you will smart for your deviltry." Neither he nor old Chief O-lou-wa-li knew who had accused Gooma and me.

The council consisted of all the matchmakers and the chief witch-doctor, who presided. Gooma and I were ushered before the council. We sat directly in front of our fathers, but dared not look towards each other. We sat in our masks, and oh, how I should have liked to speak to Gooma and ask her what it was all about!

You could have knocked my poor old father over with a feather when he saw my own brother accuse me before the council. My brother saluted everyone in the usual manner; then the witch-doctor chanted a song, supposed to exhort the spirits to clean the tongue of the accuser to enable him to tell the truth. My real accuser was the boy, but no boy can accuse another boy before a council; he must state his case to some adult, and if the adult thinks it proper to believe the boy, he makes complaint. Everybody present was thunderstruck to learn that it was my own brother who accused me.

When one accuses another before the council, he never jumps into the business right away, but makes a long speech and repeats a number of native sayings before he mentions the subject of importance. That was the way my brother proceeded. " Gazelles are fleet of foot, always," he said. While he talked, everyone repeated what he said. He continued: " A snake is slow, but I do not know an animal that can outrun a gazelle, nor a reptile that can fool a snake. It is sad when a bird tries to mate with an elephant; it strikes me the poor thing must waste a lot of energy. Have you ever known an elephant who could fall into water without making

115

a splash? I am sure a lizard would know that it is impossible for a monkey to become a zebra. Buffaloes are hard-headed, and so is the son of my father hard-headed. I am convinced that even our laws must be obeyed, or we should never have goodness in the land. But how can you heal a sore before it has become worse? When the evil spirit told my father's son to break his vows, he did so, and he should accept his punishment. One whom we all know, and whose father has given him wonderful girls to wife, has sorely pledged himself to save our good and holy law from being profaned; that person saw with an unsleeping eye an act that makes the blood of our fathers jump. A female knows no better than to be loyal to him whom she loves; therefore I feel that Gooma also has an evil spirit. I say that the son of my father is guilty and that he deserves the punishment of fire, lest the spirits avenge themselves upon our families. Burn them! Bata Kindai and Gooma! Burn them!''

I was dumbfounded, because I knew that neither Gooma nor I had committed an offence. Poor girl, I see her now as she sat gazing with her brown eyes, eyes that did not belong to people like those around her. Gooma wept, because she knew that all the charges were lies, wicked black lies. The entire council rose and held up their hands, and the

116

chief witch-doctor screamed aloud: " Fathers of your children! Put this to the test! This must be so!"

When old Chief O-lou-wa-li and my father jumped up to protest, because they knew what such action by the council meant, the chief witch-doctor asked my father and O-lou-wa-li this question: " Did you ever know anyone that is accused to tell the truth?"

These men were guided by the heathen religion of a primitive and ignorant people. Our fathers had to abide by the decision, which was final.

Gooma and I were taken to our homes and put through a kind of third degree to make us admit the charge. We were lucky, because our own fathers did the testing, and not the devilish witch-doctors. When a case of this kind is given to the witches and witch-doctors, the poor victim seldom lives to admit anything. My father, I know, was sorry, but he could not show it. If he had cried, that would have been unpardonable, because a man should never be so weak as to cry; if he wishes to cry, he gets his women to cry for him. My father acted harsh and cruel in order not to break down, but I know that his heart nearly broke every time he hit me.

The women in my father's compound were

commanded to come forth and to weep and wail. If a woman does not feel like crying or cannot cry, there is always a certain preparation they find that makes the tears fall like rain, and then all the women have to do is to scream. That is why we say, when we see a woman weeping, that it is only *maskara,* meaning " crocodile tears." No one, therefore, ever sympathizes with a woman in tears, even if the tears are real.

Old Chief O-lou-wa-li loved his child beyond the understanding of his own wives, but he had to torture her to make her confess. Gooma took the greatest oath that could be taken in my country, to prove that she was innocent. She said that she would stand upon the head of the crocodile, our sacred animal, to prove she told the truth. Gooma was only a little girl, and I a little boy, barely thirteen years old. Poor Gooma was tied to stakes, stretched out flat on the ground, and whipped and whipped and whipped; her eyebrows were burned off and she was starved, to make her admit that she had broken her vows; but she stuck to her denial, and so did I. Old Chief O-lou-wa-li did not administer the punishment to Gooma, but he witnessed it. His wives did the torturing, so the poor child suffered greatly, because the women of the old chief did not like Gooma, and they heaped curse upon curse on her head. The names they called her made the blood curdle.

It was my father who punished me, and I believe that I made him more cruel, because every time he struck me with the stick over my bare back, I said that I would go back to my white father in Scotland, and I continually called on him and on his white son, my friend. I bear the marks on my back today from the severe floggings that I received.

The severe beatings, and the torture of hot needles in my tongue, stopped, but my statement was still a complete denial, and it was the same with Gooma. My eldest brother began to feel worried, because it looked as if he were to be laughed at as a false accuser.

The council was called again, and poor Gooma and I were dragged to the place of meeting. My brother explained how he came by the tale. He said that he loved me, his father's favourite son. At this my father objected and said: " Principal son." My brother continued, saying that it pained him to accept a story against his good little brother, and he could even then hardly believe such a thing. He warmed up and tried once more to force the case against Gooma and me and continued talking. He added that his information had come from a reliable source, a small boy, and that it is as impossible

119

for a little boy's mind to tell a straight lie as
it is for a leopard to drink with a lion. "Therefore," he said, "this pair deserve to be burned."
He stopped talking, because he had again demanded that Gooma and I should be tortured.

Old Chief O-lou-wa-li could bear no more. He
jumped up and answered by saying: "We must
leave this case to Oro!"

No one dared to oppose this, because everyone
knew that it was just. Oro is a native fetish-super-
stition; the people believe that the Oro god can find
out all wrong-doers, because everyone who has committed wrong of any kind must admit that wrong
to the Oro god when it is brought round, seven
times a year, and seven days at each time. No native
would think of hiding any wrong from the Oro, because he believes that in so doing he would bring
terrible disaster upon everyone. We had to wait
until Oro sounded.

The chief witch-doctor stood up and said that he
knew that O-lou-wa-li was just in wishing to refer
the case to all-seeing Oro. He added: "Woe be to
the one whom Oro puts his finger upon; it would be
better for him never to have been born." My
brother did not feel comfortable, because he knew
that he had put the devil in that small boy's heart
to say what he had said.

Chapter XIV

ORO, THE GOD OF TRUTH

The punishments of Oro. Argument about LoBagola. The special council. The meeting ends. My father's complaint. My brother's horror. Appeal to the " Circle."

In the days that followed, my brother tried in many ways to be friendly with me, but my father kept me from him as much as possible. As for Gooma, all the women who had unmercifully flogged the poor girl wanted to be kind to her, but O-lou-wa-li kept Gooma from them as much as he could. The women had not taken part in the accusation; they had done only what they had been ordered. But they had been most cruel.

The time for Oro came, and everybody prepared. Women dare not show themselves during the seven days of Oro; they must confine themselves to their own compounds until it is all over. On the first night of Oro nothing unusual happened. Gooma and I did not go out to meet Oro, because we had done no wrong. The little boy who had told the story and my brother did not appear either. The little boy who had sworn that what he had said was true was a fetish-worshipper; my brother belonged to the "strange people." The little boy had no one in his own faith to consult, because no fetish person would give him any encouragement in the wrong that he had committed. My brother had the rabbi of our own faith, with whom he could talk the matter over before going out to the Oro. Although we are a separate people, with an entirely different religion, we are nevertheless compelled to comply with all fetish-laws regarding taboos and secret organizations. One thing we did have above the other people — seven rabbis, who were the guardians of our faith and morals. Whenever difficulty arose, we had the rabbis to consult. In this business the chief rabbi was unwilling to interfere, because it would bring down severe abuse on our community if he dared to condone the dreadful evil of delivering one of his own blood up to another people. So my brother was advised to go out to Oro, after the boy had gone, and tell all he knew of this affair, and let all be the truth.

The next night Oro sounded and it was louder and more weird than ever. Three men went before Oro on complaint of their wives. Every one of these men had ten wives, and the complaint was that

122

every man had visited the last wife too long. One man had refused to go with any of his other wives; another had taken his bride into his own house to live with him, saying that she was too delicate to work around the compound with other women; the third had remained with his bride all the time. All three men lost their wives, and all three were so mutilated that one of the three died and the other two lived in mockery the remainder of their lives, in a compound called "the place of the *agha*" (eunuchs). On this same night many other punishments were decreed. Two girls lost their fingers for stealing something, and a boy was ordered put to death by the Ogboni society for disobedience.

The little boy who had complained of me did not appear before Oro that night. On the third night the boy appeared and related his story. He said that he was not friendly with Ibn LoBagola; neither were any of the other boys, because of the strange way that Ibn LoBagola had of talking with girls and playing with them, and because Ibn LoBagola had brought forbidden ways into the land. He said that he had told the brother of Ibn LoBagola how he had seen the girl Gooma and me in each other's company many times, and that the brother of Ibn LoBagola had urged him to repeat his

123

statement over and over again and had added a few words every time.

The case became controversial, and therefore no punishment could be given until ordered by the particular council where it was first heard. My brother appeared before Oro, and his statement was brief, saying that he had no evil intentions, and that it was justice that prompted him to bring complaint against the son of his own father. During all this time my father was not asleep, nor was old Chief O-lou-wa-li. Both had received the report of the findings of the guardians of Oro, and they pushed the matter ahead quickly.

It was the day just before Oro ended when my brother gave his statement to Oro. I can never forget that day. If the case had turned against Gooma and me, it would have delayed my marriage another year, because of the burning that I should have suffered.

The meeting of the special council was called. Oh, what a meeting! Gooma and I cried! We pitied each other's state. I was still tender, and so was that flower Gooma. Tears bring no pity in my country, but usually scorn, but we cried nevertheless. I am crying now, as I write about it. I honestly believe that my brother was prompted by a sense of duty, not by spite. Although my brother had me tested by ordeal and torture and had me flogged, he was prompted by his natural sense of right. Had I not learned many strange things during the four years that I had been out of my country? When the meeting was over and we were vindicated, my father gave me his hand to kiss; and how I kissed it! Never before had I clung to the hand of my father as I did then. Gooma kissed the foot of old Chief O-lou-wa-li and washed it with her tears. We kissed the hands of all the adults present and then sat down greatly relieved.

I was willing to take as many wives as my father desired me to take, which was a task, because he had already chosen six girls for me to marry at the same time, which was a little out of the ordinary; but my father was eager, so I bowed to his will.

My father stood up, which meant that a storm was brewing in his breast, and addressed the council in the following manner, saying: " It may be that the father to the mother of that son who calls me father ran fast after the woman that bore the mother who gave birth to the mother of the son that calls me father. If he only ran after her, let us rejoice, but it is plainly seen that he caught her, and I have my hairs to witness that the female was a monkey."

This was a terrible statement. My poor brother

shrieked, and he dripped with perspiration, and he cried out to the chief witch-doctor to save him from harshness from the lips of his own father.

Old Chief O-lou-wa-li rose and began to talk. He started slowly, but he became excited and screamed. He demanded that this affair be left to the " Circle." Now, the " Circle " in my home is a bad thing. Anyone who is accused in a " Circle " is always killed in a horrible way for the pleasure of the King. The " Circle " is an ancient custom seldom followed. Its purpose originally was to discover those who had evil in their hearts and who conspired against the King. The witches and witch-doctors had charge of the " Circle "; it was their business to smell out the guilty persons. This practice had been abolished. It could be revived, however, at any time, but only at the pleasure of the King. Now when old Chief O-lou-wa-li called to the chief witch-doctor to let the " Circle " decide the case, he surely had it in mind to have my brother killed.

The chief rabbi of my people forced my father to oppose the terrible suggestion. My father said aloud: " Not a drop of my son's blood shall run."

Chapter XV

WHEN A MAN MARRIES, HIS TROUBLES
BEGIN

The council decrees punishments. A child marriage in Africa.
Public nuptials. Gooma, the impulsive. Gooma disgraced.
Gooma the Amazon.

The statement of my father that not a drop of
my blood should be shed meant that he did not
wish that my case should cause the death of me or
of anyone else of his family. In order that the de-
mand to call a " Circle " might be carried out,
O-lou-wa-li, the old chief, had to obtain the consent of the King, and it was not likely that the King
would revive the old custom unless he himself were
directly concerned; and then another thing, the
life of a member of the family of one of the King's
noblemen was at stake, and that nobleman had
opposed extreme measures. As O-lou-wa-li knew
all this, he contented himself by asking that the
council have its wish.

The council did not take long in deciding the

case. The result was that my poor brother had his beard plucked out in public, and the little fool boy had his tongue slit for telling a malicious lie. My father held a three days' festival over the outcome of the case, because Gooma and I were vindicated and permitted to continue preparing for our marriage.

My back was still sore from the severe floggings that I had received in the ordeal. At that time I soon forgot it. Was not Gooma to be my bride? But now I can never forget.

I had become eager to leave my country again, because everything offended me. The difficulty arose as to how I was going to get out safely. My father would never give me safe-conduct, and I was sure that he would oppose anyone who tried to help me go away, but I did not worry much about it then. I had to wait for marriage, at least, before I could even think of leaving home again.

I acted as if I were going on a picnic when the time came for my marriage, with its trials and feasts. Little did I dream that it was for a funeral that I was preparing. Yes, a funeral, indeed, for did they not murder the flower of womanhood? Was I not the innocent cause of breaking the heart of a true man through our barbarous, brutal fetish-custom, which seemed to prove that his daughter had

128

anticipated her marriage vows? Natural causes, and not infidelity, as they all thought, gave grounds for the accusation. But you cannot convince the people in my country that nature does things; they are too suspicious to understand natural effects.

When a boy takes a wife, he must establish her virginity in the open before the people. Now, Gooma had no mother waiting at home for the familiar sound of rejoicing that all mothers love to hear, when their daughters have been proved pure; no mother to have a broken heart if the contrary report came; no mother to allay her fears or to comfort her.

The fatal night came, after fourteen long months of waiting and wearing the mask of chastity. Gooma passed the preliminary test of the match-makers, and so did I, but it was generally thought that the girl would be more than a match for me.

There was one strong reason why my father was anxious to get me married, and that was to save me from disgrace. According to my people, I had disgraced myself by going far away across the sea and then returning, wearing clothes that came from another people. My father had a difficult task to convince the fetish-doctor that I was his son, and that I did not have evil spirits. So his first step was to get me married to the girls to whom I was already

129

betrothed, and he set the beautiful Gooma to be my last, called "the bride."

Of course I went through the ceremony all right, but I hardly realized what it was all about. After the modesty of a Scotch home I was hardly ready for such brazen acts as confronted me. I was too young to dispute with my father; in fact, too young even to ask why. The crowd gathered and I prepared for my part. The first girl was so wild that she broke her bonds, and the old men had to hold her, but finally she was conquered. Then there were the beat of tomtoms and the chanting of the old hags who had matched us, each one separately! It was all bewildering, so that I did not realize what I was doing.

The young maidens stood waiting, ready to hasten away to the girl's mother, who is not allowed to be present, but waits patiently at her own house for the welcome sound of the words: "The Spirit has given you a true daughter. Bravo!"

It is not always that a boy is given six girls to marry at the same time. With me it was different, because I had been out of my own country, and my father was not quite sure about my intentions; therefore he was eager to bind me tightly to maintain the respect of the fetish-people. So my ordeal was quite a strain, considering everything.

The next four girls were led forward. Then everybody stopped to eat and feast. Remember, I had one more to wed, and she was like Katharina the Shrew, many thought. No one expected anything startling to happen; in fact, when the matchmaker reported Gooma's attitude, she said that the girl was very happy and was talking of what she was going to make for her husband's first meal, and how eager she was to live with him. Gooma showed no sign of fear or embarrassment, which made everyone respect her. The moment arrived. When the big gong and the tomtom, covered with human hide, sounded, some rushed about the scene, while others kept on dancing.

Then the music and singing ceased, and the place was quiet; I remember distinctly that a sort of fear crept over me, for I could not understand what it was all about. No speaking, no jokes. When some young fellow began to make a little fun, they all glared at him for it. Just like a funeral! What had happened? What was going to happen? I couldn't understand.

But I soon found out; how, I don't know; but I found out just the same. It was the lovely Gooma who was being led into the circle. One old man said she would attempt to kill me, so I would have to hit her to quiet her. They all tried to impress on me

131

how difficult it would be for me to rule her. As for me, I thought different; I don't know why, but I felt that I should be able to live with this flower better than with any other. I was inclined to be soft and tender with this particular girl and always to treat her kindly. Perhaps I was inclined to love her; who knows? I was too young to know what it all meant. Gooma leaped out, laughing merrily; usually when a girl is so cheerful at that particular time, everyone else feels good also. But this time not one remark was passed.

The old chief, O-lou-wa-li, had great things in store for his favourite child, whom he claimed as his own, but who was nevertheless no blood kin to him whatsoever. He roamed about the compound, arranging to hear the welcome news of the child's marriage. He had to take the place of both father and mother, for Gooma had no mother. He was not present during the ceremony, but he was very happy. He had planned to set a precedent in the marriage customs in our country by giving me a present, instead of my father's or my sending one to him, as is usual.

Who would ever have dreamed that I, the black boy who was getting married, one day would be telling the whole world about Gooma? She had many names, some of which are: " The Evil One ";

"The Enticer of Goodness"; "Kin to the Female Monkey"; "The Cunning One"; "The Temptress"; "The Bold"; "The Brazen"; "Faithful Enemy to Good" and "The Amazon." These and other worse names had been thrown at this splendid girl.

She took her place as the other girls had done, and waited for the ceremony. I can't say just what it was, but some force moved me on; and yet my cheerfulness was affected, for I was heavy-hearted. When I took my place with Gooma, the good girl actually embraced me! Now, this action was against all rules of native etiquette. What girl would do such a thing, even if she felt affection, except Gooma? This girl was always doing something different from other girls, but always before she had kept within the bounds of the taboo-laws. Then Gooma stood, and moved no more. To the people her act meant that she could not be a wife, that she was not a virgin — in their eyes Gooma had fallen! Gooma, poor Gooma! The sweet, gentle, loving Gooma was lost — at least, lost to me! When I learned it, I wept; I don't know why, but I cried hard.

Picture the scene: the people, the matchmaker, who heaped curse upon curse on the head of the impulsive girl, barely eleven years old, so different from all the other girls of our race. All the women-folk were bitter in denunciation, while the men contented themselves with the remark: "What is a woman but a feather, beautiful to look at?"

The men took me back to the house and explained all that had happened, and how Gooma had broken the great fetish-law. I cried and repeated, and shall do so until I die: "*Da ke-dep,*" meaning: "It is a lie!"

I believe that I was the only one that kissed the hand of old Chief O-lou-wa-li at this hour of anguish for him. Of course I was not able to do anything. I had to listen to the older men, who condemned Gooma. It never dawned upon these thick, ignorant, stupid heathens that they might be wrong. They were our leaders, our wise men. I did not know then, but I know now, that Gooma was as innocent and as pure as any girl that ever walked. At that time I was only thirteen and I knew only what I had been taught by the older men and my father. I believed the men, and I believed my own father, but something within me impelled me to say out loud: "It is a lie! Gooma is a good girl for a wife."

The old chief killed himself. Gooma was unsexed and put into the King's compound. She became one of the King's chief Amazon fighters and counsellors. I still say I had six wives, but only five lived in my compound; Gooma lived with the King. Gooma was a princess by birth, for her real father, the chief of his people, had fallen under the assagai of old Chief O-lou-wa-li.

Chapter XVI

WHY GO NATIVE?

Followers. Disgust with native life. My children. A story by the village fire.

After my marriage I took my five girls to my compound, and my father secured fourteen " followers " for me, according to custom in my home. Now, in all justice, I could not very well leave these five wives of mine before at least a month had passed, so I settled down to domestic life, as best I could. My father did not live long after; he felt that he had completed his share when he had me, his strange son, safely married. But he little knew what thoughts and aspirations were nursed in my bosom. He had not weighed in his mind the change that I was undergoing and had undergone. He little dreamed that when I looked at his naked body (for he, like others in the village, went round quite naked), I felt a kind of disgust.

I had been out of my country for four long years, among other people, and the change in me was no-

136

ticeable. I wore clothes — scanty, of course, but clothes nevertheless. These and many other habits made everyone look on me with distrust and superstitious fear, and it was that superstitious fear that saved me in many disputes with the fetish-doctor, who tried to make it taboo to enter my compound or to listen to my talk.

But, after all, I am of my father, and he was a man of distinction and of noble birth among his people, and I was also a part of the people of my country; therefore it was impossible to taboo me. I admit that I provoked hostile feeling through indulging in my civilized habits, such as sleeping on a cot-bed, sitting on a chair, wearing trousers instead of a caftan, and burning a lamp, which I kept on a camp-table. All these things I had brought with me from Europe. I ate my food in the presence of my women, for I had become used to the company of women, having lived in Scotland, where the woman is the head of the house. I ate from a plate and used a knife and fork, all of which was strange and foreign to my people.

Being the youngest son of my father's bride, I have the birthright of my father, and I am allowed to use his name, and may call myself "chief," under native law. If I had never left my country again, I should have become a community chief.

My brothers and sisters are all in Africa, and I am sure that they have no desire ever to leave there; but I am more of a stranger to them than to anyone else. I have never regretted the loss of any of the wives that I married, except Gooma, who, I still feel, is my bride, my last and my principal wife. But the children of these wives are my chief concern, and I often yearn to see them. I am the father of fourteen boys. My children I love, but I never did love my wives. Who could love six?

Sometimes, even now, my thoughts go back to the stories we used to hear about the village fires at night, with the wild light leaping up and making dreadful shadows. Here is one of them:

HOW A MONKEY SHOWED LOYALTY TO HIS TRIBE

Once upon a time, there lived far in the bush an old ape. This old ape had been a guard for the tribe for many a long moon. It was said that he had once been chief of the herd, but through indiscretion he had fallen from that high station. It was known among all the animal people that he had no male offspring, and this was one of the reasons why he had lost his high place. Even the young monkeys treated him with scorn, because their parents had taught them to look down on him. To remedy the

138

wrongs of this old monkey would have been like trying to pick up scattered feathers that the wind blew about. His age no one could guess; he seemed older, and yet appeared younger, than anything else that lived in the bush. He was able to do anything that another monkey could do, and do it without effort, although the others were younger than he. He was noted for wisdom above all the elders in the tribe. His memory was like the rubber, going back further than the memory of the elephant. Who really knew this fellow? No one did. Who ever knew as much as this chap? No one did. He was referred to in every dispute, and his opinions were taken as the final word. Yet he was the butt and sport of all the monkey people. When he tried to gain praise for some wise suggestion, it brought upon him abuse and ridicule from every monkey in the tribe. His names were many, such as " The Wise Fool," " The Cunning Fraud," " The Make-Believer," " The Wicked One," " The Seducer," " The Liar," " The Friend of Man "; and for a monkey to be a friend of man is considered, among the monkey people, to be on the lowest level, because monkeys hate human beings.

After a time the monkey people became so cruel to the old monkey that he had to find another place, but one monkey tribe will never show hospitality to a monkey from another tribe. So it was useless for him to seek a home with other monkeys. They drove him away and some of the females tried to encourage the males to put him to death, because they said that no good could ever come out of anything so evil as that old deceiver. Every day the women spied on him or sent children to spy on him, so that they could report all his actions to the men in the tribe. If he was seen speaking with the elephant or the lion or even the innocent gazelle, they pretended to the tribe that he was plotting against them.

So one day, out of despair, he wandered quite a distance away and became so tired that he climbed a large vine and began thinking of his former state and of all he had lost, and he began to weep. He felt as if he would like to give up all and die; but he said to himself that he would like to do something first, in order to prove to his tribe that he still loved them, and that he was not so bad as he was made out to be. While he was thus thinking, he heard some talking, and he lay quiet and listened. It was the voice of the snake, and by it he discovered that he was resting just over a house of horned vipers.

It appeared that one of the snake couriers had brought news and orders from the chief of their tribe, saying that all snakes should muster together and be ready to make a raid on the village of the great apes. He heard one snake say that it would be a good thing to drive these cowards from the bush, as they were getting so bold that they began to think they were the owners of the bush. And another snake said that this was the best time for the raid, because the great apes were unguarded; for one of the young snakes had said he had seen the old guard wandering away, far from his village, all by himself. If that were so, he must have been driven away, for no monkey would venture away from his people, alone, otherwise. Now was the time to strike, and to strike hard.

The old monkey, hiding up in the vine, heard all this and wondered what to do; for he could not get away from his hiding-place without being seen, and he knew that if he was seen by a snake, short work would be made of him. But he thought that if he could just give the alarm to the tribe, that would be sufficient to save all his people from the horrible death that was planned for them. By this means he could show his loyalty to them. So he made a dash to get by, but he was detected at the first move he made. And in his excitement to get away, his arm was caught in a vine and he was overtaken by a young viper, who struck at him.

141

But you know that when you are frightened, your strength becomes double. The old monkey pulled and tugged until he got himself loose, but not before the young snake had struck him several times, which meant that he had to die.

When the old monkey had freed himself from the vine, he ran as fast as his legs would carry him, screaming the warning, and yelping with pain. The warning, you know, is " *Oo-lou-wi!* " meaning: " I see danger! " Now, he had to run far, and when he reached the camp, all the monkeys had prepared to flee, because they had heard the warning yells from afar. When the old monkey arrived, just at the opening of the village, he dropped down from exhaustion and from the effects of the poison that had been sent through him by the stinging he received from the young snake.

In the mean time the whole snake family came on the run, for they believed that they could overtake the old monkey before he arrived at his camp. On the other hand, all the other monkeys in camp derided and abused the old guard and accused him of playing a trick on them to get back into the tribe for shelter and protection. One monkey said that if they had known that it was that base faker who had given the warning, they would not have prepared to break up camp and run. While this was

142

being said, the snakes were near the monkey village, but no monkey cared to heed the warning of the faithful old guard.

Then the chief monkey came to question him before he died, and the chief was inclined to believe his story about overhearing a plot by the snakes. But, as always in such affairs, a woman must interfere, and so a female monkey, who saw the chief interesting himself in the old guard, cried out loud to the chief: " Father chief, do come away from that friend to man! What mother was it that gave birth to such a one, so full of devils? Why, he even tells you a lie without blushing! " This derision made the chief turn his back on the old guard; and the old chap bit his arm in anguish, until the blood ran, and he sprinkled it at the entrance of their village, which means a curse on those inside. This is customary among native people as well as monkeys. And the old guard died, without a friend and in disgrace with his people.

The snakes came in upon the tribe from all sides, and not one of the monkeys escaped being stung. All died horrible deaths. When the chief snake saw the old monkey guard lying in his own blood at the entrance to their village, he remarked: " It is just like a monkey to cut off his nose to spite his face."

Chapter XVII

LOST IN THE BUSH

Plotting with five wives. Even five wives are jealous. A faithful follower. No turning back. Tropic storms. Enfiki tells a story. Appeasing angry spirits. Lost in the bush. Fever. The boa constrictor. A drum. King Kof-fi's land. In the vines. More folk-tales.

I longed now to get away from the horror of savage life, but I dared not tell my father of my intentions, and it was not safe to confide in any one of the villagers, because my father would have been called upon to make a feast in honour of my departure.

The only thing left for me to do was to confide in my wives. Giving such confidence is a thing that a man can do in my country very easily because he can trust his wives with a secret, trustworthiness being a redeeming feature among our women. I called my five wives together and told them that I had to make a visit to another community, and that I should not return before several moons, as the way

144

was long and dangerous. One of the girls said: " I knew that he had wives somewhere else "; and the other girls cried out: " Salute your other wives for us; we hope that you find your children well."

I was flabbergasted, because I had not imagined my wives' thinking such a thing. However, that is the native way of thinking, and I was not sufficiently advanced to teach the girls anything different.

I asked my " followers " to guide me, but they were afraid at first. I explained that I had to go, and that I did not ask my father for an escort because he would be afraid of losing me again and might refuse. So the " follower " whom I had made headman in my compound volunteered to take me out of the country, as he said that he knew the bush well, and to see that no harm befell me.

We started away from our village of huts in the morning. My head " follower " really did not know the way out. He planned to lead me to the border of our country and then to let me pick up an escort from there to the coast, but he got his bearings all wrong. He first led me in the opposite direction to the coast, because he did not want to arouse suspicion at my leaving. For that reason, too, I did not take anything with me, other than a mat to sleep on and one or two personal effects

145

that I should need when I reached civilization, and my " follower " carried them for me.

Now, in my anxiety to get away, I had forgotten the time of the year, and it was only after we had walked two days away from the village that I thought about the weather. It was then near the rainy season; in fact, the rainy season was only two days off, and then the rain would pour down in torrents and flood the land, as it does at that time of the year. The rain commences about the first of June and lasts till the end of August.

To turn back would have been stupid, because my father would have known by that time that I had intended to leave the country, and he surely would influence my wives to complain of my going away from them. A complaint of that kind would spoil my chances, perhaps, of ever leaving my country again.

The rain did not frighten me so much, but the thunder and the lightning did. The thunder and lightning in my country are much more dreadful than here. After a rainy season a man need go only a short distance in the bush to see what damage the lightning does. The lightning strikes often and destroys large trees, and kills many animals, because the animals love to take shelter under trees and clusters of bushes; and so we are always able to

146

find dead animals lying about throughout the bush after the rainy season.

The rain came. I must say that my " follower " was very faithful to me; he did all that was possible to make me half-way comfortable. He collected and prepared the food; he made a hammock in the vines for me to sleep in; and, in fact, he treated me as if I were his relative.

The " follower " was a native and had his superstitions, like all other natives. He told me many stories on that journey, about animals and birds and fish. I was only a young boy and so I listened to his yarns with rapt attention. Here is one of the stories:

THE LIZARD AND THE LEOPARD

Once upon a time a lizard said to a leopard: " Come, let us see which of us can kill more people in one day." The leopard felt sure that his power to kill was far above that of the little lizard. So the leopard said: " If I kill more than you, then you must become my slave and do whatsoever I wish you to do."

The lizard said that was all right, but that he also wished to gain something if he should win. So the leopard said that he was willing to be the slave of the lizard if the lizard should win the wager.

Now, who was going to keep correct account of the killings? They decided to ask the elephant to keep the records. They were to start on the next day.

They began by making an early raid on a village, and the leopard killed seven children and one man. By sunrise the lizard had killed only three children and a woman. The leopard was so full with the blood he had drunk that he could hardly keep awake, so at last he lay down and went fast asleep.

In the mean time the lizard was very busy, and by the time the sun had set, he had killed twenty-four. Then the leopard woke, and still believed he had killed more than had the lizard. When the elephant informed him that he had lost the wager, he became furious and insulted the elephant and accused him of taking the side of the lizard and of cheating.

Now, if there is one thing that makes the elephant angry, it is to be called a cheat. Everyone knows that the elephant is no cheat. The elephant hit the leopard with his trunk so hard that the leopard became dazed. When the leopard recovered, he began to curse and rave, and he attacked the patient elephant and almost killed him, biting ferociously, but the lizard came up and stung the leopard good and hard, sending so much

148

poison through him that the leopard shouted with pain.

Nevertheless, the leopard fought on, for, as he said, he would rather die than be slave to anyone. The elephant picked up the leopard and threw him so high into the air that when he fell to the ground, he died at once. But the elephant was so weak from loss of blood that he died soon afterwards.

So the lizard said: " The leopard's death is the outcome of being a bad loser and not being a good sport; but the elephant died from being truthful; hence I am never going to tell the truth."

Whether the " follower " did not know the way, or whether his eagerness to entertain me and keep me from being afraid made him forget his direction, I cannot say, but I saw that he appeared to be in a quandary. He stopped every now and then and held his ear against a tall tree, and then he would put me away up on a vine and tell me to wait for him. He would climb ever so much higher up and look out far away at something. He would then descend to where he had left me, put me on his back, turn round several times, and then start out walking again, climbing over this and crawling under that obstacle. When he had to crawl under

149

something he would put me down on a vine or fling me, catapult-fashion, across a heap of brush so that I landed on vines. Then he would crawl under some object and I would not see him for a few minutes, and then all of a sudden his head would bob up above the tall grass, some distance away, and he would be puffing and blowing, saying, as he approached closer to me: " *Allah o akbar,*" meaning: " God is great."

I often wondered why he disappeared in this manner, so one day I asked him who it was that he was visiting on these little journeys, and he replied: " The spirits are angry with us for our acts, and I have to appease them before we can continue our journey."

In the mean time the rain poured down. I was only half clad, but the " follower " had nothing on. I was drenching wet, as the rain soaked through my clothes to the skin, whereas the " follower " kept himself well greased with some stuff that he squeezed out of leaves, and the rain just bounced off of him. I was continually wet, because I slept in my wet clothes as well as walked in them. The consequences were that I became violently ill with fever and could not go on any farther. The " follower " laid me in vines and doctored me. He prepared some kind of hot potion, the very smell of which made me vomit, but he forced me to take it.

Oh, how terrible it was out there in the bush! Lost! Yes, lost! My "follower" had lost his direction, but he was trying to keep going until we could reach some habitation. Malarial fever, which I had, is a most weakening sickness, especially when accompanied with ague. I shook my little body almost to pieces.

I remember that on one occasion when the "follower" left me alone and went to find more medicine and to commune with the spirits, he stayed away much longer than usual. I was still ill with fever, and the heavy rain was still pouring down. I lay up in the vines where he had put me, because I was too weak to move. I called and called in my weak way, but he did not answer. Then I became alarmed, for the thought came to my mind, like a flash, that he had abandoned me and left me in the middle of the bush at the mercy of animals and reptiles. Until that time I had not given snakes a single thought, but then the awfulness of my plight dawned upon me and I cried long and hard. I really wished then that I had never started out on the journey. I became delirious. What I said while I was in that state I cannot say, but I do know that when I did become rational, the first thing that

151

caught my eye was a monster boa constrictor hanging from a branch of a tree not a yard away from me. Now I could just see the thing, but that was enough for me. I screamed: *"Oo-lou-wi!"* as loud as my lungs permitted, and then I heard a voice saying: *"Yek-ras,"* meaning: "Shut up." The voice was that of Enfiki, my " follower."

Enfiki said that when he returned, he found me in a pitiful state of delirium, and that I was calling on everybody to save me. He said that it made him wonder why I should be asking to be saved, as he had seen no danger near me then. He said that he climbed up to where I lay, and then he looked up over me and saw the snake slowly uncurling itself; and he added that if he had not acted quickly, that creature would have dropped down on top of me, and I should surely have been squeezed to death. But he had snatched me from where I was and flung me over to the spot where I then found myself, and he had jumped away quickly before the thing could fall on top of him. Well, that may be so, or it may not be so, but there was the snake, hanging just where I saw it, twenty feet long; but it was dead. He said that he had killed it and had left it hanging there so that when I returned from the spirit world I should be able to see for myself how near death I had been.

I had been sick four days and we had not made a step of advance during that time. It was still raining hard. I have often wondered how we escaped being struck by lightning. My fever was gone and I was still weak, but we had to move on, even though it was now well understood that we were lost.

After a time I heard a drum-beat. I told Enfiki and he laughed and said that I was trying to make him the same as I had been, seeing and hearing things in the spirit world. After a while Enfiki stopped suddenly and asked me if I heard anything. I laughed loudly, for I was beginning to think and believe that Enfiki and myself both were losing our minds. We both heard the drum-beat, but neither of us heard it at the same time. When I heard it, Enfiki could not hear it; and when Enfiki heard it, I could not hear it. So Enfiki, although a very brave bushman, became afraid and began calling down the judgment of the spirits on my head for inducing him to help me deceive my own father. He began to rave, and I thought that his mind was surely unhinged, and so I cried all the more. I implored him to take me back, but he said that he did not know how. He said that he thought that we were coming into a strange country, by the look of the trees. He could not guess where we were, but hoped that we should not fall into the hands of King Kof-fi's people, for if we did, it was good-bye for both of us.

Just then a clap of thunder and a bolt of lightning made both of us jump up and scream. That bolt of lightning struck just behind us, tore a tree to pieces, and threw the parts crashing down into the forest. You would have thought, from the deafening noise it made, that it tore up nearly the whole earth. We were truly in a sorry plight. At the mercy of storm, lightning, fever, and frightened animals, and, worse than all, in danger of walking into the country of a hostile king.

Now the drum beat again; this time we both heard it. We were near some habitation, but where, we could not guess. The drum-beat now was long and loud. Enfiki said that it was a message, but he was unable to decipher it because it was in a different language from our own.

We sat up in the vines, where I had spent many days and nights, and while we sat there, we saw animals go to drink. It was remarkable how Enfiki knew the nature of all of these beasts; he was actually able to tell what each one would do, before it ever did it. I was amazed, because he could talk for hours about animals, and about what they thought and how they planned. I could not doubt him when he said that he killed the snake that would have killed me, because he knew the nature of snakes so well. He entertained me nearly all the time with his fund of folk-tales and animal stories. I never tired of hearing them.

This is one of the tales that Enfiki told me on that journey:

THE ZEBRA, THE LION, AND THE LEOPARD

Once upon a time, there lived in the bush an old female zebra. She was too old to bear young, and too ugly to mix with the younger females of her people, but she had wisdom.

Now, you must know that a zebra is always a dainty and gentle animal; and it never gives trouble to anyone. Its greatest dread is the lion and the leopard.

One day after the animals had all had their drink, this poor old creature sat down and began to weep because she had been snubbed by her kind. While she was thus brooding over her ill fate, up ran a lion and patted her on the back. This frightened Mother Zebra so badly that she screamed. The lion laughed and said: " Just like your kind, being

155

afraid and screaming before you are hurt. What are you doing here all alone?"

The zebra, trembling from head to foot, told the lion her story, and the lion said: "Well, since you are of no use to your own people, I suppose I had better eat you. Think of the great honour it will be for your people to give such a nice feast to their King."

The zebra pleaded with the lion to spare her life, but the lion just laughed at her and said: "You should be proud that I give you fair warning that I am going to eat you, instead of having me sneak up on you and kill you without notice, just as that sneaky leopard would do."

Just then the leopard came up and began to address himself to the lion, saying: "Just like you, brave King, to be intimidating poor innocent women and children; if you are so brave, why not choose someone who can answer you, and not take advantage of the weak." Thereupon the leopard jumped on the lion and killed him.

The zebra thanked the brave leopard and started to leave, saying that she would be glad to meet the leopard again. But the leopard said: "Wait a minute, Madame Zebra; I saved you from the lion only in order that I might have you to feast upon myself."

The zebra knew then that her time had come, and that no end of pleading would save her, so she said: "I admit, Mr. Leopard, that the lion is a coward, but he never takes advantage of his inferiors, so your saving me from the coward lion for your own brave self proves you a coward of the worst kind, for you have made of a virtue a fault."

At this the leopard ate the zebra.

I remember another story that Enfiki told me. This one is about

THE SNAKE AND THE MONKEY

One day, when the troop of monkeys tired of doing its mischief, and all the monkeys were lolling about from vine to vine and tree to tree, making up their minds for some further mischief, a young snake came passing by. Now, of course, you know that monkeys always keep away from snakes at all times, even when they are all together in their tribe, and you also know that all monkeys are cowards.

As this young snake was alone, the monkeys began to laugh at him, saying: "Hey, you, belly-walker! Why not get up and show yourself? You sneak about on your belly all the time, unseen except by people like us who are clever enough to detect you, because we are not easily fooled. Bah on you, who cannot come out in the open as we do, and face everyone! "

The young snake, being alone, and passing by so many monkeys, was a little afraid, although he knew that all monkeys are cowards. The snake thought that even the greatest coward with sufficient backing would be a dangerous enemy, so the young snake did not answer a word, but kept on walking. The monkeys laughed long and loud and talked about the fright of the young snake and chatted much about the bad ways of the whole snake family.

While the monkeys were so happy over the tales that were being told about the snake people, the young snake had travelled fast and had reached his own village. The young snake was tired and hungry, and he settled down to have a feast off a nice young gazelle.

Now, while he was feasting, the young snake began telling the story of how he had encountered a troop of monkeys gambolling in the vines, and how they all had derided him and laughed at him as he came by. He told the other snakes that the monkeys had insulted their entire race by calling them a " sneaky people " who were only able to crawl about on their bellies, and who were not so brave as the monkeys were, who could always stand up and face anything.

This made the elders of the snake people angry, and it was proposed that all the young snakes should go out and scout around and try to capture some of those devilish imps. So all the young people of the snake family started out in search of the monkeys.

In the mean time the monkeys were busy telling jokes of how they had raided villages, had coco-nut fights with men and boys, and captured several children and torn them to pieces, before the mother monkey could prevent them from doing so. That was fine sport for the monkeys. Now, while they were shouting, for monkeys always talk very loud (a sure sign of cowardice), they did not notice that they were being surrounded by all the young of the snake family.

One young snake came out from where he was hiding and showed himself to the monkeys, and that started the monkeys laughing again, and they screamed out to the young snake: " Hey, you! Belly-walker! Why don't you get some legs for yourself, so that you can come out into the sun and

let other people see you, and be brave, as we are?"
It is always the habit of cowardly people to prate
about how brave they are.

Just then one other snake dropped down right
in front of the monkey who was doing the most
talking, and nearly frightened him to death. All
the other monkeys started to run, but they were
hemmed in on all sides and could not get away.
One young monkey tried to break through, but
he was caught by a young snake who was hanging down in front of him, who curled his tail
around the monkey's neck and choked him to
death.

All the other monkeys were taken back into the
camp of the snakes, and it was the snakes' turn
now to yell and laugh. The monkeys cried and
pleaded with the snakes to let them go. One of the
older snakes said: " Ha ha! You brave monkeys,
who are so clever and who have so much brain!
Now you have good legs, but most of the time you
use your tail! You also have a brain, but you always
imitate! Explain to us, please, which is the worse
of the two, the one who has no brain or legs and
who wishes for them, and who lives straight without them, or the one who has everything and makes
no proper use of any of them? If you answer that,
we will let you go."

160

Not a monkey answered, but they all kept on weeping and wailing.

So the old snake said: " It will be best to kill you rather than see so many good qualities wasted, for you are better dead than alive without a purpose." So all of the monkeys were killed.

Chapter XVIII

AMONG CANNIBAL DWARFS

In the land of the Fans. Enfiki despairs. Wounded by a blow-gun dart. Cannibal bushmen. Enfiki's faithfulness. The village tunnel. To be eaten? The magic of English. In the cannibal village.

Now we both heard the drum beat out its message, and poor Enfiki was much afraid; so was I, but not so much as he was, because I did not know how much danger we were in. But Enfiki did. Enfiki was sorely perplexed, because we dared not go on any farther, and we dared not stop. It was dangerous to do either. Enfiki, however, did everything that he could to comfort me.

After walking on another two days, Enfiki discovered that we were in the country of the cruel Fans, our worst enemies. My own father had gained his distinction in fighting the Fans and had won a complete victory for our country. He had brought back eighty skulls of Fan warriors, and three Fan chiefs' skulls, as a trophy of the battle. These he put in the *ju-ju* house, and our King created my

162

father *Balogun* for this brave feat and sent two of his own women to my father's compound. That was a great distinction.

There was no turning back; we just had to keep going. Enfiki seemed to know that it was all over with himself, the way he talked to me. He believed that I was doomed as well. He told me to say that I was a Moslem if we were captured, and to try to imitate the Tuareg people when they prayed.

I did not realize my full danger. I had heard much about these people, but I remembered only that they were a fighting people, and that they did not like the people of my country, because we had beaten them in warfare. But I could never have dreamed that they were as cruel as I found out they were, a little later on.

The drum-beat was very loud by this time, and we were quite close to some settlement, but we could not see any sign of life. Now we heard voices, and all of a sudden Enfiki gave such a scream that it made my blood run cold. The poor fellow had been struck by a shot from a tube assagai, that is, by a small sharp piece of steel blown through a kind of tube, like a pea-shooter. This, of course, is not poisonous, but if enough of them are blown into you, they will kill you.

163

It appeared as if all was up. Enfiki dropped to the ground, and I tumbled off his shoulders, for he had been carrying me, and I fell with a thud. My first thought was that he had been stung in the leg or foot by some reptile, and when I fell to the ground, I did not lie there long, but started hastily to jump up and climb a tree, out of reach of the serpent, as I thought.

To my surprise, Enfiki caught me and held me down to the ground. The look in his face frightened me, so I began to yell and scream for all that I was worth. Enfiki put his other hand over my mouth and squeezed my nose at the same time, with his thumb and finger. This cut off my wind, and for the moment I could not breathe. His doing that made me think that he had surely gone out of his mind. If I had only known, it would have been easy to escape many hardships that befell both of us. But the poor chap was in pain and he knew what it was that caused his pain; I didn't. He really wanted me to lie still and be quiet, and perhaps no one would ever have looked for us; but my screaming and struggling upset his plans and resulted in both of us being captured by some little short men.

I first thought that these little short men were boys, but I learned later that they were those cannibal bushmen who are the neighbours of the Fans, and who rove over the whole bush, much as monkeys do, living in the trees and vines. I had heard of these people before from my own father, but I had never seen any of them. They are much taller than the Pygmy people who live in the central part of the African continent. They have a kind of settlement near the Fan country. In fact, in time of war the Fans use them as warriors because the King of that country held them in a kind of subjection. They are a little lighter in colour than the Fans or my own people. Their religion is fetishism, but their ritual is somewhat different from the ritual in my country, and similar to that of the Fans.

Enfiki had seen these little men as soon as he had been struck by the assagai shot, but I did not see them until they were quite near us. It appeared as if there were thousands of them.

By this time Enfiki had released my arm. Enfiki was naked, but I had enough clothing on to make those devilish little men stare at me. One dwarf came over beside me and started to examine what I had on, but one of his men shouted something, and he dropped my shirt-sleeve as if it were something hot, and ran. I suppose that the other man shouted: "Look out! It will bite you!"

Now, it appears that these little people had seen white men and had noticed how they dressed, and then seeing me with the same kind of clothes on, they felt astounded because I was not white.

Enfiki could make them understand him, and therefore they were rough with him. I tried to stand beside Enfiki, but they would not permit me to do so. Enfiki told me under his breath not to oppose them and never to answer them in a native tongue if they spoke to me, but merely to gaze at them. Enfiki, my faithful " follower," was truly trying to save my life. One word from Enfiki could have had me boiled alive and eaten up before we ever reached the place where they were taking us.

After much crawling under and climbing over trees and vines and through natural arbours and tunnels in the ground, we reached a large village, the walls of which were made of native clay, a sort of mud. These walls were very high, and I could not see any place of entrance to the village. I wondered if we should be taken inside, and, if so, whether we should be thrown over the wall.

The leader of these little men began to chant and shout, and then the chant was taken up by his followers, but I could not make out what they were singing. The melody lingers in my memory.

Poor Enfiki was in terrible pain, and he looked

166

most wretched. Shouldn't you if you knew, as he did, that your doom was near? Enfiki not only knew that he was going to die, but he could guess the torture that he would have to undergo before he died.

The earth seemed to open. The bushes were pushed back as if they were on hinges, the grass was cleared away, and in front of us was a sort of tunnel, pitch-dark inside. At the opening to this tunnel stood six stalwart warriors with assagais and shields. One of them came forward a few steps and shouted as loud as he could, slowly, these words: *" Mi lor ma da yoho nidan."* Remember the words? Of course I remember the words, and so would you if you had heard them under the same circumstances. The sight of these men in this pit-like entrance struck terror to my heart, and when I saw that tunnel and remembered that Enfiki had nodded yes when I inquired if we should be taken into it, I was overcome with fear.

I should have run away, only those little men were on all sides of me, and Enfiki warned me not to oppose them; so I just stood still. When the big fellow shouted out those strange words, I began to scream, because I could not contain myself. I thought that we should be thrown into a pit and covered up alive. I began to plead with the little

167

men, but they could not understand me. Enfiki told me to " dry up." He told me not to talk to those men in the native vernacular, but to use the white man's language if I wanted to say anything. He told me that those men were not going to hurt me, and that they were merely the guards of the entrance.

I wanted to ask Enfiki a thousand questions, but he made me keep quiet. Then one of the little men gave Enfiki a blow on the nose with the little tube that he was carrying. He said something in his own gibberish, and then all was quiet. I was whimpering and trying to make out what all this was about. The little man who had struck Enfiki began to talk to the guard who had shouted, and the guard answered something; then all the little men came running over beside me, and felt my legs and arms and neck, giving each part that they touched a little pinch, much the same as one does when he feels a chicken or bird to test its tenderness.

The truth was, these little men had sold Enfiki at the price of me, which meant that if the chief of that people agreed, I should be given over to the little men to be eaten. They did not have a keen appetite for Enfiki; it was I whom they wanted. I did not know then what it all meant, but I found out afterwards, from poor Enfiki, the meaning of it all. You can imagine how near I was to being boiled and eaten by those little cannibals. Once in my life I should have been devoured by sharks in the Gulf of Guinea if I had not gone below on the steamer; now I was in danger of being devoured by cannibals — cooked first and eaten afterwards. I have often thought over the whole thing, and I realize how extremely fortunate I was to escape two such horrible deaths.

Enfiki and I dropped into the entrance pit — Enfiki was practically thrown in — and we were led through the dark tunnel by the guards. How dark it was! The brush and bushes had closed over the opening again. One of the men took hold of my arm, and I suppose that another did the same to Enfiki. The man who was leading me was saying something all the time, but I did not understand a word. I remembered what Enfiki had told me about speaking my own language, so I began to mutter some words in English, the white man's language. I did not know very much English, but it did not matter; they would not understand me anyway, so I began to say words that came into my mind first: " Porridge — bread — sit down — go to bed — you know — you understand — I do — I will — I know — stop it . . ." and every phrase that came to my tongue I blurted out.

Enfiki heard me and knew that I was talking in a different language, so he shouted to me: " Well done "; but soon after that I heard him groan. I could not understand; all kinds of thoughts ran through my little mind. But I kept on talking, saying: " Silly ass — stupid fool — you ape — you dog — you beggar," and all the bad words that I had learned at school from the white boys.

We were still walking through the tunnel. We had no light, but my eyes had become used to the darkness and I could see ahead. We walked for what seemed ten minutes, and then we stopped in front of a large gate. I heard the voices of men, women, and children on the other side of the gate.

The gate was thrown open and we walked out of the tunnel into the town. The guard who had shouted at the other end of the tunnel shouted again. I remember the words, but I never learned their meaning. The words were: *" Baba wa woho kpe nou."* The *" kpe "* is just as it sounded to me. When he had shouted these words, everybody took up the shout and began clapping hands, singing the words *" Baba wa "* every time one of their men said something. And they danced around in a circle.

Chapter *XIX*

TRAGEDY AND TERROR

Enfiki stabbed and beaten. Before the chief. A boy tortured.
Enfiki tortured and killed. The brain porridge. A mad sacrifice
to the virgins. Sudden alarm. White soldiers. The hole in the
wall. The Colonel and the chief. Raw meat. I am saved.

Just after my poor follower, Enfiki, had shouted:
"Well done " in the dark tunnel, he groaned. The
sight of him when he came out of the tunnel told
me what had happened, for he was bleeding and
in a state of collapse. When he spoke to me, he was
stuck in the side by an assagai and given a blow
across the head by those brutal guardsmen;
and this was the reason for the groaning. He
was dragged away by a number of men; where
they took him I did not know then, but I found
out.

I was led to the gate of a large compound, one
that was well guarded by a number of native warriors. We did not stand outside the gate long, but
entered, and I was led to a large hut with a wide

veranda around it. I was made to sit down. That hut was the home of the chief, and I was taken there for questioning.

Inside the compound the scene was very lively, with women flitting about here and there, and children playing. It appeared as if all the children in the world were there. Men were running up and down, now entering the big hut, and now running out again, as if they were all carrying messages of importance.

I sat with my legs stretched out, for I have never been able to fold my legs under me, in a squatting position. One man stood behind me with a long assagai in his hand, and another man stood on each side.

Then I heard voices, and I heard a boy scream. The sound came from within. I was terribly afraid. Who knew what those cruel people would do to me, a strange boy, when one of their own boys was screaming so? I could not guess. In a short while some men came out of the hut. One of them was carrying the boy, who was still screaming. I saw the boy's arm; in it were several long, deep cuts. It looked as if the flesh had been cut out in small strips. That, I have since learned, is a tribal custom, and every boy who reaches puberty is treated in this manner.

172

My mind reverted to poor Enfiki; I wondered what ever had become of him. All of a sudden there was a bustle and rustle inside the great hut, and then I heard a loud voice and a hoarse laugh. One of the guards said something and then another spoke to me. I did not understand what they said, but I remembered what Enfiki had told me about speaking any native language. So I said the first thing that came to my tongue, in English: " Sit down, you clown — I don't know — why don't you try using soap? " I kept this up until some men came out of the hut. Then one of the guards put his arms under mine and lifted me up. He tried to stand me on my feet, but I did not know what he wanted. When he lifted me up, he naturally let go of me, and I sat down on the ground again with a flop. The guards looked at one another and began to laugh.

While this fellow was trying to convince me that he wanted me to stand up, the chief stepped out on the veranda and stood gazing at the guard bobbing me up and down. One of the men shouted some order, and the guard let me drop down quickly and fell flat on his face, because his chief was present. The chief looked very stern and growled, but he did not take his eyes off me. Remember, I had on some English clothes, and I wore shoes — the same that I had worn when I left Scotland for my own country. The chief spoke to me, and I answered him in English: "You are not right — hold your row — you're blathering, you idiot — thank you — not at all — I think so."

The chief, of course, could not understand me, so he burst out laughing; he laughed until he shook.

Then the tragedy started. Poor Enfiki was brought out. I say " brought out " because he could not walk; his toes had been chopped off and he looked like a man half dead. All the women were called up by the signal of a tomtom beat, and everyone ran forward and kissed the chief, from the soles of his feet to his knees. When this was finished, a man spoke to Enfiki, and Enfiki looked at me. I jumped up and rushed over to where he was lying, and began to cry.

Enfiki told me all that had happened to him. He said that the men of the village wanted to know who I was, and that he had told them that he had been out in the bush and had seen me with a party of white men, and that I could not speak any language other than the Mohammedan language and the white man's talk. He told them that I had become lost when I went away from the other men in my party, and that he had found me and brought me to this village because he knew that the noble

174

chief knew all about the white men, and that the
chief might find some use for me. Enfiki said that
the men of the village had refused to believe his
story, and that they had cut off a toe at a time to
make him change his account, but he had stuck it
out until he had lost all of his toes. Then the chief
had decided to sacrifice him to the virgins of that
country, and to turn me over to the little men who
had captured us in the bush.

Enfiki cried when he said this, because he knew
what my fate would be. If I were left with that
people, they would cook me and eat me. He said
that he had tried his best to save me, and he begged
me to believe him; he swore by the beard of his
own father. I cried and beat my chest, and they
pulled me away from him. Then a man came up
with a kind of cutlass and cut every one of Enfiki's
fingers off at the joints, but poor Enfiki kept shouting out to me not to say any native word, but to
talk the white man's talk. Perhaps I might be
saved, because, he said, these people feared the
white man.

His shouting was soon cut short by a hard blow
over his head. Then a man came forward and cut
Enfiki's head off, dug out the brain, and put it into
a pan brought for the purpose. Then the women
took the brain from the pan and put it on a board,

and one of the women began mashing it by jumping on it. Other women brought up a large jar, filled with I don't know what, and when the woman had finished mashing the brain, they all scooped it up in their hands and threw it into the jar. Then the tomtom began to beat. Poor Enfiki's remains were taken away, and men came with water and washed away the blood. I never saw so much blood in all my life. I was too amazed to cry out, and so saddened by what they were doing that I forgot all about what Enfiki had said would happen to me.

The tomtom beat drew many people, but everybody stood afar off, while the warriors, with shields and assagais, came up to the veranda and prostrated themselves before their chief, and then stood back in line again. The jar into which the women had put the mashed brain of Enfiki was stirred up, and the chief began to chant. When the chief finished chanting, the song was taken up by all the warriors, and they all began a very wild dance. While they were dancing, everyone came up and took a sip of the stuff from the jar, a man dishing it out to them in a kind of ladle. This stuff seemed to make them more fierce; they jumped and shouted and screamed and danced around like madmen after every sip. Women and even children came forward and sipped the horrible stuff. This

176

was the sacrifice to the virgins, according to what Enfiki had told me before he was killed.

In the excitement of that wild, savage gathering I had completely forgotten what was to become of me. The chief looked and acted as if he were drunk; probably he was. Who knows?

Then suddenly everybody's attention was arrested by loud shouting outside the compound. Several men burst in as if something were after them, shouting peculiar words as they ran. The people understood what these men said; it must have been very serious, because everyone stopped dancing and singing. The warriors who had been made wild by sipping the awful stuff in the jar became calm, and a hush came all over the place. The chief, who had appeared drunk, sobered up instantly and jumped up and brushed himself. He had on some kind of regalia, as if he were going to meet a superior. He gave orders, which caused confusion in being carried out, and then he sat down again. Some warriors hastened away, and others took up their stand around the chief, guarding him closely. In a short time the compound was cleared of everyone except a few tomtom-beaters. One of the tomtom beaters beat loudly on a tall tomtom. What did this all mean? I tried to think.

Then came to my mind what Enfiki had said

about the little short men, and I remembered all that he had told me. I was going to be given over to them to be eaten! I started to cry, and the chief beckoned to me to come over to him; but I was afraid, and a guard pulled me over to the chief. They sat me down near the chief and left me unguarded. My first thought was to jump up and run, but you can see how foolish that would have been, because I should have been struck down by an assagai before I could even reach the compound gate. I did not reason this out then, however, and my mind was set on getting away, anywhere, to keep from being given to those little men for a feast.

Now the tomtom beat became more rapid, and there was a stir and commotion outside the compound gate, as if someone was clearing the way. I thought surely that the little men were coming in for me, and I screamed for all I was worth. The chief put his arm over me and held my mouth.

While, inside the chief's compound, Enfiki was being killed, about two hours before, outside of the village walls, in another direction from that in which we had entered the village, were about forty white soldiers who had journeyed up from the Gold Coast. There was an officer with them — a Colonel in the British Army. The soldiers were a detach-

ment of troops who were garrisoning that part of
the country to protect Europeans employed in the
gold industry, not far from where we were. I have
since learned that this Colonel had set out to make
friends with this chief.

When the white soldiers and their officer first
came up to the walls of the village, with a native
guide, they were surprised to find that the place
had no entrance. The soldiers, of course, carried
guns, and when they discovered that there was no
visible entrance to the village, they fired a volley
into the mud wall. The firing broke the mud and
helped them to make a hole. The native guards
made the hole bigger by chopping away the mud.
The Colonel did not wish to take his troops inside,
and yet he did not wish to walk into a trap himself;
so the troops at once made the hole in the wall so
large that it would be impossible to keep them out
in the event of their Colonel's falling into treacherous hands. They had already heard about the
treachery of the Fans. Naturally, the volley
from the rifles of the soldiers attracted the attention of the guards inside the village, and they
thought the place was being attacked by white soldiers; so they immediately sent messengers to the
chief to inform him of what was taking place.
Those two messengers were the two men who came

running in at the time of the ceremony for the virgins.

The Colonel entered the village by way of the hole in the wall, followed by a native guide who had escorted him and his troops from the coast. The guide told me afterwards that he did not like the people up in that country, although he belonged to the same race. I am positive that if he had really guessed who I was, Ibn LoBagola, he would surely have delivered me over to them, whether he liked them or not. He had become civilized and made his home on the coast, serving Europeans as guide for long journeys.

When they reached the compound of the chief, the Colonel and the guide were halted outside by the guards, who began to question the guide. Naturally the Colonel's appearance in the village caused commotion, and there was a crowd of women, children, and old men around him. The Colonel's intentions were good, but no native knew what his intentions were. The guide was busy saying: " Peace, peace " in the vernacular of that country, which he knew very well.

The native guards permitted the Colonel and the guide to enter. The Colonel was unarmed, and so was his guide.

Now to go back to the time when I screamed with

fright. After the chief had quieted me, he stood up, and everyone who had been sitting did likewise. Then I saw a tall, stately, well-dressed white man, with a sharp-looking face, and wearing a British officer's uniform, walk towards the veranda where the chief and his elders were standing.

I stopped crying for the moment, wondering what this white man was doing in that village. The moment I set eyes on him, I jumped up and ran over to him as if I had known him all my life. I did not stand before him, but I fell down by his legs and wrapped my arms about him, which stopped him from going any farther.

He spoke to me and I tried to talk with him. He appeared to understand what I said, because he stood still and listened. He knew that I was afraid of something, and that I was a stranger to those parts, so he patted me on the cheek. I responded instantly to his kindliness. No one dared to interfere with me, because they saw that I could talk with this white man, which they could not do; so they were afraid to pursue me.

The guide went forward and saluted the chief by prostrating himself. The Colonel managed to get away from me and walked up in front of the chief.

Then I saw a thing that I have never seen since, and that very few people have ever seen: a

European official bow before an African chief. The chief himself, I am sure, was surprised, and he appeared to be much excited. Can you imagine that! A high British official bowing before a savage ruler? You must know, by this one act alone, that the Colonel meant good. The chief extended his hand to the Colonel, and the Colonel actually kissed it! I saw all these things, but I could not understand them at the time. It was many years later that the truth dawned upon me.

Now the chief was cheerful, and so was the Colonel. The next move did the mischief.

It is customary among native rulers never to accept the word of guides about the peaceful intentions of those whom they lead. The people who go about must themselves show that their intentions are peaceful. In the country where the Colonel then was, the chief offers his visitors a symbol of war or of peace: raw meat. If you eat a piece of raw meat with the chief, your intentions are not peaceful. That is the way these people have of determining whether you mean peace or war. The chief clapped his hands and called for raw meat.

In the mean time women were screaming outside in the village. The soldiers had become anxious about their Colonel and had entered the village through the hole in the wall. When the women saw them, they naturally thought that the soldiers had come to capture their chief, so they began to scream and to beat their breasts, the custom of native women when they are in trouble.

The Colonel's guide heard the screaming and guessed what it was about. He jumped up and ran into the village, shouting as he ran: " Peace! Peace! "

What a serious blunder! He had left the Colonel all alone and had not told him what to do next. Until now, everything had gone well. The chief was pleased, and so were his councillors.

While the foolish guide was trying to pacify the women, and explaining to the soldiers that all was well with the Colonel, the raw meat was brought forward on a large brass platter. The platter was placed on the ground between the Colonel and the chief, who sat facing each other, both of them smiling.

The chief picked up a piece of raw meat and bit it, and then he offered a piece of the meat to the Colonel.

If the Colonel had known, he would have taken it from the chief and thrown it down on the ground in front of him. This action would have pleased the chief and all his councillors, and everything would have been all right.

As the Colonel was ignorant of the customs of these people, and as the guide was not present to instruct the Colonel about the meaning of the raw meat, the unfortunate Colonel accepted the meat from the chief and began eating it. It must have been hard for the Colonel to do this, but I suppose that he thought that if he refused to eat it, he might offend the chief. So the Colonel ate the raw meat, and by so doing he innocently declared war on the chief.

As I have said before, a native never takes anything for granted. A native has no sense of your honourable intentions. A native judges you by what you do. Therefore amongst native people there is no excuse for ignorance.

I was watching every move. The chief clapped his hands, and now he was not smiling, though the Colonel was. A man came in answer to the hand-clap; the chief gave an order, and in less than a minute the man returned and handed a small assagai to the chief. The chief took the weapon and stood up quickly and shouted some words. The Colonel started to stand also, but before he could straighten himself up, the chief struck him with the assagai, which must have been poisoned, because the Colonel dropped to the ground and did not move.

When I saw this, I screamed, but no one noticed me. Everybody was too excited. I rushed from the veranda, not knowing where I was going. When I reached the compound gate, I met the guide rushing in.

The soldiers outside had not been easily convinced that their Colonel was all right and they had insisted on going to the chief's compound. The women made so much noise that all the guards came running up to the soldiers to find out what the trouble was. Just then a tomtom boomed out one beat. Its boom sounded different from the beat of any of the other tomtoms that I had heard in that village. It was the great war-drum, and it sounded the signal telling the native warriors to muster. All the guards cleared away from the soldiers, and the women stopped screaming and stood gazing as if something terrible had happened. In their struggle to enter the compound where their Colonel lay dead, the few soldiers were annihilated. Only two shots were fired.

I have learned since that those native people who killed the English soldiers and their Colonel were duly punished through one of the famous British punitive expeditions, in reprisal for the folly of the Fans. I say " folly," but the white man calls it treachery. I cannot honestly say that, because the tragedy, as I remember it, was purely the result of misunderstanding.

The guide, knowing the meaning of the tomtom, rushed back into the chief's compound. As he was coming in, I was running out. He caught hold of me, put me on his shoulders, and ran. Now, I had seen runners before, but in my whole life I have never seen a man run so swiftly as this guide did. When he got some distance from the village, he stopped, put me down, and sat down himself and cried. I heard two shots from a rifle, and then I heard no more.

The guide did not rest very long; he took me up on his shoulders and began running again, but this time not quite so fast; he simply kept up a trotting pace for ever so long a time. Night began to fall and it was getting dark, which meant that I should have to spend another night in the bush, sleeping in the vines. But by that time the guide and I were far away from the village, and fairly out of danger.

Chapter XX

A DISGUSTING SAVAGE LEARNING DECEIT

Again among white people. In Dahomey. A first-class passenger. Glasgow again. A disgusting savage. I learn there are white Jews. A fight. I learn deceit.

No one dared pursue us, because all knew that the guide would make for the nearest English camp. They thought right. Before the sun was up the next morning, we came in sight of the first smoke of a gold-miners' settlement. The guide related his story to a white man and then I told, as best I could, about seeing the Colonel slain.

I was taken to the coast and put aboard a steamer bound for the Gabun, which was in the opposite direction to where I wished to go. When the steamer stopped at the next port, I got off. The place was Kotonu, the principal port of Dahomey.

It was there that I had my first experience in being put ashore without going in a surf-boat. A

187

cable was rocketed from the mast of the ship on to the shore. It was made fast there, and I was put into a kind of basket and bolted from the ship to the coast safely.

I did not have any money, and I had to get to Whydah before I could get my ticket to return to Scotland. All arrangements had been made for my return, through the steamship company's agent at Whydah, whose name was G. Goedelt.

I managed to convince a native Dahomeyan that I was telling the truth, and he advanced the fare to me to ride on Dahomey's narrow-gauge railway, along the coast, from Kotonu to Whydah.

I reached Whydah without any mishap, and after a little difficulty I finally received the ticket for my passage, and a ten-pound note that had been made to my order, and also a trunk full of new clothes.

I waited two weeks, and then I got a steamer and once again was bound for Scotland. It had been arranged to put me off the steamer at Liverpool and then let me continue my journey by rail to Glasgow.

It had been exactly ten weeks from the day I had left my community until I boarded that steamer. How many things can happen to one in so short a time! It was exactly two years and three months that I had been away from my white father in Scotland.

Not many unusual things happened on the journey back to Scotland. What a difference from my first passage! On that first trip to Scotland I ate my meals from the floor, slept on the floor, ran into the corner of the cabin every time the door opened, and cried a great deal for my mother and for my companions. On this trip I was petted by the stewards and passengers, who were surprised at seeing a native boy travelling as a first-class passenger.

The passengers were white men employed as clerks for trading firms on the west coast of Africa, and government officials on their way home on leave to Great Britain. Most of them knew a smattering of the coast languages, but none of them could speak to me in my own tongue. They all knew of my people by report, but they had never encountered any of our men because none of our men dared to go near the sea or to do business with the people of the coast. It would have been a great shame for any of our people even to speak or look at a Kruman, a defiled creature without caste.

This passage was not nearly so long as the other had been, because this steamer was a fast passenger ship, the *Elmina*. Before I knew it, I was in Liverpool. I journeyed from Liverpool by train and arrived in Glasgow on the morning of July 27, 1902. After making a few inquiries I managed to find my master's house, out on the Drive.

When I had reached my own home in Africa on my first return there and had seen my own black father, strange as it may seem, I did not run up to him and offer to kiss him, nor do I remember having experienced any especial delight at meeting him. On the contrary, when I arrived at the house of my "white father," I was very glad to see him; in fact, I was glad to see everyone, and the whole household appeared very glad to see me. Perhaps my black father was not so demonstrative in his affection as my white father was. I know, however, that a different feeling took hold of me when I arrived in that home in Glasgow. Everyone, servants included, embraced and kissed me profusely, as if I were one of their own.

The strangest thing about all this was that I do not remember having shown any resentment at such demonstrations of affection. In my country it is a great shame for a father to kiss any of his children, but he sometimes will permit the child to kiss the back of his hand. Even mothers discourage the act of kissing on the lips, although some children do before the mothers can stop it. There is really no demonstration of love or affection among my

190

people, because their religion does not teach it to them; so you will understand how singular it was for me to permit the people in the Scotch house to fondle me as they did.

I had forgotten many of the English words that I had learned before I had left for my African home. Therefore you can understand my bewilderment at hearing many names for the same thing, and at hearing some names that caused offence in different grades of society. There were a number of things, as well as words, that I had forgotten, through disuse, and it was necessary to refresh my memory. For several days I was strictly guarded, to prevent me from breaking something or from doing some disgusting act, for I had again become a savage.

My young master got chummy with me soon, and it was he that got me released from the vigilance of the household. That Scotch boy was truly patient with me and spent his whole vacation period teaching me, once again, the things that he had so painstakingly taught me before I had left Scotland for my own home.

It was embarrassing to the household when company was present, and they had me on exhibition, as it were, to have me, in the middle of endearing remarks and conversation, do some strange, unexpected thing, or speak vulgar words that shocked everyone. All these things were soon corrected by my young master, which truly made me quite comfortable.

The young master was quite a big boy, much larger than I, although only two years older, and of an entirely different stature. All my young master's mates were away, and it was lonesome for him to stay at home with me. Somehow he always contrived to think up some amusement for both of us, so we were often together in the parks, gardens, and playgrounds of Glasgow.

One day while we were in Kelvingrove Park and my young master was busy playing cricket, I sauntered off because I was attracted by a band of music. I stood by the bandstand ever so long, simply charmed by the music. When at last I remembered my young master and tried to find him, there were so many people about that it was impossible for me to distinguish one from another.

I picked up a piece of black liquorice, and after examining it, as I did everything that I got hold of, I started to eat it. A little tow-headed girl, rather shabbily dressed, ran to me and tried to take it from me. I did not understand all that she said because she talked too fast, but I knew that she did say " Blacky." I began pulling her hair and scratching her, and she pulled my hair and kicked me on the shins. She screamed, and I screamed also. Just then a boy came up and parted us, and the girl told him what it was all about. He took the piece of liquorice from me and held it behind him. Then he stood between the girl and me and did not shout or make any noise whatever. He was quite silent. His silence frightened me a little, because it lent strength to him. I always fear silent people.

When the girl had finished her complaint, the boy turned to me and asked if the liquorice were mine. I shook my head no. It was not mine; therefore I could not say it was, because I should have been telling a lie, and at that time I had not acquired the habit of telling deliberate lies. I have often wondered just what a civilized boy would have done if he had been in my place. I have seen, since that time, things claimed by right of " Finders keepers," and the thought has often occurred to me whether I should not have been justified in saying that the liquorice was mine because I had found it.

When I said that the liquorice was not mine, the boy who acted as mediator gave it to the girl. The boy exacted strict respect from the girl before he gave it to her, however. The girl literally grabbed it out of his hand and started off, but the boy caught hold of her, took the liquorice away from her, and said something. Then the girl said: "Thank you." This impressed me greatly, and I therefore did not mind the loss of the liquorice.

I stood close to that boy because I somehow felt safe with him. He tried to talk with me, but it was difficult for him to make me understand. He took me to his house, and I saw his mother and a man. What relation the man was to the boy I never found out, but it was at this boy's house that I discovered that there were white people who were Israelites. The name of this family was Ansel, and they were Jews. For a long time I could not believe it possible that a white man could be an Israelite too.

The boy led me back to the park, where we found my young master still playing cricket. I came eating a large piece of cake that the woman had given me. When my young master saw me eating cake, he ran to me and attempted to take it from me. The Jewish boy prevented him from doing so, not knowing who my young master was. Of course that started a fight right away.

How my young master could fight! The Jewish boy could fight also. I ate the cake and laughed at the fighting. I shouted, as all the other boys did, and said what they said. I repeated all their coarse words: "In the jaw! On the smeller!" and much worse. I screamed with delight and rolled on the grass in joy, not realizing that the fight was on my account.

My young master never permitted me to eat anything that he had not examined first. I had a habit of picking up anything and everything, and smelling and tasting it. My young master, knowing all this, naturally thought that I had found the cake on the ground. The Jewish boy, on the other hand, did not know that my young master was my guardian. He thought that a rude boy was trying to steal my cake so that he could eat it himself.

So over a piece of cake a battle was fought, and my young master got a bloody nose, the Jewish boy a black eye, and I a piece of cake and a lot of fun. I laughed so much at my young master that it annoyed him, but I do not think it necessary to repeat the vile uncomplimentary things that he said to me.

My young master told his mother that a cricket-ball had hit him on the nose and caused it to bleed. That was a deliberate lie, and I often wondered why he had to lie over such good sport as a fight; especially when it got him a bloody nose. It was only because I was not asked that I did not tell the truth about the affair. I did use some of the words

195

that my young master had used while fighting, and shocked the butler by using such "gutter language," as he termed it.

The house was not attractive during the summer months. My young master took me to every place of interest. He took me to a place called Laird, a provost seat in Ayrshire, and then to Addrossan, and to many places down Wemyss Bay. At Rothesay we ran into the Jewish boy again, the lad who had bloodied my young master's nose, and whose eyes my young master had blackened. Strange to say, I recognized him first. When I saw him I began to laugh. For the moment my young master was puzzled, because he did not know what made me so gleeful. Then the Jewish boy ran to me, and talked so fast that I could not understand a word he said. I was glad to see him and wished that he and my young master would fight again. Such fine sport!

The Jewish boy began to talk to my young master, and it appeared as if they were going to be friends. They shook hands, and the Jewish boy went away and spoke to a man with whom he had been walking, and then ran back and joined our company. We walked along together. They laughed and joked, and although I could not understand their humour, I laughed and frolicked and ran and

196

screamed, to the delight of my young master and his new companion and everyone else who saw me.

When we arrived home, I tried to rehearse everything that had happened, and I told, as best I could, about the new friend my young master had made. I never knew what the trouble was, but something displeased the madame, who scolded so that my young master cried and went to his bed, and I to mine, without food. He found me during the night and took me down the back stairs to the pantry, where we ate to our heart's content, oatcake, shortbread, milk, and everything.

These little deceptions on the part of my young master made a deep impression upon me, and I wondered about them. It was not long before I tried to practise them. The difficulty I had was not in performing such acts, but in explaining them when I was caught. My young master always knew just what to say, but I invariably admitted the offence after I had been detected. I was not anxious to admit all the wrongs that I was caught in, but I could not get it into my head to deny the truth when I was asked for it. I had never learned words in my own language for making excuses and evasions, let alone in English. For a long time I was constantly getting into hot water.

For example, I was forbidden to go out alone,

197

but I tried to go out, as I had seen my young master do, by going quietly upstairs, making a little noise, then keeping quiet for a time, and then putting my things on and walking out the front door instead of the back door. All of a sudden a stern voice would shout: " You're going out alone, young man."

I would answer: " Yes, yes; out alone; no, yes; I'm not; I am."

I was confused and at a loss what to say. Although it always caused me to be deprived of my meal in that house, it nevertheless caused a great deal of laughter. On such occasions my young master always saw to it, after the lights went out, that I got plenty to eat.

Chapter XXI

SAVAGERY VERSUS CIVILIZATION

The call of the Hebrew blood. The synagogue. The music-hall. Should a savage tell the truth about civilization? Men and ideals. Two boys and one a man. Excesses begin.

One night my young master himself took me out. It was a virtual crime, one of the seven sins, for us to leave the house after dark. He took me to town on the tram-cars. I was bewildered. We walked through " Sauchi," down " Buccy," and along Argyle, seeing the sights of a lifetime. (These abbreviations are the first names that I learned for Sauchiehall Street, Buchanan Street, and Argyle Street.) Almost at the end of Sauchiehall Street we ran into the Jewish boy again. As he came out of a tobacco-shop, my young master saw him first and hailed him. I was glad to see him; I don't know why. It may have been the call of the blood; who knows? He was glad to see us and led us back into the tobacco-shop. The people inside laughed. Perhaps they saw humour in me, seemingly a black imp.

The Jewish boy took us to his house, but we did not stay there long. We got on a different tram-car and rode over a bridge. Now I know where we went; it was on the south side of Glasgow, a place called Govan. The Jewish boy led us into a large room. There were inside only men. To me it sounded as if the men were crying, but it soon became clear that they were not crying, but singing. I heard the word "Ishrael" so plainly and so often that I began repeating the word myself. Some old men tried to question me. I could not understand then, but I know now what their curiosity was about. They had heard me mumbling the word "Ishrael" and were curious to know if I could be an Israelite.

They pointed their fingers at me, saying: "Ishrael! Ishrael?" I repeated: "Ishrael" and said my " *Schma*." When they found that I was really a Jew, they talked so much and made such a noise that my young master and I became afraid. We ran out, not waiting for the Jewish boy, and made our way over the bridge.

Before we went home, my young master took me into a music-hall, the first I had ever been in. There I saw so many people and heard so much singing that it astounded me. In that music-hall I first heard the song "Stop yer ticklin', Jock." I never forgot the tune, and for the longest while I hummed it. I soon learned the words, because I liked them very much, and I sang them in the house. No one of the older people could understand where I had picked up such a song, but they were highly amused at hearing me sing it.

We arrived home safely that night, but, needless to say, we both did without our porridge the next morning, because we slept past breakfast time, which was seven o'clock in that household.

I have often wondered, since I have become somewhat modernized, just what would be the reaction if I should be inspired to write "What a Savage Really Thinks of the Civilized World." My first conclusion is that the Church would rise in arms against me. The Jews would resent my "presumption."

A few years ago I was taught to be a follower of the crowd, susceptible to influences; and so I feared to tell the truth about what was brewing in my mind. Now, since I have been scientifically imbeciled, legally pauperized, and theologically jailed, I am free to utter a few facts from a "savage's" point of view, without bitterness of heart or malice. I have suffered, and lived the life that I am recording, and I think that I am amply equipped with data to express an opinion on the subject. Opinion! Yes, only an opinion, because, after all, since I am veneered with that coating of "justifiable hypocrisy called civilization," I have been left only with an opinion, and permission to express it.

Let me begin by making a very familiar quotation: "All men are liars." In my country, from a Western point of view, "black is white," and therefore a lie is justifiable, in the sense that I wish to convey. I mean by that that what you in your land think wrong we think right.

We believe in early marriage and marry at puberty; you do not believe in early marriage, but you desire its rights. We think it perfectly moral to go about nude; your standard of morality teaches that it is improper to expose the body, but you worship the God that gave you the unclothed body—a singular inconsistency, to be ashamed of that which was given you by the One you revere.

We believe in polygamy; you openly oppose plurality of wives, but secretly condone multiple relationship. We marry for progeny; you marry for love, a word greatly misused and misunderstood. I have been informed by the newspapers that a judge here sentenced a man to have no more children, rebuking him for the number that he already had.

Oh, your one-sided civilization with its deceits, taught from the cradle! Its delightful living of a lie! Its self-satisfying debauchery in impurities of word, of thought, and of deed! White men often delight in the discomfort of neighbours, and laugh in the faces of their brothers when they ask for food! Civilization is not civilization without its mixed cargo of rum and good works!

I know what some will say when they read my last statement: " He is against white men." Is that so! Well, nothing could be further from the truth. I am not against good works; neither am I against the white man. I am against the mixture, good works *and* rum; white man *and* hypocrisy.

We, in my home, are licentious, just as are many people in the Western world, but is there not an excuse for us? We do not live a lie; we sincerely believe that we are right. We have no higher guidance to tell us anything different.

The white man has every advantage of culture, training, and, above all, religion, whose principal precepts are faith, hope, and charity. Spires point to the Deity of the white man at every corner in the towns of the white man, preaching hourly the doctrine of brotherly love. There is no excuse for a white man to be less civilized, in the proper sense of the word, than we savages. Railways, motor-

203

cars, lighting systems, town-planning, huge buildings, bring you no closer to real civilization than does the yawn of a crocodile bring a tsetse-fly, sleeping on its nose, to its mouth. It is not the white man that I criticize, but the white man's " civilization "!

I remember that it is the white man whom I have to thank for everything that I have and that I know. I thank him for my being alive today; so do not misjudge me and think that I am against the white man. I wish, however, that all men would practise their ideals.

When the summer was over and the time had arrived for my young master and me to return to school, the question arose as to what to do with me. I had been away over two years, during which time I had stopped book-learning and had forgotten almost all that I had learned before I had gone away. My young master had been advancing all this time and knew considerably more than I did, so it was impossible to send me with him to school. That same problem has followed me all through life, to know just what to do with me!

I had been home to Africa, had married, and, in truth, was a real man. My young master was still an unsophisticated wee boy. He asked many questions about my being married, and I told him, the best I could, about my wives, and about Gooma. He was interested in the story and expressed a strong desire to go to my home with me on my next journey and get himself " a few wives," as he would say.

He was a splendid boy, of excellent character and of fine stature, physically fit and well matured. He belonged to a family that had stifled every reference to the subject of sex. He had been taught to consider sex affairs as unclean, whereas I had been taught to understand that sex matters were as natural as eating or drinking. I did not know that sex is a closed book or an open secret; so I acquainted my young master with all that I knew of sex.

Under the circumstances the reaction to such open and frank treatment of this forbidden subject bewildered my young master. We spent many hours together talking about my wives and about the vows of girls in my country about to be married. It surprised me to learn that the young master was so ignorant of the subject.

Our custom in Africa tends towards discouraging secret, depraved actions, but in the Western world, I learned, real vices are indulged in secretly and vigorously opposed in the open. My young master had been taught that a woman is to be desired, but to be avoided. I was differently taught. My view was that a woman is not only to be desired, but also to be possessed, and that relations with her are of a lasting beauty. Woman, with me, in other words, has a definite place, a reality; with him, she was a fantasy.

Here was another instance of "the sins of the fathers." He was only a cog in the wheel that grinds out the destinies of men in Western civilization. Excesses are always sweet when indulged in, like the proverbial stolen fruit, so you can understand why I followed readily and wondered all the time why my own father had not told me about any of these things before. My young master truly needed a wife, and it was not long before I discovered this.

It was decided to send me to board-school — that is, a city public school, under the Glasgow school board — and my young master to a school called Allan Glen, both in Glasgow. We met frequently and often spent the week-end together.

Chapter *XXII*

FUGITIVES IN ENGLAND

Impossible in school. Tutors. Impossible at home. An insulted maid. Running away. Birmingham. Coventry. Lady Godiva. The paint-shop. Indignant labourers. The repair-shop. I act the savage. Gorgonzola, the Celebrated African Cheese.

Time passed, and nothing unusual happened except the unexpected death of old Dr. Dobbie, who must have been over eighty years old then. I am sorry to say that I rejoiced at the news of his death.

The boys in my new school were different from the boys I had met at school in Edinburgh. Most of these boys could not understand my being black and frequently asked: " Did you ever try using soap? " That was thought quite a joke, and so the whole school called me " Soap." This annoyed me, and I complained to my master about it, with the result that he took me from that school and engaged private tutors.

I had three such tutors in all, one for mathematics, another for civic studies, and another for

English. The last also acted as a kind of nurse. This combined nurse and English teacher, a maiden lady, Miss Cranston, from Ayrshire, about fifty years old, was quite stylish in her make-up and spent much time in front of the mirror. I believe she said she had met, or taught, or seen Florence Nightingale, because she frequently held forth on the many adorable qualities of that lady.

The three tutors did not last long with me, because I was not easy to control. I was sent back to board-school. There I was almost always in a fight. I would bite anyone who disturbed me, even my teachers. I was frequently paddled, but that did not do much good. When four years more had ended I had not gained much school-learning. I had, however, learned a good deal from the tutoring of my young master.

I have always been wilful and somewhat hard-headed, and I was more so in that house in Scotland than ever before. The truth was, I was becoming too wise, and, as you all know, a little knowledge is often dangerous. I did not know much English, nor was I particularly bright in school-learning, but I thought that I knew everything. That, with my naturally over-bearing disposition and my constantly increasing vanity and conceit, made things somewhat difficult at home.

My young master contributed his share in moulding me into the character that I was fast becoming. I copied from him all the impudence and effrontery that I could. You can hardly blame me, for was I not a man already? Had I not actually married five wives in my own country? My own father had no legal jurisdiction over me, because in my own land I had become a man at the age of thirteen. My self-assertiveness, therefore, was partly due to my natural position, and partly to the example set by my young master. When he rebelled, I rebelled; what he was satisfied with, I was satisfied with; and vice versa.

One day I received a severe scolding because of a complaint made by one of the maids. The maid was a new one and it seemed she did not relish working for me. Perhaps she came from a country district and had never seen a native black boy before. My master had brought her from the " feeing market " in Glasgow, where servants were usually engaged. I had noticed my young master's free and easy ways with her, and of course I thought it quite proper for me to do what he did. She did not take so kindly to my attentions as she did to those of the young master, and so she complained to the madame, who in turn reported me to the master.

When the master spoke to me about my rudeness to Agatha, the maid, I replied, as I had often heard my young master: "She is only a servant."

The master was greatly annoyed, and scolded me severely. He added: "She is not your servant, anyway." With that he boxed my ears good and hard.

I screamed, and thereupon told him a good many things that I had heard and seen my young master say and do. The master was not pleased at this, and when the young master came home, there was a terrible row. The poor maid was sent away, and my young master was in disgrace.

All of this happened in April. My young master was still going to school. The Easter holidays had not long ended, and he was again hoping for the next holiday. It appeared that the trouble that I had unwittingly got him into was more serious than I could imagine. He took me out one afternoon, not saying a word to anyone, and we went to the railway station. Where we were going I did not know; he bought tickets and off we went. We had no luggage with us, so I thought that we should come back soon. We did not, however, for we slept on the train all night, and in the morning I heard the guards say "Leicester." Even then we did not get off. We continued travelling and the next place that I remember hearing called out was Birmingham.

There we got off the train and walked. We soon came to a busy street called the Bull Ring. I remember Bull Ring Street, because a large church stood in the centre, with a tower and a clock. We stopped to eat in a place built like a ship, called, if I remember right, Nelson's Cabin. I cannot easily forget the place. I was sad and half afraid of what my young master was doing; so I began to cry. I aroused the sympathy of one of the girls who was serving, and I remember hearing a man say to her: "Look after him, Alice!" Then she was extremely kind to me.

Up till now my young master had not told me his plans. In fact, he was quite surly. He and Alice began to talk, and finally he wrote something on a slip of paper and thanked Alice. She washed my face and patted me when she said good-bye. My young master laughed. That was the first time I had seen him smile since we had left Glasgow. How good it made me feel! When he looked down at me and smiled, I simply threw my arms around his neck and cried more and kissed him much. That was unusual for me, because even when we had slept together at his home or anywhere else, I had never done that. As for him, he was always petting me or someone else, for he had a most ardent nature. It must have been a pathetic scene to the onlookers, and especially to Alice, to see us standing there in Nelson's Cabin restaurant, me weeping on the shoulder of my young master and kissing him, and him holding me and smiling.

I said to him after I saw him smile at me: " Why don't you kiss Alice? " He replied sharply: " What for? For you to go home and tell about?" Then for the first time it dawned upon me that my telling things had brought my young master into a lot of trouble, and I really had done him much harm. He kissed Alice good-bye, however, whether to please me or to satisfy his own nature, I don't know. At any rate he kissed her as if he had known her before. I told Alice that I would come back some time to see her again.

My young master had written at Alice's dictation the address of a place where we might lodge for the night. We arrived at that place all right. There, later, when we had gone to bed, my young master told me everything that had happened and said that I had brought him into trouble with his father and into disgrace in the eyes of his mother, of whom he was very fond.

I could not appreciate the seriousness of disgrace in the eyes of his mother, for I had been taught that a mother is only a mother, and merely a woman, so I could not grasp, at that time, the seriousness of his feelings. On the other hand, to merit his father's scorn was a most serious thing in my opinion. That is the way my savage training made me think.

Where my young master got the money for travelling I do not know. I did not ask him, because I never once thought about it. All I knew was that we travelled. He talked with many people, but I never, or at least very seldom, caught the conversation.

Finally we left Birmingham by train and travelled to another place, called Coventry. Something seemed about to happen in Coventry; the people were all talking about a great coming event when the whole town was to be decorated with banners and streamers. I soon learned what was going on. Coventry was once the home of a famous woman, a certain Lady Godiva. From what I understood, she, or someone representing her, was about to ride through the whole town without any clothes on. Of course to me that did not seem a remarkable thing to do. I had always seen people without clothes.

Coventry was so full of life that we stayed there. The thought of Lady Godiva attracted my young master and made him lose sleep. The procession was not to take place until a month had passed. I am not certain what day or month it was, but I know that we had to wait ever so long before anything happened. I must admit that I would not have missed the excitement for anything. My young master mixed freely with people and took me with him. It caused curiosity to see a black boy taken round by a white boy. Most people thought that my young master was a rich tourist who was visiting Coventry to see the great Lady Godiva procession.

One night we were sitting in an inn. A young man, whose name I afterwards learned was Maude, became interested in my young master and me. He arranged to show us all over the town and to take us through the motor works of which he was either manager or foreman. That was the Humber motor-car factory. Coventry then was the home of the English motor-car industry; many of the bicycles and motor-cars used in England were manufactured there. We were taken through the factory, and my young master was offered a job. He accepted it, perhaps for the novelty of the thing.

At once the question arose, what was to be done with me. After much talk it was decided to give me a job also. I was put into the paint-shop. I do not remember which shop my young master entered.

The men in the paint-shop did not take kindly to me, and they did everything they knew how to annoy me. My particular job was to rub the bodies of motor-cars to make them smooth, with a piece of pumice-stone. I simply did what I was told. It was fun for me, and perhaps I might have stayed there a long time if the men had not annoyed me by throwing pieces of pumice-stone at me, invariably hitting me on the head or in the face. That, of course, hurt me, and naturally I did not like it. When the head man came round and asked me in a kindly tone how I liked the work, I complained. He roared and swore at all the men. I had heard my young master use the same words when he was angry. The men were most indignant at me for telling the head man about their hitting me with pumice-stone. They signed a paper saying that they would not work in the same place with me. The head man appeared holding the paper and said to me in the hearing of all: " Well, my boy, the men won't work with you and I'm sorry that I'm an Englishman. You'll have to go."

My pay was sixpence ha'penny an hour. After I received the money due me, I went outside the building and waited for my young master to call for me, as he had done every day.

When I told my young master what had

happened, he did not like it and complained at once to Mr. Maude, who had me put in the repair-shop, where the men were a little more tolerant. I did not do much work in the repair-shop, but I was kept there as a sort of novelty.

I learned a good deal about the particular motor-car made in these works, but my young master learned a lot more than I did. He did excellent work, so I heard men say. I also learned more English during my stay in Coventry than I had learned in the whole time that I had been in Scotland.

We met a man named Sumner, owner of an inn. This Mr. Sumner became interested in me at once, because he had been in Africa. Mr. Sumner was eager to have me with him all the time, so that he could put me on exhibition before his customers. One of his customers happened to be chairman of the Godiva procession committee, and it was suggested to him to propose me to the committee, to ride in the procession as an African chief.

All parts of the world, so they said, were to be represented in the Lady Godiva procession, but I was the only black person to be had. The proposal was accepted unanimously and I was advertised to ride horseback, dressed in so-called African costume, through the streets of Coventry, as Amgoza, the Celebrated African Chief. Many people twisted my name and called me Gorgonzola, the Celebrated African Cheese.

My young master was thoroughly delighted by this new development of affairs and was inspired to write home to Glasgow to his mother and to tell her all about it.

In the mean time Mr. Sumner managed to get hold of a kind of African native costume, with an elaborate head-dress. Whatever the costume represented, it did not have anything to do with my part of Africa. After I had been fitted out, they had my photograph taken and copies made on postcards, with my name printed at the bottom. These postcards were sold to the public for threepence each.

The day of the procession arrived. Coventry was overcrowded with people from all England. The procession formed in a place called the Pool Meadow. I was placed on the back of a black and white, or piebald, pony. The march began at ten-thirty in the morning. My young master ran beside me in the procession all the way, selling postcards and holding the money for those that I sold. I screamed and made all kinds of noises, with my finger in my mouth. That lent colour to my make-up. I had no pockets in my costume, and so my young master carried all the money. I had brass curtain-rings in my ears and in my nose. One jolly fellow who had been drinking ale from a great mug shouted to me: " Hey, chief, I bet you have more brass on your face than you have in your pockets."

The procession ended at six o'clock in the evening. I was sore from sitting astride the piebald pony so long.

When we returned to Mr. Sumner's inn yard, my young master counted the money we had made selling postcards, including those sold by Mr. Sumner himself to his customers, and there were twenty pounds! Mr. Sumner said that it was all for me. Everybody tried to talk to me, but I was so tired that I could not remain there and finish the night in their company.

Chapter XXIII

A FLIGHT ACROSS EUROPE

Birmingham again. A day like a crazy dream. A slave of passions. The Dover boat. Boulogne. Paris. A Dahomey woman. Antwerp. Cat meat. Russia. Germany. Shipped back to Africa.

My young master took me to our lodgings in Payne's Lane, if I remember right. When we arrived at the house, there was a message for my young master, a telegraph dispatch. What it said I never learned.

Instead of my young master's giving me food and putting me to bed, he gathered up what little luggage we had acquired, jumped into a hansom cab, and hastened off to the railway station, dragging me with him. Thousands of people were at the station, waiting to get away. The next thing I knew, we were back in Birmingham.

We got out of the train and walked up and down the platform. I went everywhere my young master took me. I could not help myself. He held me all

219

the time by a hand or an arm. I told my young master that I felt sleepy, and he said that he did also. We finally found the place whose address he had written on the slip of paper, when he was talking to Alice of the Nelson's Cabin restaurant.

The proprietor of the place opened the door and greeted us as if we were relatives of his. He remembered us. We went to bed in the same room where we had slept two months before, when we had first landed there. I was indeed tired, and it was two o'clock in the morning.

What a day! The excitement of preparing and dressing for the procession; the confusion of the line-up for the march, down on the Pool Meadow; the difficulty of inducing me to mount the gentle piebald pony; the procession through every street of Coventry; the screaming, the shouting, the laughter of men and boys; the giggling of girls and of women; the stopping at every inn; and the passing around of a pot filled with good ale; the selling of postcards with my picture as Chief Amgoza; the hubbub of the crowd at Sumner's inn; my fainting condition — all that was like a wild dream. Just when I had been about to have a hearty meal, the first that day, and then a good sleep, my young master had rushed me off to the station, taken me on a train, and ridden four hours or thereabouts,

220

and then hunted for the address written on the slip of paper. That day was the most eventful day in my career.

I slept, and so did my poor young master, but only for a time. He suffered mentally, and I suffered physically. It is a problem which one of us suffered more. Our minds were on entirely different things. He feared his father, I think, though 'I have never learned definitely what made him toss the way he did. I feared him. I began to think that he was losing his mind, and did not know what he was doing. I wondered if I had done something to upset him. I could think of nothing.

Today as I sit alone and look back over those days, I boil with indignation. I was not to blame, neither was my young master. The stupidity of his parents was to blame. Shut off from every contact with truth, the poor boy had become the innocent victim of his passions, all because of forced ignorance. How many young men, even today, labour under the same yoke! I bleed when I think of the suffering of one of the best boys that ever lived. You might have thought him guilty of murder if you had seen his depression. Yet he had run away from home and from school only because of a slight indiscretion of which his parents had learned.

I woke up many times during that night and

found my young master in tears. I kissed him; I tried to kiss away his tears. Finally we both slept soundly, and then the morning came. Another day. What would happen? I could not guess.

We left that place and found Nelson's Cabin, so that we might eat. There we saw Alice, who greeted us warmly, but I had to tell my young master to kiss her before he attempted it. That made him smile with the same happy smile that I had seen before when I had first told him to kiss Alice. We ate, and Alice talked long with my young master. Then he wrote something more on a piece of paper and gave it to Alice, and she went away. When she returned, she gave my young master a lot of money, all in gold. We left Nelson's Cabin and Alice, but I noticed that now my young master kissed her without urging.

That night we left Birmingham for London and took train for Dover, at the Victoria Station. Of course I did not know the names of any of these places until my young master told me. I had to ask him everything, because he did not talk to me much. When he did say anything, it was very short and usually an answer to some inquiry that I had made. Half the time I did not understand his answers. All that made me miserable, and I wished

222

that I were back in Glasgow, in the home out on the Drive.

At Dover my young master ran here and there, talking first to this one and then to another, showing some papers and giving away money. It was all most mysterious. We finally sailed on a boat at night. I did not dream that we were leaving England. Going where? I did not know, and I honestly believe that my young master did not know either.

In a comparatively short time we reached the other side, and I discovered that we were in Boulogne, France. The whole scene changed. We were in a strange land, which had a different language from any I knew. I did not know a syllable in French. Perhaps my young master knew, for he seemed to get along nicely and to make himself understood. Before we left Boulogne, a kindly woman washed my face and put clean things on me, things that my young master bought. The woman's name was Eshkanas, and she was an Israelite, the first one that I had recognized since I had seen the Jewish boy Ansel.

The little sea journey had done me good, and that, with the washing that Madame Eshkanas gave me, made me quite cheerful. I began to hum " Stop yer ticklin', Jock," and actually made my young master smile. I had no curiosity to learn what he was doing. I thought I had better not learn; I might tell it when I got back to my white father in Scotland.

We left Boulogne, and before I knew it, we were in Paris.

As I said before, I never knew where all the money came from for all this travelling, but we went about everywhere, it seemed to me. My young master must have had money. I had a little, but I had no chance to use it. My young master paid for everything.

I had lost my bonnet on the boat coming across the Channel, because I had tried to stand out on the deck in a strong wind. Consequently I went about bare-headed. My young master liked the idea, so he threw his own bonnet away too.

We stopped at a hotel, where the maids made a great fuss over my young master and me. I usually did everything that he did, if I had time. When the maid came into our room in the morning, my young master caught her and gave her a kiss. To be like him I tried to do the same, but I got into trouble.

My young master took me to see an exhibition going on at that time in Paris. To my surprise, I saw there, for the first time out of my country, a real native Dahomey woman. There she was on exhibition! I could hardly control myself or keep from rushing up to her at once. The white women had not interested me at all, but the native woman fascinated me. I did not speak to the Dahomey woman, however.

After remaining in Paris two weeks, my young master took me to Brussels, and then across France to Marseilles. From there we went in a steamer to Antwerp. In that city I saw people eating cat meat, and we ate it also. It was then a common food in that country, just as rabbit is in Great Britain and the United States.

We left Brussels and started by train for Saint Petersburg, in Russia. To my young master's surprise, we were not allowed to enter Russia. From what I could understand from a kindly gentleman who was willing to explain everything to us, no one was permitted to bring into Russia any black, or any Chinaman, and I believe he said Jew as well, without giving a heavy bond. He said that he was a Jewish lumber-merchant from Riga. My young master asked why they permitted him, if he was a Jew, to enter. The gentleman explained that he had access to any place in Russia, and that he was a large property-holder in a part of Russia called Kurland. My young master expressed the wish to travel with the Jewish gentleman. That recalled the scolding that my protector once got from his mother when I told her that we had been in company with the Jewish boy Ansel, at Rothesay. When I told the merchant that I was an Israelite, he was naturally surprised, but was extremely kind both to my young master and to me.

When we reached the place where the man lived, we discovered that most of the people spoke German. I knew no German, but my young master again got along all right. We stayed with the stranger nearly two weeks. My cup was running over. I was sorely homesick, and I cried often, but I did not say what was wrong with me.

My young master took me from Riga to Berlin. We did not have such an easy time entering Germany, but at last, after being held in a kind of barracks for several days, we were permitted to proceed on our way.

I fretted, and teased my young master to take me " home." He must have thought that I meant my own native Africa, because at last he went to an office and arranged for me to go back to my own people.

We waited a few days in Berlin, and then travelled to Hamburg. There my young master received a long letter from his mother. How she knew where he was I cannot say. He cried a great deal over the letter, and yet he told me it was good news. I could not understand.

Finally he put me on a ship of the Woermann Line and promised to see me again some time. We kissed good-bye on the dock that day, and both cried. I was on my way back to Africa and he was on his way back to bonnie Scotland. I did not have much luggage and so it did not take me long to get settled. I am sure that if the steamer had not pulled out as soon as it did, we should not have parted at all, because we both cried and wished we were not separating.

Chapter XXIV

''ONLY NIGGERS''

Two labourers. A modern slave-ship. Heartless treatment. Buried alive. Better the jungle beasts than white men. " Only niggers." I swell with pride. Trunks and box capsize. Whydah. A friendly agent.

The steamer stopped at Sierra Leone, and then I discovered that my passage was booked only to that place. I got off to wait for a coasting steamer. The fare from Sierra Leone would not be nearly so much as it would have been if I had remained on the German passenger ship. I did not have enough money anyway, although my young master had said that he would have five pounds waiting for me when I landed.

After waiting three days amongst the Krumen of Sierra Leone, I boarded a coasting steamer bound for the Congo River, but the vessel would stop at my port in Dahomey. The ship was loaded down with a mixed cargo and carried a number of natives, but none like me. The ship carried provisions

228

and stores to the various trading stations along the coast.

The other blacks were contract Kru labourers, from Sierra Leone and the vicinity, on their way to a destination they did not know, to work on plantations, as they believed. They were a happy lot of people and all Christians. On deck they sang sacred songs. They were all deck passengers, huddled together at the stern of the ship. The crew was unpleasantly rough with them. They consisted of men, women, and children who had been picked up by agents, hired, and promised, by blank contracts, return passage, free of charge, to their own country after the season had finished. Of course they never returned. In other words, these poor unfortunates were being shanghaied, as they frequently are on the west coast of Africa.

I was a cabin passenger, my ticket having cost thirty pounds and sixteen shillings, but I mixed much with the Kru people during that trip.

The crew, all white, was good to me, making a pet of me. The chief engineer and another officer were especially kind and often had me in their cabins. I suppose the white crew could not afford to treat me unkindly because I was a cabin passenger. They called the Krus " niggers," and I heard the word " nigger " so much that I, too, began to address them as " niggers." I am not sure that I was ever addressed as " nigger." I may have been, but I do not remember it.

I had much chance to learn about the Kru people who were being shanghaied. What I gathered was that the Krus would be landed at a place called Fernando Po, a Spanish colony, and the moment that they set their feet on shore, they would be virtual slaves, without any avenue of escape. They had signed contracts thinking that they were securing for themselves good positions and a sure passage home, but they had really signed their lives away. They did not know how to read or write and signed by making a cross-mark.

One night one of the " nigger " men fell down a hatchway. He fell from the main deck through to the bottom of the ship. I understood that his back was broken, and I heard much wailing and screaming among the women all through the night. There was a doctor aboard ship, who had evidently qualified as a bridge-player and whisky-drinker. I remember noticing that he was much annoyed at being disturbed, when he was told that one of the " niggers " had fallen down the hatchway. I heard him say: " Couldn't he just as well have fallen overboard? It would have been a softer landing for him."

I followed the doctor when he left the saloon to go below to examine the man, who had, by that time, been brought up out of the hold and stretched out in the anchor room, on the floor. I shall never forget the expression of suffering in the face of that poor wretch. The doctor told the sailors that the man was dead, and the crew at once sewed a canvas bag. I watched them put the dead " nigger " into the bag. It was morning. That poor man had been left suffering in the anchor room all night, without anyone to give him a cup of cold water.

A hatch cover was placed on the side of the ship, by the rail, from which a section had been moved. The body was laid out on it, and the crew tied heavy pieces of lead to each leg, and then put him into the canvas bag they had made and sewed it up. The captain stood at the head of the hatch cover and opened a book. What he was doing and saying I did not know then, but I know now; he read the last rites for the dead. Horrible as it seems, I know that that man was not dead, because he moved his head when one of the crew put the canvas bag over it. He groaned audibly, and I shouted that he was not dead. A white man said: " If he isn't, he soon will be."

I could not understand why the man was put into the bag for having broken his back; so I said to the

231

chief steward, over and over again: " Not dead, not dead."

He replied: " That's all right; he's only a nigger." I was contented, believing that all was as it should be. The canvas bag containing the man who was not dead was thrown into the Gulf of Guinea. The " nigger " was buried alive. *To this I solemnly swear.*

I was so eager to get off that ship that I was extremely pleased when it reached Whydah, in Dahomey. The white men offered to take me to Kotonu, in order that I might have a better landing-place, but I vigorously declined their offer. I preferred taking all the risks of landing in a surf-boat and getting drenched to spending another day in the company of those very " civilized " white men. I could not explain at that time why I was so eager to get away from them, but I can fearlessly give the reason now. I was better off at the mercy of the beasts of the Ondo bush than in the company of that pitiless crew of potential murderers.

Scenes of that kind were frequent along the west coast of Africa. Ships transported their cargoes of human souls from different parts of the coast down to Fernando Po, for the purpose of supplying slaves to the Portuguese. The " niggers " were free people until they landed, but no sooner had they stepped on shore than they ceased to have names and became slaves, with numbers or brands. All that I heard from the crew of the ship. They treated me far differently from the other blacks, who were only " niggers," as they said. I really thought then that what they did was proper and quite in place, for, after all, as the white men said, they were " only niggers."

It was many years before the awfulness of it occurred to me and I began trying, like a fool, to better the condition of the Krus. My poor efforts were quite futile. I became another martyr to the cause of justice for all people. The more civilized I became, the less willing I was to be a martyr for any cause. Life offered much else for me besides being flogged to death or poisoned or allowed to rot in some tropical prison, merely to help " niggers." I became more and more convinced that the European powers, which had partitioned among themselves a continent larger than the combined areas of their European possessions, without so much as a " by your leave " to the people most intimately concerned, would not be willing to have their pet schemes upset or interfered with by an insignificant " savage " like myself.

The surf-boat in which I left the ship neared the coast. The men stopped paddling and began shouting at one another in their own tongue. One would have thought that they were going to fight. I had two steamer-trunks full of who knows what, and a large wooden box filled with household effects. No one paid any attention to my luggage. A heavy double surf hit the boat and threw it up on the shallows, although it was still far out in the water. A man grabbed me, threw me across his shoulders, and ran out of the water. There was so much shouting and screaming that I did not notice what the other men were doing. I landed, without mishap, with my legs and feet a little wet, but I did not mind that, so long as I myself was safe.

The surf-boat had capsized, my trunks and wooden box had been dumped into the water, and everything had got wringing wet. One man was struck by the overturned surf-boat and killed, but that did not worry me. I remembered, for the moment, the poor black man who had been buried alive in the Gulf of Guinea, but no sooner had that thought come than another flashed through my mind: the steward had said that the man was only a " nigger." So was this man who had been killed by the overturned surf-boat. Why worry?

The coast became alive with people, and many gathered around me. There were some white men, dressed in white, the French customs officials. They did not know any English, and that really surprised me. I was not surprised that the other men who stood around did not know English, because they were all black, but I could not conceive of a white man's not knowing English.

They made me understand that I should have to open my trunks and the box so that they could examine the contents. I was angry at once, because my trunks and wooden box were soaking wet. Everyone laughed at the hasty, angry way in which I handled my things after I had opened my trunks. The customs men indicated that they were satisfied with their search, and that ended a disagreeable job.

Now I tried my best to locate the native Dahomeyan whom I had met on my previous trip home, but no one knew him. No one knew me either. They just stood and gazed at me. I had to leave my luggage on the coast and walk alone, about five miles inland, to the town of Whydah. The going was easy compared with the journey that I should have to take before I could reach my own home.

When I reached Whydah, I found the office of G. Goedelt, the agent of the steamship line. He said that there had been five pounds sent there for me, but that I should have to pay two pounds and ten shillings for something, I didn't know what, and of course I had to consent. He gave me the remainder in German marks. Therefore I lost another ten shillings, because of the rate of exchange. It was useless to try to get the agent to have someone bring my luggage up to Whydah. He would not even give me a place to stop in overnight in his compound.

After walking around for a long time, looking in at every place, I came to the depot of an English trading company, John Walkden and Son, of Manchester, England. As best I could, I explained my plight to the agent of that company. He was a gentleman, as I have invariably found real Englishmen to be. He immediately dispatched native workmen to the coast and had all my luggage brought into the company compound. He told me to open up everything and said that he would see that one of the native servants put my things in the sun to dry. Most of the stuff had been ruined because of the salt water, but it was easy to dry it, for the sun is very hot on the coast of Dahomey.

The English agent gave me supper, and after the meal he had me sit down and answer questions, because conversation was impossible, as my English was too limited. He was quite amused with me and much interested in my story about my first departure from Africa. He said it would not be

wise for me to go up to my home the same way that
I had come out. It was impossible for him to induce
men to guide me so far, because whenever a coast
man gets caught up there, the inland people are
so cruel to him that it makes coast people afraid
to go near the bushmen.

I knew this, because I remembered what had happened to the crew that had taken me up home on my
previous return. The agent suggested that I go
by canoe to Porto Novo and try to pick up guides
there.

Chapter XXV

A WILD JOURNEY

*A caravan. The guides. Up the Weme. Killed by a hippo.
River spirits. Carried on a hammock chair. A porter's story.*

The next day I started from Whydah on an entirely different route to my distant village near the Sahara Desert, by the way of Porto Novo. When I reached Porto Novo, I met a family of Portuguese Negroes who wished to befriend me. They gave me hospitality, and finally made up a caravan for me to travel with from there, but it took them a whole month to do it, because it was a difficult task to induce enough natives to accompany me.

If the native Dahomeyans had known that I really belonged to the people where they were guiding me, they would have taken me a little way into the bush and killed me, because they hated my people as much as my people hated them. We had always beaten them in warfare, even though they copied us in putting women on the field of battle.

The difference between their Amazons and ours was that their women were flabby and fat, while ours were firm, hard, and strong. When we caught one of their men, we always mistreated him.

The Portuguese Negro family had represented me as an English subject, from a different land, who did not know any language but English. They told the men that were going to guide me up-country that I was going up to settle some affairs for my English master. It took a whole month, however, to get eleven men to believe the yarn; that was the number that had been selected to take me up, nine carriers and two guides. One of the guides was a Kruman, and the other a Dahomey warrior. The others did not matter much, as everything depended upon the guides. I pledged the Portuguese Negro family that I would protect all these men when they arrived in my country, and that I would see that they left safely for their return journey to the coast. It cost me exactly thirty English shillings for the trip up-country, from Porto Novo to my home village, about seven hundred miles, or from sixty to sixty-five days' walk.

We started off, the nine carriers taking turns in carrying me and my luggage, for, however spoiled the luggage was, I clung to all of it. The Portuguese Negro family had supplied me with a hammock and a mosquito-net. We started at night and travelled by canoe up the Weme River as far as a place called Biagra, or some such name as that. From there we struck out for the bush.

Even on the river it was dangerous, because of the crocodiles and hippopotamuses. We lost one man to a hippo, but it really was his own fault. He happened to be the liveliest one of the whole crew. On the night after we had left the river, this poor fellow wanted fish and said that he knew how to get them, in spite of the warnings of his companions. The guides did not trouble themselves in the least about what he did. I did not understand the argument. All I knew was that we were going to have fish to eat, because I caught the word for fish in their tongue, which is *" a-wa."*

We had halted for the night, a little way in the bush from the river, every man holding a torch, and with fires lit all around us for protection. The fellow took a torch with him and paddled one of the canoes out into the middle of the river; then he leaned over the side of the canoe with a small handmade net, watching for fish. A hippo is always attracted by a light, especially on the water. The poor chap was so intent on his job of catching a few fish that the splash of the big beast in the water did not attract him. The hippo made for the light

240

that he was holding, upset the canoe, and threw the fellow into the water.

We all heard the screams, and my blood ran cold at that unearthly cry. Everybody rushed towards the river's bank. We could see the hippo making its way up the other bank, and we all could hear its jaws, grinding the bones of our poor unfortunate carrier. Oh, what screaming and moaning!

You would have thought that the other carriers were going to kill the guides and me, or grind us up in their jaws. It was the hardest job I have ever seen to keep those men from turning back and abandoning us there in the bush. If they had really dared, the guides and I would have been left alone from that night on. One of the guides was quick-witted enough to rush to the river's bank and destroy the other canoe, in order to prevent the carriers from slipping away from us during the night. That was really their intention; one of the men came running back to the fires, while we were asleep, and woke us up, screaming that someone had taken the other canoe. He was too dense to understand that it had been punctured by one of the guides, who had caused it to sink.

The guides thereupon built up a fantastic yarn about the river and the evil spirits where we were, and made those poor chaps almost change colour.

If I had not been as "civilized " as I was, I, too, should not have retained my blackness after hearing the stories that the guides told to the carriers. Whether the guides made up their story, or whether they believed it themselves, I really can't say, but I do know that it saved the situation for us. Instead of sleeping any more, the carriers insisted on pushing farther into the bush, away from the river.

" Why, don't you know," one of the guides said, when all was nice and quiet, " that this river lets out a host of serpents that have green eyes; and when your foot has been wet by the water of the river, these serpents surround you with long tentacles, which stretch out ever so far and draw you to them, and then the snakes just take you down into their bellies whole? One of the tentacles may be reaching out now, just ready to twist around your neck and choke you! Who knows? "

Just then a piece of vine dropped down on the head of one of the carriers, and Lord! didn't he scream and jump! He thought the vine was one of the tentacles reaching out for him.

We broke camp that minute and started trekking through the bush. We did not stop until the next night. That was a long time to keep going, without food, and hardly stopping for water. At any other time the carriers would have wanted to stop and rest every two or three hours, but now they were willing to keep on and never stop, even to eat.

I had to ride in a hammock practically all the time, for not to do so would have spoiled the morale of all and would have put me in danger of being left alone. Among native people kindness is weakness. I rode and listened, but I dared not be so familiar as to join in conversation or even to express pleasure. It was not easy for me to understand all that the men said, because their language was different from mine, and unless they talked slowly, I could not catch the gist of their talk.

Because of the state of mind, everyone in the party tried to relate a harrowing experience of his own, or of someone whom he knew. None of the stories was true, but they made us shiver just the same.

I here relate, as exactly as I can, a story told by a carrier during one of the halts or rest periods.

WHY WE EAT FISH

" In the days when there was no river, and the seas were masters, there was a woman, named Arifa, who had been abandoned by her husband because she could not bear a child. Now, you all know that a woman without child is like an elephant without a trunk. This woman, it was said,

243

had mated with all the beasts in the bush, without success in becoming a mother; and Husni knew her well!''

Who Husni was, I do not know, but I believe that he was a great story-teller, whose word was beyond reproach to those natives; to mention Husni was to make a sort of oath as to the credibility of the yarn.

'' Husni knew her well. He even tried himself to take the witch curse from her; and you all know what Husni can do with any woman. Why, women have triplets when he merely looks at them. Even Husni failed to cause the old woman to become a mother.

'' One night, while the woman was lying on the coast and trying to sleep, after having tried everything that she knew to be with child, she dozed off. While she was sleeping, a strange monster rose up out of the water, for the sea knows everything and has the key to all secrets. This monster crawled up on the shore beside Arifa. The creature was like an elephant, except that it had a tail instead of feet. It lay down beside the woman and then at last went away. When the woman woke in the morning, she knew she was to bear a child. Everyone was surprised when she returned to her former home. Her husband made a feast in honour of his wife and

244

there was much rejoicing among all her people. The news was told by tomtom, and pledges were made to the fetish-gods in honour of Arifa.

" Just before the time had come for her to bear the child, she acted strangely, by going outside her village and weeping and moaning. No one paid any attention to her sadness, for all women weep at such times.

" One morning, just at the time when the women-folk draw their water for cooking, a girl ran into the village and shouted: ' Arifa has given birth to a litter of fish! ' Everybody laughed, and a woman said: ' Don't talk silly, child; no fish can be a hus-band. How can she have borne fish instead of chil-dren? Then, too, there is no water near here, and fish live in water! '

" The whole village, out of curiosity, ran to where Arifa had been lying, and there they saw her throw-ing water into a ditch. When they asked her what she did that for, Arifa answered: ' To give a home to my young.' At this, she produced a palm-leaf full of little fish, alive and wriggling.

" The people were afraid and ran to the village and told the husband of Arifa the whole story. The husband hurried to the scene, with the whole village behind him. They could not go the whole way, because the water that Arifa had thrown into the ditch was now deep, and they had to stand where they were. To their surprise, Arifa appeared in the middle of the water and spoke to them, saying: ' From now on, this will be the home of my young. Woe betide any of you that shall disturb them.'

" That is the reason why we have rivers with sweet water, but with evil monsters like crocodiles, hippopotamuses, and snakes. Beware of rivers. Fish were first put into all rivers by a woman. Therefore the water has a mysterious depth, just as does the nature of a woman. Then, too, fish are good to eat because they contain the brain of a woman, the craftiest of all creatures."

I did not believe that ridiculous yarn, but I was amused at the looks of interest on the foolish faces of that baby-minded crew. The story took my thoughts away from real dangers. To make people forget danger is the object for which all such stories are told, I believe.

Chapter XXVI

The hostage. Village festivities. An old companion. Again into the bush. Chivalrous defence of a woman. Sacrilege. Saved by a white man.

After ten days of fast travelling we arrived at a village. Upon our arrival men met us just outside, as is the custom of people in that part of the world. The object is to find out who it is that wishes admittance, and to learn whether the travellers wish to remain in the village or merely to pass through it. If it is, as with us, merely to pass through, the strangers are not forced to go through any ceremony of purification, in order to drive out of them all evil spirits. They must leave one of their party, as a sort of guarantee, in the event of plague breaking out because of the party.

Here is where the evil crew of devil-men and witch-doctors have a picnic. If anyone at all falls sick, it is attributed at once to the evil influence of the party that passed through the village. Of course the poor unfortunate fellow who was left behind has to stand the blame. The witch-doctors and medicine-men take him and try to remove the evil in order to appease the anger of the spirits. I never knew anyone to survive being made pure in that manner.

For us it would have been more terrible if the carrier we left behind had known the whole truth. A person of his kind seldom knows the customs outside of his own town and away from his own people. Of course, you hear many things, but tales are conflicting and none are very complimentary to any village. The poor fellows believed what they were told by the guides — that their companion would remain in the village and would be given back to them upon their return to the coast. Needless to say, they never saw him again. Still, we had to leave him for the safety of the rest of us.

During the night, festivities were held, which included wild dancing and getting drunk by drinking palm-wine. The village was not illuminated, save by fires that were lighted to keep out beasts; therefore I could not get a good look at any of the faces and figures of the people as they danced and jumped about. I drank so much palm-wine that it made me dizzy; so I sought out the place where I was to sleep and tried to hide myself, but that was useless. All the people went to their homes, and

248

my carriers and guides, all except the one who was remaining behind in the village, came into the large hut with me, and there we all lay on great grass mats.

Early in the morning we started off again, but we did not stop to say good-bye or to thank anyone for hospitality. It is not customary for our people to go around and kiss everybody good-bye when we go on a trip. Again, had we not lost one of our carriers to that village? The guides knew that they would never see him again; they also knew that if anyone in the village fell sick or even complained of a strange feeling, that carrier would be blamed for the trouble and would be sacrificed by some savage form of mutilation.

I was two carriers short. That made the going a little more difficult, because the remaining carriers had to stop more often from fatigue. I rode in the hammock. It was then September, and the rain had stopped. The bush at that time was beautiful, with a riot of colours, known only in a tropical forest. Birds with lovely calls and gorgeous plumage made us forget our sorrows for the time being.

The route that the guides took was different from that taken by the guides who had taken me home on the previous journey. This was a much more delightful way, so it seemed, for every ten or fifteen days' journey we came to a village, and at every village we had a different experience. The other route would have been much better for my poor carriers, because they suffered most.

I almost fell into danger in one of these villages, through my own foolhardiness. We had circled far away from my land and had entered another territory. We were approaching a village called Illorin, in Nigeria. This is a town on the Nigerian railway, but there was no railway leading from the direction in which we approached it. My guides' intentions were to go from this place as far as Kano and then turn due west, which would bring me within two days' journey of my own village. It was there that the guides intended to leave me and let me walk into my village alone. I could easily pick up carriers from there to my own home, because I should come to many communities.

The distance from Kano across to my country is about twenty-one days' walk, or about three hundred miles. If the guides had brought me home by the other route, I should have been home long before; but the other way is dangerous, because of many things, including reptiles and beasts. It was not long before I discovered that we all should have been better off at the mercy of beasts

250

than we were in some of the places that we passed through.

The town that we were now entering was under British rule, and one or two white men resided there. Of course, natives under British rule never interfere with people passing through their territory, because of the influence of the British officials.

I had never heard of this particular place before; therefore I was ignorant in regard to the customs of the people. It appeared that some ceremony for girls was going on when we approached the place, because we saw a young girl, probably not more than eleven years old, running at breakneck speed out of a compound and screaming at the top of her voice. After her ran an old man, seemingly trying to catch her. He brandished a red-hot iron above his head.

I had been in Europe and had learned to dash to the aid of women when I saw them in difficulty. I jumped from my hammock and shouted at the old fellow. The guides trembled from head to foot and begged me to let local affairs alone. But I had forgotten myself and started once more to interfere in the affairs of someone else. If I had done such a thing outside of Africa, I might have escaped with a good beating, but in the country where I then was, among a lot of fanatical fetish-people, my punishment promised to be more than a beating. It might have cost me my life by a very cruel death. I was not prudent enough to think these things out at that time, so I did not heed the guides. I simply ran to the aid of the girl who was screaming.

I caught up with the girl and took hold of her wrist, trying to make her understand that I wished to help her. She struggled and fought as if I were some monster. In the mean time the old man, who could not run so fast as I, came to where we were struggling. When he saw me holding the girl by the wrist, he dropped his hot iron, put both his hands to his face, threw his arms towards the sky, as if exhorting the gods, gave one awful yell, and dashed away, as if someone were chasing him.

I could not understand this. Why had he run away when he saw me holding the arm of the girl? Why did the girl fight me all the more fiercely after the old man had run away?

The confusion, the girl's violently fighting me, and my trying to defend myself — a difficult matter because the girl fought me as if the Devil himself possessed her — all this frightened me. I let go of the fiend and ran back to where I had left my guides.

Meanwhile my guides had rushed to a store and

told the story of my foolishness. An Englishman, who was in charge of that station, for the firm of John Holt and Company, overheard the guides tell the story in their noisy way. As he knew a few words in the language of Nigeria, which is Yoruba, he became interested and asked the native clerk to tell him all about the affair.

As it was afterwards explained to me, the clerk conveyed the idea to the Englishman that another Englishman was in trouble. The guides really said that a man who spoke English — not an Englishman — was in trouble. The clerk put his own construction on the story and told his master that it was an Englishman in difficulty.

The guides knew what folly I had committed. According to the rites of the people in that region, I had injured a maiden, at the time when she was going through a barbarous test of virginity, by putting my hands on her undefiled body. The old man had been secured by the father of the girl to go through with the ceremony. To interfere with such a sacred rite meant death both to the offender and to the girl. It is strange that, even in that part of the country, where white men go and where missionaries have churches, such savage customs are practised. I did not stop to think of all this. If I had known what I was doing by my interference,

I surely should not even have looked at the wench, not to speak of touching her. I was prompted to do what I did only out of pity for her. Certainly I did not wish to ruin her for life among her own people.

When my guides ran to the store to get help, they thought that all was over with me, and probably with themselves. I ran from the girl, who had fought me so cruelly after I had tried to save her. The old man dashed away screaming, and calling out something in a loud voice. What it was I never found out, but it must have been curses on my head and on that of the girl.

He aroused much commotion. When I came back to where I had left the guides and the carriers, all the women in the world appeared to have congregated on the spot. If the Englishman had known who had fallen into trouble — that is, if he had guessed that it was a black, just a " nigger " — he would not have moved a step to save me, whether I spoke English or not. Since he thought that a white man was in danger, he called out all his men and rushed to the spot where the host of angry women surrounded us. He had a revolver in each hand, and his men had short guns.

The Englishman came just in time, for the old man who had run after the girl with a smoking hot iron pushed his way through the crowd of women, pointed at me, and said something in his own language which I could not understand. At that the women rushed at me and would have torn me to pieces except for the white man, with his men, all carrying guns. They burst into the crowd and held things in abeyance for the moment.

When I saw the white man, I cried out: " Rescue me! Rescue! " That was the only English word that I knew at that time for " save." That is, I did not know the word " save," so I screamed the more unusual words, " Rescue me! "

In the mean time the men who had come up with the Englishman drove the women and the men back and one snatched me from a fat woman who had my head and neck under her left arm, in a position to choke me to death before any of the others could get hold of me. There I was, snatched away from her, and there she was, pushed back by one of the men with fire-arms. The men who drove the angry people back belonged to the white men, and the natives dared not show hostility to anyone acting under a white man's orders. They remembered punitive expeditions, with burning and bloodshed. How could they forget? Those expeditions remain as blots on the annals of European intercourse with Africa.

Chapter XXVII

DISBELIEVED AND FLOGGED

A prisoner. " A coast nigger." Disbelieved. Flogged. A kindly storeman. Obstinate carriers. A close escape. The lost carriers.

The man who had snatched me away from the fat woman ran faster than I could and literally dragged me behind him. It was not far to the place where he took me, so I did not mind it much. I was only too pleased to be rescued from the mob.

The Englishman appeased the women and the men by saying that he would have me punished after he had learned how I had interrupted one of their most sacred customs and defiled a virgin by my touch, thereby rendering her liable to be put to death by the council, which exacts the death penalty for any breach of purification laws. My carriers and guides were driven like cattle to the grounds of the white man. I was not put with them, but was taken to the Englishman's house and left on the porch, waiting to be questioned.

Another white man, an assistant to the Englishman, tried to influence his chief to hand me over to the natives. He said: " This fellow is only one of those arrogant coast niggers."

The head white man was not convinced that he should give me up. He argued long with the other to change his opinion. I was bleeding from the scratchings that I received from the girl in her resentment at my interference. I had on English clothes. I told the head white man that I had been in England, and that I was just returning from there on my way home. The second white man would not believe me. He said: " You are a damned liar!"

I said: " You can see that I know the English language."

He laughed loudly and replied: " You are only a coast nigger who has learned a little English from the traders."

He asked some questions in English, to test whether I had been in England or not. I could not understand what he said. That confirmed his opinion of me and influenced the head white man a little. Both men thought I had never been out of the country.

The Englishman was so blinded by narrow-minded prejudice that he could not accept the truth when it was given to him. Both he and his assistant felt sure that I was deceiving them.

It is the same in the United States today. People

all over the country try to show that I am deceiving people in this story of my life. They have told me to my face that I never saw Africa; that I was born somewhere in western Pennsylvania or in some place in the South.

I had a most uncomfortable night in a hut all by myself. During the night, while I tried to get some sleep, but couldn't on account of mosquitoes, native men entered and began flogging me. Of course I screamed, and the assistant ran down. Did he help me? No! He actually told them to give me more. I heard him say: "Lay it on good." He gave the natives a bottle of trade gin for their trouble. That is what I got for telling the truth.

When the agent's man left, one of the native storemen came to my hut to comfort me and tried to assure me that he was my friend. He said that he had overheard what the assistant had told the head white man about me. He added that he knew that it was all false, but that he dared not say so to them.

The kindly storeman told me that the assistant had said: " That coast nigger is trying to spoil the other niggers we have here, with his coast talk, saying white men are afraid to touch him. Why, when the boys wanted to lead him to his hut for the night, he began to scream. Then when I went to find out what the trouble was, he was actually cheeky to me! I won't let a nigger talk back to me, you know.''

The native storeman said that the assistant had induced the other white man to have me turned over to the native women in the morning. Since the storeman knew the treachery of this one white man and hated him, he had come to help me to get away before morning.

I asked this kind native about my guides and carriers, and he promised to bring them to me. He told me to prepare to get away immediately, while everyone was asleep. I asked about the men who had flogged me, and he said that they were all as good as dead men, from the effects of the gin that the white man had given them.

I collected my carriers and guides and proposed that we should all leave separately. Of all the dumb creatures that I ever saw, those carriers were the dumbest. They insisted that we should all stick together. I could not persuade them to separate. The guides and I gave up trying to reason with them. There was no time to lose, because in all native villages women rise very early to draw water before the sun comes up. It would be fatal to be seen leaving the village so early. Natives have no secrets. They scream what they think.

259

The good storeman led me out of the white man's compound without difficulty. Then he returned and led the guides out also. He could have led all of us out without mishap except for the stupidity of the carriers. Their obstinacy balked his plans.

In all European depots in Africa there is a night-watchman, usually an old man not fit for anything else, but faithful nevertheless. His job is to see that no one goes out or comes in during the night, and that everyone is in his proper quarter. The friendly storeman held quite a responsible position compared with the other natives. In fact, he was much superior to the others. Everyone showed him respect, even the old watchman, whom he had often favoured with a bottle of trade gin or with some tobacco. For that reason the old chap did not challenge him when the storeman took the guides and me out.

At the same time it was not easy for the storeman to foretell the actions of the night-watchman. It is true, he succeeded in getting me out, but it made him sweat to get up courage to lead out the guides, and especially two of them together. A native mind is so simple that it is really honest. Like a child, as long as suspicion is not aroused, the native is perfectly safe. The moment he begins to suspect, he cannot hold his suspicions to himself. He just *must* blurt out what he has on his mind. He has not trained himself to deception.

We were fortunate to fall in with such a friendly person as the storeman. He belonged to Lagos, in southern Nigeria. I heard afterwards that the same young fellow, after having shot some white men who had had him flogged, turned the gun on himself.

The watchman let us pass without challenging us. When the fool carriers started out together with my luggage, the watchman became suspicious and at once sounded the alarm. That woke up the whole place. Even the women, who had not started to draw water yet, were awakened by the alarm that the watchman set going. They tried to run after us, but that was useless. We had slipped out into the bush. Even there, out in the bush, we heard the sound of fire-arms and cries.

We had soon left that place behind, for we made every effort to escape. Death was looking for us. The guides travelled in a different direction from the one they had originally intended. They were expert in finding their way, so there was no danger; they always knew just what to do.

Needless to say, I lost my two trunks and my wooden box. If that smart white man had caught me then, he would have accused me of stealing my own luggage.

Natives alone will not pursue one far in the bush. Natives are too superstitious to leave their own locality for such things. If we could get far away, we should be fairly safe, for the time being, anyhow. Goodness knows what became of those foolish carriers! I have never heard of them from that day to this. What does that matter? They were " only niggers "!

Chapter *XXVIII*

WANDERING IN THE BUSH

*All baggage lost. The Kruman versus the Dahomey warrior.
Lonely journeying. The Kruman's story. Fright. The boa constrictor. A despised Good Samaritan.*

I did not trouble much about where the guides
were taking me; what worried me was that the
little bit of money I had was in one of my trunks,
and they were lost to me. I was sorry also to lose
all the clothes that my trunks contained, and the
necessary things that were in my wooden box. If it
had not been for the good feeling of getting away
from the devilish white man, I surely should have
cried hard, but it was consoling to think that my
life had been saved and that no one was pursuing
me.

My guides were faithful and even offered to
carry me on their shoulders should I become tired.
I declined their offer and walked with them, following their instructions. Since I wore shoes and
stockings, the ground did not trouble my feet much.

263

There were only three of us, and therefore it was not difficult to get food.

One of my guides, the Kruman, was a handy-man and he prepared all the food. He sang often and entertained us delightfully. He was a better man than I had been taught to believe Krumen could be. It is easy to distinguish a Kruman from other natives because the Krumen generally have wide tattoo marks down the middle of their fore-heads. Because of our small number and the happiness of the Kruman, we became more friendly than usual.

My other guide, the Dahomey warrior, was of just the opposite nature to the Kruman. He was inclined to resent any familiarity with the Kru-man, but we finally got him to be sociable.

It is the custom amongst native peoples never to trust themselves, in travelling, with two guides of the same people, or who are friendly. The reason for this is that when you have guides of two opposite characters, you can always depend upon one of them to be in accord with you.

So it was with me. The Dahomey warrior looked down on the Kruman and felt himself superior; therefore he never treated him as on equal footing. On the other hand, the Kruman, although a human being like the rest of us, had mingled with white men — had worked for them, indeed, in the capacity of servant and cook — and therefore thought himself more civilized than the native, who had never mixed with white men or worked for any man for money. If he had worked for another, it had been for one of his own kind, as a courtesy only.

Krumen are usually descendants of slaves, who in former days were bought and sold by the other natives. They have no caste; they eat any food and they mix in any company that receives them. You can see what a breach there was between my two guides.

The Dahomey warrior could truthfully boast of service in the Dahomeyan wars, but the Kruman could glory in nothing but in having served the white man and in having worked for money, and not as a courtesy, for any native who would employ him. Really, it was a hard question to determine which was the better of the two. My prejudice arose, of course, from what had been taught me by my father, for I knew nothing against the Krumen beyond the fact that they were the offspring of slaves, and that they laboured for money, which is the cause of dishonesty, my people believe.

The Dahomey warrior became friendly, and because of this I found out both of the men's names. The Kruman called himself Toby, and the Dahomey warrior called himself Bambo. I could understand the name Bambo, because that is the name of a powerful family, but I did not know anything about such a name as Toby. From my point of view, that name had no history at all. I suppose some white man gave the Kruman the name, just as he might have called a dog Prince or Jack. The Kruman, if he ever had a family name, probably never knew it himself.

Toby and Bambo were my sole companions, and they made the trip as comfortable for me as possible.

We walked on and came into marshy territory. I could not understand it at all. The warrior disputed with the Kruman as to just which course to take when we hit the marshy land. Both agreed that we were in dangerous territory. The Kruman said that we should soon be out of it, but the other thought that we should find marsh all the way until we hit the belt of the desert. It turned out to be as the Kruman argued.

We made our homes in vines and took turns watching for beasts and reptiles. I never saw so many snakes anywhere else in all my life; it seemed as if we were followed by snakes. Of course we were not, as no snake ever follows a human being. The danger was greater now than when we had the carriers, for then one or two of the carriers went a little ahead of the party, acting as beaters, to stir up anything that might lurk in the tall grass and bushes. Now there were only two guides, and they nearly always stayed together, one of them walking in front of me, while the other followed in the rear.

The most difficult task was to keep my men entertained. I made up a tale about white men, and how I was born amongst them. I really surprised myself by telling such a convenient lie. It was only a few years previous that every time I tried to imitate my young master in telling a falsehood, I would be caught in it instantly; but I convinced these native men that all I said was Gospel truth.

We passed days and days in this manner, first one, then the other, telling some yarn. Then I would tell some weird tale about the white man's land.

One night, after eating, while we were resting in a vine, the Kruman was smoking a pipe, a habit that he had acquired from his contact with white men, for tobacco had often been his only pay. I had not learned to smoke at that time, but I had often seen my master smoke, and also many of the men who visited our house in Glasgow. While resting, the Kruman told a story. I shall tell as much of it as I can remember.

THE WHITE HUNTER

" Once upon a time a white man came into the
country of the lion " (meaning the hinterland of
Sierra Leone). " He came alone. No white man
ever knew how to stalk a lion; so he asked the chief
of a village to give him some men to follow the
lion. The chief was afraid of the white man, since
his own daughter had been bewitched by one. So
the chief consented, because he was afraid to refuse, for fear that this white man would bewitch
more of his family. The chief offered the white man
food and gave him one of his own women to please
him.

" The white man accepted the hospitality of the
chief. During the night the chief felt unwell and
complained of pains in his head and a loud drum-
ming in his ear. He thought that the white man had
put some kind of charm on him; so he ordered all
his huntsmen to appear before him so that he could
pick out the craftiest as well as the most formi-
dable of the group to guide this white man to the
hunt and, as he hoped and believed, to his death.
He instructed the two men he had chosen to guide
the white man into the path of the elephant and to
see to it that he be mashed into the earth; and if
they did not succeed in doing that, they should lose

him in the path of the lion, for, as he said: ' The old lion will enjoy the flesh of a white man better than it did that of the monkey.'

" In the middle of the night the white man was awakened and told that his escort was ready, and that it would be best to start then, because the way was long and they wished to reach the place where the lions drink together, before the sun appeared.

" The white man, not knowing anything about the lion and its habits, believed the story; so he too was anxious to start off at once, not suspecting treachery. The escort and the white man started off, he carrying his guns, and the escort carrying the supplies.

" Well, before they had walked three hours, the escort lost the white man, by a very simple ruse. They left him standing, to wait until they should return, saying that they were going just a little farther to see if there were any dangers immediately ahead, and to learn if they should change their course. After waiting some time, the white man became suspicious and began trying to find his own way out of the bush.

" In the mean time the escort returned to their chief and reported what they had done. The chief was pleased and gave a feast and dance in honour of his deviltry. It was useless for the white man

269

to try to get out of his difficulty, because even natives lose their minds when they are lost in the bush. The white man was left all alone, and even his guns were of no use to him then.

" Now, as you know, I, a Kruman, know the bush from Gambia to Calabar, and I frequently travel alone in those parts. It so happened that I was out in the bush that day and I heard some noise that was strange to my ears. I know every sound in the bush."

Just then a lion actually roared out so that it startled all three of us. Even the brave Dahomey warrior jumped because of the suddenness of that roar. The Kruman beat us all in jumping; he actually jumped out of the vine altogether!

So there the story ended; the nerves of the Kruman had been so badly shaken that he could not think of the rest of the story. We should not have believed the story anyway, so it was just as well that the lion did roar and bring his impossible story to a close. It was not even interesting.

When we all had settled again in the vine, the Dahomey warrior began talking for the first time, but there was such a noise and so much threatening from the voices of animals and he spoke so slowly and so quietly that it was hardly possible to hear a word that he said. His words were well weighed before he uttered them. He began by saying:

"Lions have large hearts and pretty manes, but they are cowards nevertheless. I know some people who resemble the white man, the nearest thing to a snake, who are very brave until they are in danger; then, like the monkey, they turn tail and squeal.

"Our friend, this Kruman, would have us believe that he was the saviour of his *bakra* [white master] in the face of the lion and in the face of an angry chief of a wild people who eat babies as their chief article of food. Now this brave man trembles and falls at the sound of the voice of the hyena. In the days when I ran in the wars, taking the heads of savage bushmen, whose country we are now approaching, nothing stopped me or made *me* tremble. I wish that I could see a bushman now; I could just chew him."

At this point he stopped to demonstrate just how he would handle one of those bushmen, who are my people. He was too stupid to guess who or what I was, but you can imagine how uncomfortable it made me feel while he talked of chewing one of us if he saw one.

The noise of the different beasts made it impossible for him or any of us to talk any further. So while our brave Kruman watched, we tried to snatch a little sleep. Did I sleep? Never. How could I sleep? The Dahomey warrior was supposed to sleep also, but I do not believe that he got much sleep either.

Morning came and we were ready to start again. The Kruman prepared a delicious mash of *fou-fou,* a favourite native dish in my land. It was as good as one could expect, out in the bush. I had no idea in which direction we were travelling; I followed my guides. We turned off our course once at the approach of a tribe of monkeys, about three hundred and fifty in all. It was easy enough to tell that monkeys were in the vicinity because of the noise they made in their talking. We soon lost them, however, and nothing further interrupted our journey until we reached the Ou Gourma country, a desolate place with a wild people. The intention of my guides was to drop me when they reached the region of Dari Dare Salem and then let me find my way home from there.

Now, while we were passing through the Ou Gourma country, the Dahomey warrior was caught by a boa constrictor, by his leg, and his leg was broken by the tightness of the grip of the snake, but his life was saved by the Kruman, who was extremely clever with the javelin. He almost cut

272

the big snake in two. Strange as it may seem, the snake did not loosen its grip on Bambo's leg. The Kruman cut away the part of the snake that held Bambo's leg, and then he tried his best to heal the break.

In my country it is taboo for anyone to minister to any disabled person, but the Kruman had not been taught that. He believed that it was his duty to help any man who was in pain or trouble. Perhaps the Kruman was right. He may not have been, however. I shall not say that it was right or wrong. I shall only say that where one is in trouble or pain, I shall be inclined to shut my ears to any appeal, remembering that there is a law of average; as I have appealed and not been heard, I shall feel justified in not hearing anyone else. Very unchristianlike, isn't it? But it is the way of my people.

The Kruman was prompted differently, and he carried the Dahomey warrior from vine to vine. We lost much time in waiting for the man to recover. It was his own fault that he came to the end that he did, all because of his haughtiness.

When such kindness is shown to a native of good breed, as that warrior was, by one of inferior birth, as the Kruman was, the words that are used by the superior are not complimentary. For example, when the kind Kruman was trying to tie up the broken leg in order to set it, the warrior felt pain, and he cursed the Kruman and his family and wished that his house would burn. He called him every disrespectful name, from " pig " to " offspring of a monkey." The Kruman paid no attention to the abuse, because he understood the customs of natives, even though he was not born among the wild people. Abuse continued until the Dahomey warrior was able to move without assistance. It was several weeks before he could support himself.

Of course it was out of the question to expect me to help him; both men were dogs in my sight.

Every time the Kruman tried to hold the Dahomey warrior up while he was trying to walk, the Dahomey man would say: " Now, you donkey, go easy! You fool! What a pity such a dog as you ever was born! Be careful, you low-down! I should wring your neck! Oh, why didn't the snake take you by the neck and strangle you? Then we should not have such carrion as you to put up with! "

But the kind Kruman ministered on, showing no resentment whatsoever. The action brought back into my mind what the white men had often said: " He's only a nigger! What does it matter? " Perhaps the Dahomey warrior thought the same as the white men, although I never heard him say so.

274

Chapter XXIX

A DEATH AND A DYING CURSE

A hostile guide. Under suspicion. My death proposed. My view of woman's proper position in life. Unpaid guides. A quarrel. We kill the Dahomey warrior. A dying curse. In my own village.

The Dahomey warrior was openly hostile to the people amongst whom we were to go, and he continually made insulting remarks about them. I could not get it out of my head that he was directing his words at me. In the first place he had been convinced by the Portuguese Negro woman that I belonged to the white man's land and was going up to that country on business for my white master. Finally he became so open in his hostility that both the Kruman and I had to speak to him about it.

My interference was not welcomed, and he asked me for the first time, directly, from which people I really came. It so unnerved me to be questioned directly that at first I was confused and did not

275

know what to say, but I soon composed myself and
started to make up a lie about a people who live on
an island and who are all black. I said that my
father was a great chief of these people. That my
discomposure had not been overlooked by the Dahomey warrior I could tell by the way in which he
eyed me. At that time I did not know of any black
people in existence other than those whom I knew
in Africa, so you can imagine how difficult it was
for me to frame a reasonable lie. I had just been
initiated into the new field, the civilized art of
lying, by my young master, and of course I was not
well equipped in it. The Dahomey warrior noticed my nervousness and questioned me all the
more closely. I felt annoyed and on any other occasion might have answered him in a manner that
would have shut him up, the dog! How dare he
talk to me, to one who was the son of my father,
carrying his name, and of noble birth, one not even
to be looked at by one so base as he! He was only a
" nigger " to a white man, and a " dog " to me!
Such impudence!

These thoughts rushed through my head, and I
was about to burst out and begin cursing him,
when the saving thought occurred to me that if I
should talk in that way, I should surely reveal to
him exactly where I came from. I should have to

use the words and the manner common to my people, and he would detect me the instant I opened my mouth. There I was, suspected by one of my own guides of belonging to a people whom he hated, and I did not fully know the mind of the other guide. If I could have divined the mind of the Kruman, I should have been relieved, but he came from a sort of scavenger people, and even though I knew he would fly to the rescue of any white man, I was not sure how he would respond to the cry of a native of my part of the country.

I remembered also that my people were always most cruel to Krumen when they got hold of any. It was never a shame nor a sin nor a crime to skin a Kruman or to boil him alive. The great shame was in touching the dog, "for fear of contamination," as my father or my brother would have put it. You can understand why I did not expect that Kruman to defend me against the Dahomey warrior if it had become known to them that I belonged to the people of the country where we were then travelling. Fortunately the Kruman was more gullible than the Dahomey warrior, and he felt convinced that the other was all wrong in his suspicions.

One night, while I was asleep in a vine, as usual, I was suddenly awakened by loud talking. I listened.

The Dahomey warrior was trying to induce the Kruman to abandon me and to go away with him. He offered to kill me before I should awaken, but the Kruman opposed him strongly. That made the warrior angry, and he threatened to kill both the Kruman and me together. The Kruman was not afraid of the warrior and talked back to him roughly. I heard the Kruman say: " If you touch that *pickin* [child], the birds will have a feast unexpectedly."

The Kruman was skilful with the javelin, as the Dahomey warrior knew. Was it not by his skill that the boa that had broken the warrior's leg had been cut in two? Yes, he was skilled as a hunter and a fighter, but, as we say in my country, his blood ran wrong. Therefore I could not respect him. It was that same Kruman, " the servant of a white man," " the toiler for money," " the nurser of wounds," " the unclean," " the defiled," the " nigger " — it was he who, in the end, saved my life on that journey; and in return I saved his; but I let the Dahomey warrior die.

We were within the border of my land, and it was only a matter of a few hours before I could tell these men who I really was and then trust to fate to escape the poison from the tongue of the Dahomey warrior.

It has been women who have come to my rescue on more than one occasion. I cannot help feeling that it is only their place and their duty to protect a man, for a man, after all, is the one to whom they must look up. I do not mean that man is superior to woman in the physical sense, but I do believe that, as the Scriptures say, man was the first to come on earth, and that woman came last and as his helpmate. She should continue in that same position throughout her entire life. When man shows weakness or abdicates his throne of manhood, I cannot encourage woman in taking his place. I feel that she should support the man and help the man to hold the fort, and not try to command it. A real woman is genuinely happy in fulfilling her role as helpmate, because it is the woman who loves, and hence she takes any position to help the one she loves.

So it was woman, ever talkative, ever gossiping, ever screaming, ever loving, and yet ever vigilant, who came to my rescue. It happened when my guides were about to leave me and return to the coast. The few shillings that I had had when I started out on my journey from Porto Novo were in one of my trunks, and my trunks had been lost with my wooden box back in the village in Nigeria. Therefore I did not have the required thirty shillings that I had agreed to give the guides at the end of the journey.

The Kruman was reasonable and did not complain, although he needed that little bit of money more than the Dahomey warrior did. He could not go, as the warrior could, into any family and obtain hospitality on the strength of his being a warrior. In his own country every door was open to the warrior. The poor Kruman was more familiar with the white man than with anyone else, for no other native would be familiar with a Kruman. A white man, of course, would never offer him hospitality. So far as money was concerned, the Kruman might get a part of what he really deserved, if he worked extremely hard for it, but in all probability he would then be accused by a white man of stealing that for which he had worked so hard. Do you wish money from a white man in Africa? Well, as the Americans say, "try and get it." That condition exists, I think, because the white man usually believes that a native is trying to "put something over on him," and of course in order to protect himself from being hoaxed the white man steels himself against charity or sympathy for any native. On the other hand, because of the white man's natural stinginess towards natives, especially those who work for him, the native who must work for him is forced to become crafty, sneaky, and, often, dishonest.

Such was the position of the Kruman out of his own country. My Kruman guide did not say anything, but stood listening to the poison from the tongue of the Dahomey warrior.

The Dahomey warrior said: " Of course, I must expect from one who is connected by blood with a noble family, and whose father is a great chief amongst the Black Islanders, from whom you tell me you come, nothing but acts of honour." He then continued: " But if your father came, for instance, from these people up here, and if he were even a chief amongst them, why, I should step on his head with my heel, and that would pay me for my trouble."

I did not let him finish that sentence, for I could not contain myself any further. I broke out and said: " God should burn your house! " That is a terrible curse amongst my people. I went on: " If He did, He would rid our noble land of obnoxious vermin, your people! "

At this, the Dahomey warrior screamed and tore his hair and began a dance, which meant that he was going to kill me.

I was so excited, and so angry over his shocking insult to the head of my family, that I had to have my say out, so I kept on talking. " Your people are not a people! They are a plague! It was the curse on our good land, for some reason, that your people were permitted to breed, for I can't say born, because all pestilences breed, and your kind came by filth!"

Just then the Kruman saw that the Dahomey warrior was taking aim to thrust at me with his javelin. Quicker than a flash, the Kruman sent a javelin straight through the warrior's ear, but not through his brain. Then we killed him. So the Kruman saved my life.

I was still so angry that I did not even feel sorry at the death agony of the Dahomey warrior. He died hard, but he was brave to the last. He cursed me with his last breath. He said: " Every step that you take in life, may you be followed by Ba — " and then he died.

I think he was about to say Ba Gag Goa, who is an evil spirit of the Dahomey people, I suppose. I had heard something about that devil, but I did not fear it so much as one of his own kind would. I have come to the conclusion, however, that whatever the name of that evil spirit was, it surely has been close on my trail, even to this day and here in New York, far away from the bush. That curse meant something.

The great problem arose how to get the Kruman out of trouble, because he was alone and had no one to help him to fight his way out of the difficulties that surely would come. Not one of my people could mistake a Kruman; therefore it would be futile for me to say that he came from another people, especially since he bore a horrid Kru tattoo mark down the middle of his forehead. Well, he had saved my life, and it was my place to try to save his. Here is where the woman came into the picture.

I arrived in my own village about one hour before sunset. When the sun goes down in my home, it is dark at once. That is, we have no twilight; it becomes dark immediately.

Chapter XXX

A HOSTILE HOME

Recognized. Family matters. A lying story. A new wife.
The witch-doctor thwarts escape. Defending a kindly woman.
Poisoned. An unfriendly home. Yearnings for civilization.

When we arrived in the village, I was surprised at the number of people who remembered me. Even boys knew me and referred to me among themselves as " the mate of Gooma," or, in my vernacular, " *Gauz il Goomah.*" I knew by the salutations that I received that I was recognized. There is a special saying due to one who has been away for a long time, and the one saluted must answer in a particular way. There is no hand-shake, as among the civilized; therefore no one ran up to me. A group of men would be standing off somewhere, and when they saw me, they would shout: " Welcome from having been away," and I would answer: " Thank you for knowing me." That is not the literal translation of the words spoken, but it is as near as I can translate them. The native words are:

"*Ah qua ti jo,*" and the reply is: "*A ku lai lai a ku lai lai.*"

This form of salutation is also used in the Yoruba language. My language is a dialect of Arabic, mixed a great deal with Hausa, Yoruba, and Benga vernaculars. Many of the words used by those people are used by us, but we do not use them all in the same way.

Now, hearing so many people saluting me, I was quite pleased, and I managed to go to my own compound — or, at least, to the compound that I had run away from, four years before — safely, and without being questioned then about the Kruman, who stuck to me closely.

The poor Kruman confided to me that night that he was afraid for his life. I did everything I could to make light of his position, although secretly I was as scared for him as he.

My father had died, I learned at once, but my eldest brother still lived with his twenty-one wives, and, as rumour had it amongst my own women, he was contemplating taking another two, his reason being that he wanted more sons.

My own five wives should really belong to Enfiki, but that poor fellow had gone to his reward long since, over in the Fan country. The wives were the sole property of three of my followers that I had

285

left behind; and now they all lived in one compound.

By native law I was not allowed to marry again in my own country, because I had stayed away from my own wives over the stated time, a native year. I could go back to my own wives if I cared to, provided I could arrange it with them and with my followers, to whom they now belonged. That was an easy matter to settle, but it was difficult for me to explain what had become of Enfiki. Here is where the science of telling a good lie saved me a lot of trouble. Believe me, I surprised my own self by the way I did it, being so new to the civilized school of thought.

I said that when we had reached the place where I went to visit, Enfiki became infatuated by the charms of the women of that place. I said that I begged him not to think of them, but that he would not listen to me. I said he had abandoned me, and that I had had a most difficult job to get anyone to guide me back home. I had been lost and had been stranded amongst a different people, and my life amongst them had been very miserable.

I got sympathy by that remark, so I piled on more. I did everything but weep, for if I had done that, it would have changed pity to scorn. I said that I finally had induced a Dahomey warrior to guide me back, but that I had not let him know that I belonged there. That made them all laugh, for it always pleases my people when they know that anything is " put over " on one of our proudest enemies. I told them about his questioning me, and about his insults to my people. I explained that I had intended to bring him there and then feed him to the hyenas. Then I said that, as I had nothing to carry, I was willing to travel with one guide in order that I might get back to them all the quicker. That also " washed." But on our way, I said, we met another man, and the Dahomey warrior was anxious to draft him to help guide me. He had tried to plan, I explained, with this other one, to kill me before I finished my journey, and to return to his people and say that he had been forced to kill me because I had attacked him. The new man, I said, had not liked the evil in the heart of the Dahomey warrior and, being a skilled man, had prevented the Dahomey warrior from carrying out his wicked plan. Then, I said, we had reached the border of my own noble land, where men are good husbands to their own wives. At this all the girls beat their breasts on the ground, a sign of deep respect for the narrator.

The base Dahomey warrior, I said, had so insulted my honourable people that I had spat in his

287

face and had cursed him. He had been about to kill me because of his anger, when this brave one, this true man, had walked up to him and had struck him dead with his javelin.

Up to that time no one seemed to have noticed my poor Kruman, but when I referred to him in such noble terms, everyone's curiosity was aroused. A Kruman in my country is about as safe as a honey-bee in a nest of hornets. We do not like Krumen, that's all. Whatever good they may have, we scorn that good and turn it to evil, because we simply can't see why such people are allowed to live anywhere. Is that savage and barbarous? May I be permitted to ask, does not race hatred exist in places outside my savage land, amongst people who are not savage? Ask yourselves!

One of the men said sneeringly: "What is this that we have in our midst?" He left immediately after he had said this, promising that I could choose any one of the girls that I wished to have for a wife.

I knew what deviltry he and others had in their minds when they left, and so did the women. I chose one of the women and immediately tried to influence her to help me save this man who had saved my life from the Dahomey warrior. She gave me her word that she would help me. We had to plan quickly because before long everyone in the whole community would surround the compound and take him by force, which meant good-bye to him.

All this time the good Kruman had not said a word, for I had told him to keep silent. He did not know much of our language, but he scented danger when men left the compound.

The plan I made was to go out and hold the attention of my people by telling them about the difficulties I had had in the country I had been visiting. The woman then was to lead the Kruman out of the compound from another side, talking to him all the time. She intended to lead him out on the side of the river, for she would be sure not to meet anyone coming from that direction, since the river in my home is taboo. From that place he could strike out for himself and travel in any direction that suited him.

The men had been gone only about fifteen minutes when the sun began to settle and the fires were lit for the night. One witch-devil-doctor happened to see the woman with the man, and, being curious and full of mischief, he rushed over to see who the man was. He afterwards said that he knew that no man from his village would be walking in that direction and especially in company with a somewhat

289

sick woman. No one had thought of that at first, and even I had not given it a thought when I had chosen the woman, who was anxious to help get the poor fellow out of the country. Even she herself had overlooked her sickness, knowing that she was not going to wife the man, but to save him.

When the witch-doctor came up to where the two were walking, he screamed and dashed away. That meant that he was giving an alarm, but not shouting the word "danger." He hastened to tell his elders what he had discovered — a strange man walking away with one of our women; and that woman in sickness, which tabooed her from the company of all men in our land. The Kruman did not realize that he was breaking one of the most sacred taboos in our country. The woman, on the other hand, thought that she could get the man outside of the community before anyone could see them, and that no one would be the wiser, except me, to whom she had been promised as wife.

The evil witch-doctor caused a commotion. I was busy telling the men some impossible lie, in order to hold them, so that the woman would have time to get the Kruman out of the village before those dogs got to the compound. The best-laid plans of mice and men are balked, not by blunder, but by cruel fate and by force of circumstances.

290

The witch-doctor came panting up to our group; I believe that he moved faster than he had ever moved in his whole wicked black life. He interrupted my talk by saying: " Ibn LoBagola remains strange."

I said: " We all know that a vulture is no friend to the hyena, and even the lizard dislikes being stepped upon. A man is condemned only by his kind. How is it that a father should choose one to follow his own son if he has a tongue like a woman? "

That statement ended our pleasant conversation and gave the rascal a chance to tell what he had seen, but not before he took another dig at me. He said: "When the great chief sits in council to hear one accused, he does not expect that the accused will condemn himself, for the chief is not so powerful as the mighty Oro. Here is a man who would save us much trouble if he were brought to trial, because his eagerness to ingratiate himself only condemns him, and his guilt is proved by himself."

It was true that I had spoken too hastily and had put into their minds exactly what I wished to keep from them — that I knew what the witch-doctor was going to say and about whom he was going to say it. He told what he had seen, and in order to

291

prove his point he offered to take anyone to the compound of my followers and show them that one of the women was missing. True enough, when we reached the compound, we saw that poor good woman coming in at the other side. She appeared hurried and excited. She guessed our mission and the purpose of the men.

The witch-doctor said: " It would make the Spirit angry if I were to deceive anyone, for, as you all know, to deceive another is a sure sign that we deceive ourselves."

At first his story did not apply to the woman; it seemed to hinge on me. The witch-doctor was trying to show that I knew something about the woman's having been out with a man and that I must have known the man.

The woman, brave little soul, although she knew that she was about to get into trouble through the witch-doctor, stuck to her story that I had not even seen her leave the compound. She admitted that it was true that I had been saved by the one whom she had led out of the village so that he could go home to his own children.

The follower who had given her to me as a wife became angry and said: " Have I been so long with one who shows such feelings for a base Kruman, above the respect due to her own man? "

I answered him: " I know women are weak, and I am sure that in their weakness they fall, but when the gazelle stumbles on a pebble, I will not see it down, but will raise it up again. This woman has told you the truth, and you wish to make it evil. Now, in the first place, whose right is it to judge her but his to whom she has been given ? "

That seemed to settle the question, and the men left, sorry in their black hearts that they had no one to mutilate.

Because of that affair my position was not so safe at home as I had expected it to be. I had to keep constantly on the alert for fear of being poisoned by that devilish witch-doctor, who would surely put me out of the way if he got the chance. However, that good little woman was wide awake, and she carefully examined everything before I ate. Her name was Bek-hor. What it meant I did not know. Soon after that event she died of poison and I was bereft of another true friend.

My brother acted as if I had been a benefactor to him. He actually fawned upon me, as if he truly liked me. He had fallen from the favour of most people because of having had his beard plucked, and that had made him a wretched man. I was sorry for him, but I dared not show it. If I had done so, my sorrow would have been interpreted as weakness and not as kindness, and it would have lost for me the respect of the people. So I treated him coldly and indifferently, and that harshness made him and everyone else respect me all the more.

Strange to say, because this time I had brought nothing back with me and now sat and slept on the ground, as everyone else did, I was listened to and believed. When our people believe what one says to them, they interrupt by repeating everything said, but if they do not believe, they simply sit and listen intently, just as if they were interested.

I was afraid to tell the truth, because I knew that the truth would do me harm; so I told lies about my having been amongst another native people, and about how I had fought them and at last had come off victor. I told them that a white man had wished to take me back to his village with him, but that I had refused and had said that I should never forget my own kind, but should return to my own noble people, never to leave them again. And they really believed me!

Is it not true in these so-called civilized countries that when one tells the truth, he is invariably doubted; but when one presents fraud, lies, and deceit, he is hailed as a hero? Think of Admiral Peary and Captain Cook! My experience among the civilized nations of the world has taught me that the people of those lands are more eager to accept romance than plain facts. It is the same the world over. I fooled my native people, and they loved me for it. I was safer in my own home at that time than I had been at any other.

My daily life there was miserable because I did not have such company as when I had had Gooma. Gooma had gone. I suppose she had died, although no one knew. She had run away from the King's Amazon women, and no one had heard any more of her. She may be amongst her own people in the desert; who knows? O-lou-wa-li was gone. My own father had been poisoned, according to my brother. I do not believe such tales as that. When anyone of distinction dies in my country, no one believes that he died a natural death, especially his own relatives; they always say that he was poisoned. Sometimes it is true, but it is the native custom to believe evil in all cases.

I had no one to run to if I fell into trouble. I could not trust my eldest brother, because he might plot against me, and I should have no one to defend me if I were called before a council. So I was alone, and more of a stranger at home than I had been in any other place.

Of course I had women. In fact, I had the companionship of all the women in my compound, and I knew I could depend on their assistance. My risk would be great, but life and happiness would not be worth having if there were no risks.

I fell ill with fever, and then I was compelled to leave home earlier than I had intended to. However, I stayed there in savagery eleven months.

I had no luggage and no money. I was not sure that my passage back to Europe had been secured, because I had come home from Hamburg that time, and I had not seen my white master for ever so long. Goodness knew what had happened to my young master. I did not dare to think about him; yet it was difficult for me to dismiss him from my mind, whenever I thought of his strange actions, for I feared that all might not be well with him.

So I arranged to leave my African home again. This time I did not fear leaving, because I had no father to oppose me. If I had chosen to go by way of Timbuktu, it would have cost me money after leaving there, and money I did not have. And, again, the way by Timbuktu was unsafe for a bushman, like me, to take, since I could never disguise myself sufficiently to prevent my being recognized by the Tuaregs.

Chapter XXXI

STRANGE STORIES AND SONGS

Boy guides to the Egba. A folk-tale. A native trader. A native preacher. The Al'ake of Abeokuta. "Stop yer ticklin', Jock." In Lagos.

I finally got two young men to guide me as far as the border of the Egba country. Their names were Kplowo and Yashiadi. Both of them were fetish-boys, and unmarried by choice. They had chosen a hunting life to married life. That, of course, tabooed them both, but it did not make it a crime, under native law, to travel in their company. Both were very lively and acted like small boys, frolicking and jumping about like young animals. Both were skilled with the assagai, and I felt safe in their company.

I did not talk much to these boys because I did not wish them to know where I intended to go. I had to walk all the way, although I did not feel much like walking, because I had hardly recovered from a severe attack of malarial fever.

One night, during a halt for rest, while we were all lying in a vine, one of them began telling a story about an experience out on one of his hunts. What he had been hunting for I do not know, but the story sounded as if it were folk-lore and not a true experience. In the story, he made the animals talk.

THE LION AND THE LEOPARD

One day, just after the lion had left his wife (and you know the nature of the lion, how he always acts shy when he has been wifing), he ran up to the water-hole. It appeared that he was late. Madame Gazelle, the elephant with her brood, the prancing, dainty zebra, and even the giraffe were all at the hole, with all the other people.

The giraffe caused commotion by her presence, because she is very seldom seen in those parts, but she had been a long way off to a picnic, and she had been caught by thirst before she could get back to her own country. Everyone began teasing her because of her long neck, but she took it all good-humouredly.

Then up bounced the lion. He tried to get to the hole without anyone's noticing him, but he was unsuccessful.

You all know the monkey. Well, the monkey saw the lion first, and he began his usual taunts when the lion comes late to drink. The monkey said: " It is very funny when even our own King keeps his subjects waiting."

The gazelle inquired: " Which one were you with last night, O King? You surely must have liked her, since you oversleep."

The lion, being used to such jokes, said nothing, but drank on in silence. Really, he was so bashful and ashamed that he felt more like crying than laughing.

The elephant, who is never afraid of the lion, began teasing him also. What the elephant could not understand was why the animal people should keep as their King such a shy, timid, woman-loving creature, merely because of his good looks. He wondered why they had not placed himself, the great elephant, over the animal kingdom, because he was gentle, steady, reliable, and long-lived. The elephant was always gentle to the lion, but he liked to tease him whenever he had the chance; so he said: " Now, now, come, my pretty, why not admit to your loyal subjects that you were out visiting the leopard and his family, your friends? "

All the animals laughed, because they all knew that the lion did not like the leopard, because the leopard would not obey him and often gave him a good beating when the lion spoke to him.

The lion became angry at this last remark, and he shook his big head. The others plainly saw that there was going to be a fight. Now, if the lion had dared, he would have given the elephant a good bite for his impudence. But, as you all know, everyone loved the elephant, and the lion will never attack the elephant or any other beast when he is by himself.

The lion contented himself with remarking that it is no sign, because one is big in body, that he is big in brain also; and as for good looks, some people can see only their own ugliness by observing the good looks of others.

The giraffe laughed aloud scornfully at the wisdom of the lion, but that did not disturb the lion a bit, because he could always see humour in the long neck of that animal.

The giraffe then said that she had to go, and she asked the lion to escort her. The elephant said that he would have escorted her if she had not appealed to the King first. The lion could do nothing else but go with her, much as he disliked it, because it is the custom of all the animal family never to refuse to assist a female. So off the two went.

Before they had gone far, the animal people all heard a terrible screaming, and they rushed to find out who it was. Finally they came to a place where the giraffe lay screaming and they saw the lion and the leopard in a hot dispute. They all knew that the leopard wished to kill the lion.

The elephant rushed in and parted the two, asking for an explanation of such goings-on.

The leopard, who is never afraid of any animal, realized that he could not fight the elephant. He began telling the cause of the trouble. He said: " You know, Elephant, that I never mix with other people, and that I should feel sad if I had to talk with this lion, the seducer. I came along and saw him trying to take advantage of Madame Giraffe, and, as a defender of the weak, I rushed to her aid. I was busy questioning this lion when you came along."

This was a wonderful tale, and all the lion could say was: " It's a lie! I have been plotted against, for that she-devil of a giraffe began screaming without anything having happened to her. She had asked me about my wife and I had told her not to talk to me on that subject. Then she began to yell. When I turned round, this night-prowler, who does his mischief in the dark — "

At this the leopard bounded at the lion, but the elephant caught him by the throat and threw him flat on the ground, telling him not to be so impolite as to interrupt people who are talking. The elephant asked: " Did anybody interrupt you while you were telling your tale?" The leopard licked his paws and rested content, while the lion continued: " This thing came up and struck me on the shoulder. It was about this blow that I was arguing when you came along."

The leopard remarked that everyone knows that a pretty creature always tells a pretty tale, and he asked the company to leave it to him to chastise the lion for his wrongdoing. He said that he knew how to punish such a creature.

It looked as if the leopard were going to have his wish, when all of a sudden someone spoke from the trees. It was the snake, and it said: " People of the bush, the tongue of the leopard is twisted and needs straightening. All he has told you are lies, black evil lies."

The leopard started to run away, but the elephant caught him around the body and gave him such a squeeze that it made him cry out for mercy. The elephant warned him not to try to run away again.

The snake continued: " I saw the whole thing. The leopard met Madame Giraffe, and he wanted to eat her, but the giraffe pleaded so hard with him that he made a bargain with her. He told her that if she would induce the gazelle to leave the water-hole and accompany her, so that he could catch the gazelle, he would permit the giraffe to proceed on her way home unhurt. The giraffe promised to try, and she said that she would scream as a warning that they had arrived.

" When the giraffe was out of hearing, the leopard rolled on the ground with delight and talked out loud. He said that he would first feed upon his favourite morsel, the gazelle, and then he would run around and head off Madame Giraffe and would eat her also, for her trouble. The leopard added with glee: ' What a glorious world! '

" But when the giraffe returned with the lion, she told the leopard that the lion had prevented her from bringing the gazelle and had followed her in order to make love to her; so the leopard was going to give the lion a good beating. Then you all arrived."

The elephant said: " You people know now that your King has told you the truth, that he had been plotted against by the leopard, who calls himself brave; but I prefer to be called a coward rather than to be the kind of ' brave ' that he is. What shall we do with him? "

Everyone except the gazelle said: " Squeeze him to death! " The gazelle said they should tread on him and mash the devil out of him.

Someone suggested that since the giraffe had led her King into such trouble, she should be killed also. The giraffe pleaded so hard with the lion to save her that the lion, out of the kindness of his soft heart, begged them to let her go on her way to her family.

All told the lion that he was silly, to let one live who had lied so shamefully about him. So the leopard and the giraffe were killed, and the lion went back to his family and related the story.

The giraffe pleaded, before she died, that it was fear that had caused her to do what she had done, but the elephant said: " Fear or no fear, you cannot justify a lie."

That was only a folk-story, and of course it did not add at all to the merit of the young fellow who told it, because we could all tell one just as good, and perhaps better. But hearing it helped to while away the time on the journey.

Nothing unusual happened during that thirty days' trip. The two young fellows left me at a place called Oro, in the country of Abeokuta, meaning " Under a Stone " in the Yoruba vernacular.

I made my way alone to the compound of a native trader, a store-keeper. He was very ignorant, but he knew a little English. He could hardly believe that I had come from the people whom I told him I had come from.

He took me over to meet another native man, whose name was Davis. At least, that is what he called himself in English. I understood afterwards that he had been a native preacher in some church and had left to become a sort of private secretary to the King of the Egba people. That King was called the Al'ake of Abeokuta.

My English was not so bad, but my pronunciation of it was much different from that of the natives who spoke English in that region. The real language of that people was Yoruba.

The native preacher, Davis, was very kind to me. The first thing he did was to get me some clothes.

While we were sitting on the veranda of his house, I told him my whole story and said that I had learned everything that I knew in Scotland.

Naturally, that was unbelievable to him, but he was intensely interested. He had been in Scotland and had lived a short time in Edinburgh. He recalled having heard Harry Lauder sing. I told him that I had heard the same man sing, and I started to prove it by singing a song that I had learned in a Glasgow music-hall, "Stop yer ticklin', Jock."

Davis was delighted, and when I rolled my r's,

he laughed heartily. He was so pleased that he wanted me to do it before the Al'ake himself.

I promised to let myself be taken before that noble personage. He came all bedecked in a flowing caftan and aba, made of the finest silks, with a kind of crown on his head, full of tinsel. It looked to me like a toy crown. He had a husky voice, and I could hear him coming long before he reached the porch, where we were waiting for him. He was followed by a small boy, and a couple of native servants who fanned him. I sat in a large wooden chair, and by me stood Davis and another native Nigerian, who called himself David Taylor. Where he got the name I cannot say. My belief is that he was a prosperous Kruman, without the tribal mark common to his people. Krumen are usually called anything that first becomes attached to them. They have no particular language, but Taylor, like a good many more prosperous Krumen who lived in Lagos, spoke the language of that country.

Taylor stood on one side of my big wooden chair. The Al'ake sat opposite me and put his arm around a little naked boy, who was quite brown in colour. The Al'ake himself was not black, but both Davis and his friend Taylor were extremely black.

A bottle of champagne was brought in, and the Al'ake poured it into a large metal cup, took a sip himself, gave the little brown boy a sip, and then gave me a sip. The rest of it he swallowed off at a gulp. The little boy then took the cup and tried to lick it. The Al'ake laughed when Davis told him about me, for he also had been to Edinburgh, but he did not know a word of English. He could, however, appreciate a Scotch song, and I was asked to sing the same one, " Stop yer ticklin', Jock," and to put all the laughs into it. I sang it, but whether I sang well or badly I am not sure. Anyway, it went over all right; the Al'ake and the others roared with amusement.

Then everyone in the royal compound was called up to the porch, servants, followers, children, and wives, and I was requested to sing the song again. I think it was the way I laughed in the song that made them all so pleased. I made a hit.

Of course I had no money. It was only through the kind offices of Davis that I received my train fare to Lagos, on the Lagos government railway.

My life in Lagos was not at all eventful. I had to beg my fare to get out of the country.

Chapter XXXII

SADNESS AND DEATH

Again in Glasgow. A sad household. A son in disgrace. " The devil that is in me." Perverted instruction. A loving master. " You are human." Misunderstood. My master's dying advice. A doting mother. Distrusted. An inheritance.

When I arrived again in England, I had to be carried ashore from the ship, because on the way I had had a severe attack of malarial fever. I was put in the infirmary for tropical diseases and, when I became better, shipped directly to Glasgow, where I had said that I wished to go.

When at last I arrived in my old master's home, in the house out on the Drive, everyone was astonished. My master was ill, and the mistress seemed in mourning. The help were all newly hired people, who were shocked when they saw me. I learned afterwards that my master had thought that it would be advisable to have all new help in the house after the fall of my young master.

Till then I had not heard of my young master, and I began calling him by name. What a change

had taken place in that good home! Soon after
I had left my young master in Germany for my
own home in Africa, he had arrived home, and he
and my master had had a terrible row. My master
had tried to discipline the boy, and my young master had resented it. So he had rushed away from
the house, and the last they had heard of him was
that he had " accepted the King's shilling," and
you know what that means. When that news
reached the good people in the house, it prostrated
them. " In the Army! " " In His Majesty's
forces! " " No, it can't be true! " Those were the
exclamations made by his good folk. At that time
gentlemen's sons did not join the common ranks
in the Army; they sought commissions. To think
of the young master's joining the Army, and going
into the ranks, was more than those poor people
could stand. But it was their own fault. They had
caused the breach by their prudishness. Their own
boy had been driven from his home and led to neglect his education through their misguided sense
of morality.

What was done was done. Why prolong comment about it? Oh, if I had known what I know
today, and if I could have expressed myself as well
as now, wouldn't I have talked to them! Well,
believe me, I should!

So the boy was a soldier! It would have been quite simple for my master to have taken him out of the Army at that time, so I was told, by showing that the boy was under age and by paying a small fee, of about twenty-one pounds. But my master did not move a finger to redeem his son.

The truth of the whole thing is this: when my young master had returned home after running away, they had treated him with such scorn that he could not bear it any longer; they had tried to subject him to rules similar to those he had known before he had run away; they had tried to make a small boy of him again, but that was impossible. Did he not know as much of life as they did? No, he was no longer a small boy to be dictated to, or to be chastised for every gesture; he had become a man, self-supporting in every way.

What a mistake some parents make with their children! They either indulge them too much, or are too rigid with them. A boy secretly yearns for the day when he can break his bonds and run free from the paternal yoke. My young master's actions were a direct result of such feelings. I believe that I was the only one in the world who really knew his heart, and I knew it better than did his own father. Up to the time of the incident with the maid, we had been inseparable companions, *friends*. Even

310

when he had run off, he had taken me with him, although his heart had changed towards me, because I had dragged him into such a mess.

Upon his return his mother had tried her hardest to show him that it was only through me that he had fallen from grace, and it was generally believed that if it had not been for my heathen influence, he would never have attempted to accost the maid.

Yes, it was I, that young black imp, that did it all, for how could a young innocent creature like the young master do such mischief? Impossible! Everyone thought so except perhaps the young master himself.

What if those white people had known the truth, that my first excess had been because of the boy? I am sure that if my own father had thought certain forms of wrong-doing were a legitimate part of the human scheme, he would have included them in his thorough instruction concerning sex matters. My young master taught me what he really thought to be right, but if you do not teach a child that it is not proper to stroke a snake, the child may choose the snake as a partner because of its beautiful colours. My young master was not to blame; neither was I; it was the mistake of his conservative parents in withholding instruction. God rest their souls!

311

That was a dreary house for me during that period. My master was ill, and I hardly ever saw my mistress. The servants never talked to me except in the line of duty. I had no butler to take care of me then, and I nearly always ate alone. I was miserable. I was permitted to visit my master's chamber, where he lay ill, and I got a little cheer sitting by the window, but I never looked out. I watched him lying in the bed.

One day he called me over to his bedside, pulled my head down on his breast, and kissed my forehead. He said: " Never you mind, my lamb; I love you anyway." That made me cry. My master made me sit close to the bed, and he petted me. The chamber-maid and the nurse came into the room, and when they saw me near the bed, they made a fuss and wanted to put me out of the room. My master prevented them from doing so, so they went away to report to the mistress.

The mistress came into the room and asked me if I did not think that it would be good if I took a walk in the park. My master answered her. By this time the nurse, the maid, and the butler had come into the room. My master said: " The lad is not doing any hurt; let him stop here."

The mistress told him that the doctor had left orders that he was not to excite himself, and that she was not going to have me upset him. The master replied: " I am not exciting myself, Maggie; it is you that's causing the excitement! Why worrit so sorely about nothing? Away, all of you, and dinna annoy us! "

There was one thing to be remembered in that house: even though my master was an ill man, he was still the master of his own house, and everyone in the house respected that.

What an estrangement! I did not realize it then, as I did later in life, or as I do now, but there was truly a great undercurrent of bad feeling towards me, as was quite obvious. It was then that my master said those never-to-be-forgotten words, as I stood there with long trousers on and neatly dressed: " I truly thought that you were impossible, but I found out that you are human like the rest of us."

He asked me if I did not wish to go home, to be with my own people, in my own country, and if I did not think that I could do more good there than by remaining in Scotland.

I did not understand what he meant by that, but I answered: " Yes, I think I can." I did not know the significance of my own words.

When I went out for a walk and met some of the boys whom I had known before my young master had run away, I saw that they were changed also. It appeared that they were not interested in me a little bit. I suppose that they also, like the people in my house, believed that it was I who had carried my young master away, and not my young master who had taken me away. What a misunderstanding!

I know all now, but I knew only a little at that time. What was it that made me cry so often? Was it because my young master was not at home, or was it because I felt that my real true friend, my master, was going to die? I don't know. I cried; that's all.

One day, not long after the time to which I refer, all the house was excited, and the bell rang often. People I had never seen before came and went. Everyone whispered. I wanted to go into my master's chamber, but the nurse, with the aid of the butler, tried to prevent me. I broke in, however, and there I saw my poor master. The doctor stood near a table, and the mistress stood at the foot of the bed.

My young master had come home. I was surprised to see him and to know that he had been in the house overnight, and that he had not even greeted me. How odd! Did he, too, believe that I was to blame for his folly? I suppose so; it was

314

only another instance of believing one's own lies. If ever there was one who had lived a life of lies and of deceptions, it surely was my young master. I suppose that was all right; since he was white and civilized, it was right for him to do anything. It was wrong and savage for me to follow suit.

My young master was in the bedchamber, but my master did not speak to him. He was dying. He spoke to the mistress, but what he said I did not hear. I heard her say, between her tears: " Yes, yes, George, but please do not leave us. Oh, doctor, save him." She wept pitifully on the shoulder of the doctor. Then my young master took her in his arms. I noticed that he did not wear military clothes. I afterwards learned that it would have pained his father to recall that his boy had joined the Army.

My master addressed himself to the young master, saying: " I hope you will be more loyal to your King and country than you have been to your father."

My young master cried, and my mistress led him out of the room.

Then my master addressed himself to me, saying: " I have seen to it that you will be taken care of, but my advice to you is, go, go away back tae your ain country; we have enough people in Scotland; your country needs you, my boy "; and he actually embraced me.

The doctor took my master's arms from around me, and I cried and did not wish to leave the chamber; but I had to go, because the doctor insisted.

My master died that night, and the house became a sad one indeed.

After the interment and after everything had settled again, my mistress was affected by my restlessness. I could not keep still. I was lonesome, and I could not even study the little that had been given to me to study by my tutor.

Soon after that I had no tutor, and things became worse. My young master came home occasionally on leave, but he had little to do with me on these flying trips; he was his mother's boy.

During the winter evenings the mistress sat and talked with me, and we had many a good laugh over the first days when I had come into that house. It was during one of these talks that I told about my young master's throwing me into the bed. That was the first time she had known that it was my young master who had led me from my room that night. She had had a kind of superstitious belief about the whole thing, until I undeceived her. She became so downcast and took the confession so much to heart that it came to my mind like a flash that I had told something else.

I knew clearly that it was my telling things that had caused my present estrangement from my young master. I foolishly tried to cover everything up by telling my mistress that what I had just said was not true, and that I had just made it up for fun.

She, poor, narrow-minded woman, said that she thought I was lying about her boy, and that she was sure that I had told many other falsehoods about him. Her pet, she said, could never deceive his parents, nor even disobey them, unless some adverse influence — some "evil," as she put it — dragged him into it. "How wronged my child has been! And you did it, after all our benevolence!"

From that time on, needless to say, I was never again believed by anyone in that house. Even the servants were influenced by the mistress's condemnation of me. She said that her husband had been too kind anyway, failing to remember that if it had not been for her and for her pet, I should at that moment have been back in my own country, amongst my own people, respected by them. Instead, I stood in her drawing-room, bereft of all near and dear, despised by my own people, and

317

branded as a fabricator. I had been taught evil, and now I was accused of teaching evil.

I tried to be like the loyal old monkey in the bush story. I tried to bite my flesh and sprinkle my blood over their door-steps and then die. The consolation in dying would be that I should know that I had not lived in vain. Although wicked, and a liar, I had this consoling thought; I had found the white man's civilization, and I had spanned the chasm of Darkness and Light. Today, even a quarter of a century afterwards, I honestly advise any boy in my own African home who wishes to leave for the purpose of seeing white men that the experience is worth while.

My young master never admitted any of the charges when he was approached on the subject by his loving mother. He may not have recalled it, but I remembered clearly how he had misled his dear mother on the occasion when a Jewish boy had bloodied his nose. What seemed strangest to me was that I had never been taught by my own father to deny truth, since such denial was the chief article in the faith of my young master. I loved him much, and I believe that he loved me, but, rather than displease his good mother again, he found it easier to sacrifice me.

When the time came for my master's will to be

read, it was learned that I had been bequeathed one thousand pounds sterling. My young master received a like sum, and my mistress the remainder of the estate. I did not remain in the house long enough to find out what that was.

Chapter *XXXIII*

FIRST DAYS IN THE U. S. A.

In London. Money stolen. Liverpool. A travelling show. A bicycle. I first hear of America. I plan to help civilize America. Philadelphia. "We don't take niggers." I find a keeper. A fire-walker. Playing to the galleries. Gambling. A ticket to Dahomey. A poor informant.

I went from Glasgow to London. While living in London, I made the acquaintance of a man by the name of Austin, who liked me very much and taught me many things, among which was the foundation of astrology, which he knew to perfection.

I did not realize the value of money, and so, instead of putting my thousand pounds in the banks, I carried the cash in my pockets. How the white people stole from me! They short-changed me, and they overcharged me! I know now what they did, but I did not know then.

I went from London to Liverpool. While in the latter city, I frequently crossed the ferry to New Brighton. In New Brighton I met a woman, a Mrs.

320

Collins, who travelled in a show. She owned a travelling cinematograph show and induced me to go with her to attract people to see her show. I did not see why I should not do as she asked, and, in fact, I thought it would be fine sport; so I went along. Her people taught me how to dance, and then they dressed me up in a white suit and made me dance on a platform outside the show. By travelling with the show I saw many towns in England.

I soon got tired of that kind of life, perhaps because I did not earn anything. I do not recall ever having received any money for my work. I did get my " eats," and I slept in a wagon, much as gypsies do. The lady bought me a new suit of clothes, but when she learned that I was going to leave, she took the suit away from me. I abandoned the show in a small town called Bewdley, in Worcestershire.

The folk in Bewdley liked me very much and were kind to me. It was in this town that I first learned to ride a bicycle. It happened one day that a man by the name of Mr. Jenks, a barber by trade, who, as a side line, rented bicycles, lent me a bicycle, and I went a riding. I did not know how to ride, but I was eager to learn. So I went to the top of a steep hill, got on the bicycle, and started to go down. When I reached the bottom of the hill, the bicycle was around my neck, and I had many cuts and bruises. I have been able to ride a wheel ever since.

I visited a small town near there, a place called Kidderminster. This town was then a carpet-weaving place.

One Sunday afternoon, while standing on the platform at the railway station, I saw a train crowded with cheering men and women, who were waving good-bye to their friends, who stood weeping on the platform. The boy I was with told me that the people on the train were all off for America. I think he said that they were going to " one of our colonies." The tale the boy told me about the place was exciting. That was the first time that I had heard there was a great, new land where men and women went to establish new homes. I wondered why my young master had not taken me to it, since he had taken me to almost every other place worth while.

The boy went on to tell me that in this new country most of the people were outlaws. He said that everyone walked around with guns and with revolvers on their hips. Perhaps he believed these things himself; certainly he told me as if he believed them. The picture that he drew of the new land was far different from anything I had seen in England, or anywhere else. According to him, America was a wild country. I asked him why all those people should go there if it were such a wild land. He replied: " To civilize the people there." That thrilled me, and I was eager at once to go and see that land and help civilize the people. I did not tell the boy my intentions.

I had no benefactor to dictate my going and coming, and I did have some money left; so within a week I secured my passage to that " outlaw country " America.

During the whole time that I had lived in Scotland and in England, I had never seen another black man. I remembered seeing blacks from Dahomey on exhibition in the Dahomey village in Paris, when my young master had run away with me; but before then, and since then up to the time that I am speaking of, no one had ever mentioned to me that there were black people living in the world outside my own land, Africa.

I embarked on the steamship *Haverford*, at Liverpool, in 1909, bound for Philadelphia, in savage America. I landed in Philadelphia in the spring of that year.

Now I was confronted for the first time in my life with the problem of colour. Up to that time no one had ever mentioned my blackness to me; it had not been thought of, so far as I knew, except as a curiosity. The thing that puzzled me now was that I was not spoken of in this new country as a black man; I was called a " coloured " man.

I wandered about, after having been released by the dock authorities, and at last came into a district called Kensington. I immediately thought of Kensington in London. But what a difference! I then heard, for the first time since I had been out of Africa, that familiar word " nigger." I went to about forty houses, as well as to public hotels, but everywhere the people turned me away. Some said: " We do not take niggers here "; others were not quite so harsh. At that time, however, the words did not seem harsh to me, for had I not seen " niggers " before, out on the Gulf of Guinea?

I happened to meet a kind woman who was very patient, and explained to me everything as far as she could make me understand her. It happened that she was a woman from Kidderminster, where I had conceived the inspiration to come to the outlaw country. When I told her that I had recently been in Kidderminster, she wept and said that it was her birthplace, and that she longed to return on a visit. According to her, the district of Kensington was not the place in which I should look for apartments or lodgings. She said that the people

there would not let a " coloured " man, meaning
" black man," live there, and that I should expect
to live in a black man's house. She added know-
ingly: " This is not the old country."

She started me off. I left the street car (meaning
" tramway ") at Fairmount Avenue and Thirteenth
Street. I walked into a cigar-store (meaning
" shop "), which was actually owned by a " coloured man." He was kind to me and called in another " coloured man," who, incidentally, was not
black, but white. How could they call *him* coloured?
What a mix-up!

This white " coloured man " took me to his
house in P— Street. The place looked more like
a lane than a street. It did not take me long to find
out that his house was a gambling-house. At that
time I did not realize that such a house was out
of place. It affected me as almost everything else
did that I came across that was new.

The white-coloured man became my landlord
and my keeper. He lived there in the company of
a girl. I thought she was white, like him, but I did
not know what to call her in this land of confusion.
The little house was nearly always filled with other
coloured men and women of all shades; they did
a great deal of drinking and playing some card-
game for money.

325

It was there that I got my first impression of America. I was surprised that everything was so different from what the little boy had told me at the station, back in Kidderminster. Needless to say, my money soon went in that house in P — Street. When I wanted to buy anything, my landlord did the buying for me, in order to "protect" me "from getting robbed," as he put it.

He was an excellent dresser, and his idea was for me to look spick and span also. I frequently received lectures from him as to how I must appear in America. Whenever I bought a suit of clothing, through him, he bought one also, from my money, which he held "for safe keeping." My money soon went and I had no means of getting more. My landlord tried to induce me to write to Scotland for funds. That I could not do. He became angry because I had no money to pay him for my lodging. I did not know how to work, and I had no talent; at least, so I thought.

One day I was out walking with my landlord, and we both stopped to look at a signboard. It was in front of a dime museum. The thought occurred to him that I might get a job there. I remembered how I had delighted crowds in front of the travelling show of Mrs. Collins; so when he asked me if I could do something funny, I said yes, because the idea pleased me.

Now, in my home in Africa we have a medicine made from the sap of the papaw-tree; its name in my vernacular is *throy-on*. It is chiefly used for healing open wounds and cuts. It acts like a " New Skin " solution. I have often used it, and I had used it especially on the occasion of my ordeal, when I was tested by fire in regard to my flower, Gooma. At that time I managed, through the help of one of my father's women, to smear my whole body with this stuff before the ordeal. The medicine has a milky appearance. Now, I am not certain whether it was the action of this medicine upon my skin that did it or not, but I know that when an oily torch was lighted and applied to my fingers, arms, and legs, the fire did not hurt me. That was about the strongest proof that I was telling the truth, according to our way of thinking. I remembered that I could burn my fingers with a lighted match without feeling any effect. I told the white-coloured man that I could do this. He was delighted; he took me inside and showed me to the head man. Of course the head man wanted to see me touch fire and not get burned, so I did it in front of him. He was also delighted. My keeper explained to him that I had come out of the bush of Africa.

They planned to dress me up in skins and feathers, much the same as Mr. Sumner had done in Coventry when I had ridden in the Lady Godiva procession. I was supposed to dance a native dance, but that is very difficult to do without the accompaniment of a tomtom. I was also supposed to talk a little about my native land. Now, I knew nothing specific about my own home; that is, I did not know its latitude, longitude, or altitude; I had had no real instruction about my own land. I could not talk concisely about any particular thing. I made up a nice little talk, however, with the assistance of the head man of the museum, about missionaries in my country, although there are none there. I was supposed to tell the people to keep their money at home and not to send it to Africa for the missionaries. I was advised to say that I came from Dahomey, a land which everyone had heard about, and not to talk about any other part of Africa, because people would not believe me if they did not know where the place was. I got thorough instructions.

My audience was always sympathetic, especially amongst Jews, agnostics, and working-men. Though I did not realize it then, my talk was of a highly controversial nature, and not at all a talk about the customs of my people.

One day a theatrical agent saw me at the dime museum. He thought that I would make a good feature for a theatre. He took me away from the museum and put me in a first-class motion-picture theatre. Needless to say, my native dancing was quite a novelty, but it was my talk about the missionaries and the money that made me notable at that time. To tell the truth, I had no idea what I was saying and what its importance was, for up to that time I had never seen a missionary. I did 'not know what a missionary did. So I followed instructions and simply played to the gallery. I played in that theatre two weeks, the first being the regular engagement, and the second by the request of the public. My salary was thirty-five dollars a week at the theatre. It had been twenty-five dollars at the dime museum.

From that time on I was called upon by many managers to play at their theatres, and I was quite a success as a vaudevillist. All the money that I earned I had to give to my keeper, who was supposed to put it away for me. He surely did put it away. He allowed me to keep three dollars a week, so you can see how he was prospering, and all from my labour.

I was contented, nevertheless, until the coloured man began taking me, every Saturday night, inside a pool-room and cigar-store combined. In that place I always met a crowd of men gambling. I had never known what gambling was before then, but the men soon initiated me into all the games. I remember the names of the games that I was taught to play: four-card monte, open poker, and dice, called "craps." The dice game attracted me very much, but I never won, especially then. Even now, when I stoop low enough to indulge in that national pastime "coloured golf," I never win, because I really do not know how to play it, or how to bet. I have won once or twice, but usually a little later I lose my money anyway, so it is a case of "Heads I win, tails you lose."

On the ship that brought me to America, I happened to meet a Mr. K—. He became interested in me when he heard me sing the Scotch song "Stop yer ticklin', Jock" for a benefit on shipboard. He gave me his card and told me that if ever I should come to his home town, which was Pittsburgh, Pennsylvania, I must call to see him. I had forgotten the man until one day I was engaged to perform at a very exclusive club, the Mercantile Club, on Broad Street, Philadelphia. I made such a hit there that some of the members invited me to come down from the stage and sit with them at the table and eat. It was at this table that I saw that same

Mr. K—, a Pennsylvania Senator. He was telling everybody that he had met me on the ship coming from Europe. That put my stock up a hundred per cent.

One of the members became interested in me and asked if he could do anything for me. Now was my time to complain about my keeper and to let them know that I was dissatisfied. I told them all about what went on in the little house in P— Street, and how I had to give all my money to the coloured man. The gentleman was sorry for me. He asked if I wished to go back to my own country, and I said yes. Why, I do not know. What should I do back in my own home? Whom had I to see there? I simply said yes for the sake of answering. Really, I was getting on all right in America, only my circumstances upset me — making such a lot of money and then not being able to keep what I made. That was the only trouble.

The gentleman said: " All right! I shall see that you get home." That made me happy.

After making other appearances in public I was called to the office of that gentleman, and he informed me that my passage was being arranged, and that I should sail for Dahomey, via London. I could hardly contain myself, but why I really do not know.

During my stay in Philadelphia I had the honour of meeting several learned gentlemen, among them Professor J—, of the University of Pennsylvania, and Dr. G—, of the University of Pennsylvania Museum. These men asked me to give information about the social organization of the people of Dahomey, where I was supposed to come from. Well, I supplied them with what I knew of that country, but I was not certain whether what I said was accurate or not, because there is as much difference between a Dahomeyan and one of my people as there is between a flea and an elephant. At that time I was not asked questions about my own people. I took it for granted that I was to talk about what the questioners wanted to know about. They did not know how to question me. Therefore I talked to them just as I had talked to the audiences that I had been appearing before. When they asked me questions about the Dahomey language, I told them what I knew, and added anything I could think of. I did not imagine that the men wished anything but entertainment. I had no idea that I was supposed to be any more accurate in imparting information to the men who were assigned to question me at the University of Pennsylvania than I had been when talking to a common crowd at a theatre.

Some questioners were very kind to me. One was Dr. S— and another was Mr. W—. Neither of these men asked me anything except concerning the place they understood that I hailed from. Not a word was said about my own antecedents; they asked about the Yoruba language, of which my knowledge was very limited. When I found that I could not answer about matters in Dahomey, I simply said anything that came to me, but never once did it dawn upon me to talk of my own people and their customs. Not long after that time, I was invited to speak in the Department of Anthropology, at Exeter College, Oxford. My subject was to be fetishism. Now, I have specific information about that subject, and, needless to say, I made a hit. The professor who had invited me to speak was delighted, and so was everyone else. I had been asked to talk about something that I knew about. I suppose the good gentlemen of the University of Pennsylvania discussed me, and I am sure that it must have dawned upon them that they were in error in the way they sought information. They took it for granted that I knew the things that they questioned me about.

When I left them, that good man Mr. W— gave me an excellent letter of introduction to Professor M— of Oxford University.

Chapter XXXIV

IN JAIL, AND BACK TO AFRICA

A peculiar " coloured friend." Is fair exchange robbery?
Arrested in London. Four months in jail. On bread and water.
Off for Dahomey. My Kru friend once more. In Porto Novo.
An escape. In Savage's compound. No work. A public enter-
tainer. Flogged publicly. Success in concerts. Fever. Shipped
to England.

I left America in the summer of 1910, through
the kindness of Mr. W— and a few of his friends of
the Mercantile Club. The ship on which I sailed
was the *Celtic;* I had a second-class passage.

On the voyage I met another black man who did
not like to be called " black." I wonder why. When
one is black, he should love the colour. That man
wished to be called a " coloured man "; so I satisfied him. He appeared to be a good man; so I became friendly with him.

All the money I had when I left Philadelphia
was fifty dollars, given to me by the good American
gentleman. My passage to Dahomey was being

taken care of by another gentleman in London, Mr. Joseph F—, a friend of the Philadelphia man. All my legacy was gone, because I had been cheated and robbed by everyone. I now had to rely on my own efforts. Money was becoming a great factor in my life, but I still did not know its value.

I had my directions: they were to go to the gentleman in London and to receive from him my ticket for a passage to Dahomey, but not to my home. The coloured man whom I met on the ship was on his way to Liberia, so he said, to open up some stores, so he would be my sailing-companion nearly all the way.

We landed at Liverpool. I had been there before, but the coloured man had never been outside of his own country, America. Strange that he should belong to America and be a black man too! A fleeting thought came to my mind when I asked him what was his language and he replied that he had no language. I thought to myself, he must be a Kruman, for Krumen have no language and no caste and therefore are "niggers" according to white men. However, I was kind to him. Heaven knows I was too kind, and he knew it, too. He never wished to pay for anything. I had to pay his fare to London; that is, I did pay it, and he did not give me the money back.

I introduced him to people in London whom I had previously met. That was quite a novelty for him; he had never been given hospitality by white people before. I had been brought up among them, and I had not known of any other kind of people outside of my own country, except the few blacks whom I had met in America. As for them, they had made such a bad impression on me that I did not like them. They had treated me badly.

I did not have much money when we arrived in London, and I did not know the value of what I did have. I spent freely and did not give the morrow a thought. I had not been trained that way. I did not think of what I should do when all my money ran out; in fact, I could not think like that; I was not born like that, and " What's in the bone must come out in the flesh."

In the mean time the black man was living on what little money I had. Finally my money was gone. Mr. F—, the gentleman who was arranging my passage, took his time. Meanwhile, we had to live, and the black man would not go away before I was ready to go. What were we going to do for expenses? He never mentioned the subject. He ate every day and slept every night. So one day I took ninety pounds of his money to pay the bills. I got it when he left his bag on the table in our room; I helped myself. I did not take all he had, but I took enough for our needs. He did not say anything about it, so I did not speak of it. I was beginning to think that such an action was all right. Instead of asking me about the money, he asked the police about it.

On the night before the coronation of King George V the police came to our house and asked me frankly: " Did you take that man's money? "'I replied: " Yes, I took it to pay expenses," and I asked them how they knew about it. They told me that the black man had charged me with stealing it. I laughed, but they arrested me and took me away. That is what they called it. I was away the whole night. I was brought up before a magistrate, who asked me again: " Did you take the money? " I repeated that I had taken it; why make such a fuss over it? I was using it to pay expenses, because my money had gone, and someone must pay. I had not complained when the black man from America had taken my money. I had not run to the police about it. Why all this trouble about money? I was so blind I could not understand such procedure. What was it all about anyway? My young master always took money when he wanted it. No one told the police.

The magistrate asked me: "Didn't you know that it was not your money?"

I replied: "Yes, I knew it was not mine, but since the other man had spent all of my money for our living, I did not think that it was wrong for me to use his."

The British magistrate did not view the matter in that light, so I had to be punished. I cried much and begged to be permitted to go home to my own country, for it seemed as if everyone in the white lands was against me. Even the black man was angry with me, as if I had done him an injury. I did not want his money for myself. I wished to pay expenses that we both were incurring, and he had used my money for the same purpose, and nothing had happened.

I was put into prison and kept there four months.

In the mean time Mr. F— notified the man in Philadelphia, so I was told afterwards, and the Philadelphia man sent a cablegram saying: "Do not defend him." All of this I learned afterwards.

While in prison I worked in the laundry. My job was to boil clothes. I was called out of the laundry one day by the governor of the prison. He read a letter to me from Mr. F— asking if I would be satisfied with a third-class passage to Dahomey, when my four months of prison should expire. I screamed with delight to know that someone thought kindly of me. I naturally replied: " Yes, surely; I shall be well satisfied." The governor laughed at my delight and sent me back to the laundry. I became frightfully hungry in that place, and one day I asked another prisoner for a piece of bread. Then I was put into a place by myself for a long time, with only bread and water as my diet, because I had talked.

On October 12th I emerged from my bondage, wondering what it had all been about. I got into touch with Mr. F— and with the people where I had lived before the trouble had happened. They received me once again into their home with pleasure and gave me a grand welcome. That good woman, Mrs. Martin, the mother of three fine children, pitied me, and she stuck to me to the end, although it caused some estrangement between her and her relatives.

The black man had left by that time. I did not see him again. Various people, including Mrs. Martin, tried to show me that I had been guilty of theft. I never have felt that I am indebted to that black man. Neither have I felt remorse because I spent some of his money for both of us. In the eyes of white people my honesty was at stake. As for me, I am convinced that I was within my rights, at least under the circumstances. I know that many people will not agree with my definition of honesty; but, then, was I not new to the ways of white people, and of black people who had learned white ways?

My passage to Dahomey was at last arranged by Mr. C—, the secretary to Mr. F—. I left England without even visiting Scotland, just three weeks after I had been released from prison. Mr. C— had secured for me a letter of introduction to a Mr. Deeming, the chief agent for the firm of John Holt and Sons, at Porto Novo, Dahomey. The letter was written by Mr. John Holt himself. Five pounds had been left to my credit at the steamship agent's office, and I received the usual German marks for English pounds, in exchange, from G. Goedelt.

I knew a little more on this trip than I had on the previous one when I landed in Africa; so immediately I set out for Kotonu by the narrow-gauge railway that runs along the coast of Dahomey. I remained at Kotonu overnight and planned to go by canoe to Porto Novo the following morning.

I stopped with the man who had befriended me when I had left Africa the second time. He was fond of French drinks, of which his favourite was benedictine. Before morning I had spent most of

340

my German marks treating my friend to that drink.

The next morning I started off for Porto Novo, by canoe. Whom should I meet but the same Kruman who had saved my life from the Dahomey warrior, and whose life I had saved from my own people. He was pleased to see me, but said that he would never guide me, or anyone else, up to that wild country again. I persuaded him to act as head man in guiding me to Porto Novo and promised to pay him upon my return to Kotonu, because, I said, I was going to be employed by John Holt, at Porto Novo; at least, so I thought. He agreed, and I arrived safely at Porto Novo just before dark that same day.

The first thing that I did was to try to find the Portuguese Negro woman who had persuaded natives to take me home on my previous trip. She was not pleased to see me, and she refused to admit me to her house. She told me that a price had been set on my head by the tribesmen for having done away with all the men whom she had so kindly begged to take me home.

I hastily made my way to the John Holt office and was ushered into the presence of Mr. John Deeming. I gave him the letter. After reading it carefully he turned to me and said: " You must remember that there are no feather pillows out here, and I can see that you have been used to a pretty good life at home, in England. I recommend that you go to Lagos, Nigeria, and see the agent there; he may be able to employ you. We do not make a practice of employing natives from other parts of Africa, but he may be able to use you in Lagos.''

I remained all night in that place and just caught the John Holt steamer for Lagos. As the steamer was pulling out, about forty native Dahomey warriors rushed to the pier, hoping to capture me. The engineer on the steamer was an Englishman, and he protected me from being molested. After he had heard my story, he pitied me and advised me to return to Scotland or to England at the first opportunity.

I arrived in Lagos with very little money. I hunted up the Mr. Taylor who was the friend of the private secretary to the Al'ake of Abeokuta. Mr. Taylor was not very cordial, but referred me to another merchant, Mr. Shita, who was sympathetic and tried to help me. I slept in a hotel the first night in Lagos, but I had no money to pay for staying there any longer. Mr. Shita secured me a place to stay with a very fine family of native Christians, by the name of Savage. So I took up my abode in

"Savage's compound," in the native district of Olowobowo, Lagos.

I was introduced to several distinguished native people, including a Dr. Obasa, one of Nigeria's best physicians. When it was learned that I could sing a Scotch song and one or two English songs, my company was requested by many of the native nobility of Lagos, for the purpose of entertaining their friends. I received one guinea for every entertainment.

This life was so successful that I wrote a letter to Mr. C— requesting him to send me some songs from Scotland and from England. Mr. C— did this, but advised me in his letter to try to secure some employment more stable—excellent advice!

John Holt in Lagos would not engage me, and I tried to obtain work with the government railway, but my mathematics were not good enough for a job in the accounting department, where there was a vacancy at that time. I had a chance to work on motors at the government ship-yards, because I had said that I knew something about motors; for I remembered the time when I had worked in the repair-shop in the Humber motor factory at Coventry. I failed at this because I actually knew next to nothing about motors.

Really, I was a problem. People tried to help me

by placing me where they thought I would fit, but no good came from any of their efforts, not because I did not try — everyone knew that — but just because I was a sort of round peg in a square hole. It has been so during my whole life. The only thing that I seem able to do successfully is to entertain the public.

So I learned songs and, through the goodness of the native physician, Dr. Obasa, gave one or two public entertainments. Tickets were sold to all the Europeans for my first big entertainment, with a high Nigerian government official as presiding officer. The affair was a tremendous success. I was assisted by other natives who knew how to sing, and who had good ideas for vaudeville sketches, but I was the star. I had learned new songs, and I rehearsed daily, in order to "put them over right." Judging by general comment, I entertained admirably.

My best friends in Lagos were two brothers by the name of Vaughan. These young men were the sons of a wealthy American coloured man who had gone out to that country many years before and had amassed a fortune as government printer. He left his entire estate to his three children, two boys and a girl. The two brothers were extremely kind to me, and they tried to connect me with their family, because I had said that I had been in America.

My experiences in Lagos were not thrilling, outside of being flogged publicly when I took a trip to Northern Nigeria. I was flogged because I refused to prostrate myself before a white man. In my own home natives prostrated themselves before me, and I was a man of distinction, having my father's own name, and I had even taken women to wife. How could any sane person expect me to prostrate myself before him, unless he were my superior, in age, knowledge, blood, and experience. I wore clothes, the same as a white man did. My own master, or my young master, who was at that time an officer in His Majesty's overseas forces, would never have exacted prostration. No, I did not prostrate myself. A gentleman would not exact respect in that way. But what's the use of talking about it? I was flogged; that ended it. Truly, it was my own fault. Laws cannot be changed to suit an individual, and I knew that country before I ventured into it.

My second entertainment was duly advertised, and tickets were sold again. This time the hall was not large enough to hold the crowd. The event took place in May 1912, at Lagos, at the time the rest of the world was shocked by the sad calamity of the *Titanic*. My concert was scheduled for the night after the arrival of news of that tragic disaster, but we had to go through with the entertainment because all the tickets had been sold and we did not wish to disappoint the public. Men had come from a long way off to hear the concert, and so we had to put it on.

I was taken ill just after the show and had to be carried to my compound. Through the excitement caused by the loss of the *Titanic,* and through the strain of the evening's performance, I fell ill again with my old enemy, chronic malarial fever. Dr. Obasa and Mr. Vaughan said that if I did not get out of the country immediately, I should die ultimately of black water fever. So my passage was quickly arranged, and I was carried aboard the *Falaba,* bound for Liverpool.

Chapter XXXV

A SAVAGE RUNNING RAMPANT IN CIVILIZATION

Luckless in England. Wanderings in London. First arrival in New York. Again luckless. Prospects of being a fire-dancer. I run rampant. Puzzles of civilization. A savage's view of the treatment of wrong-doing. I become a boot-black.

I lay between life and death until the steamer passed the Canary Islands. I managed to walk off the steamer at Liverpool, but I had to go straight to bed when I got to the hotel. Dr. Obasa and his good wife had given me a draft for five pounds when I left Lagos, and the Vaughan brothers had given me one for thirty-five pounds. This money, with the money that I had earned from my concerts, made quite a little sum when I landed in England.

I did not go to Glasgow, but went straight to London when I had recovered. I went to see Mr. C—. He expected me, because I had sent word to him of my intentions. He was very charitable towards me, and did everything that he knew how,

347

to find me stable employment, but he finally despaired of it.

I learned then that England has no place in her industries for a black man. After months of haphazard wanderings about London, it was decided to ship me back to America, where I had made a success on the vaudeville stage. It was thought that the same opportunity would offer itself again. I had brought from Africa many little things that would stand me in good stead in stage work. I had brought with me wearing apparel, such as a caftan, an aba, a fez, sandals, and a great deal of other paraphernalia. Mr. C— arranged my passage and gave me a few pounds to land with.

I arrived in New York in September 1912, on the *Saint Paul,* of the American line. That was the first time I saw New York. I had visited on my previous trip Philadelphia, Baltimore, Washington, and many small towns in Pennsylvania and Maryland, but I had never seen New York until this trip. Truly I was flabbergasted.

I donned the caftan, fez, and sandals the moment I had passed the immigration inspectors. I strolled out into the streets dressed in that manner. You can imagine the commotion I caused. For a while crowds of people followed me. I did not mind having people stare at me; I had become used to that from the first time I had come into civilization.

I got as far as the neighbourhood of Fortieth Street and stopped. I secured a lodging in the boarding-house of a black man in that section of the city. My room was like a clothes closet. I sat down on the cot-bed and cried like a baby. What I cried for I am not sure, but I believe that I was lonesome. In a great city like New York I did not know a soul. I was far away from anyone whom I knew. My master was gone. Who knows where my young master was then? My mistress was dead. I was truly alone. I wandered about aimlessly, without any prospects.

In my first week in that boarding-house I was robbed. I have always been robbed, and usually by my own kind. I never have considered black people in America my kind, nevertheless. The only thing that we have in common is colour, and my colour was a gift. In this New York boarding-house my very trunks and all my belongings were stolen. My landlord became annoyed when I mentioned it to him, and he said that he knew nothing about it. I did not think of telling the police, as the black man had done in London when I had taken money to pay common expenses. What could I expect but to be robbed? That was what I had learned.

My money was all gone, and I could not get work in the theatres. I became hungry. When I asked the owner of the boarding-house for something to eat, he laughed and said: "Hard times in New York will make a monkey eat red pepper." That was quite a joke to him and his kind, but I could not see the humour in it. I managed to beg something, however, and, after a little, I made myself known to a professor at Columbia University.

He became interested in me, and through his kindness I was able to earn enough to keep from starving altogether. I supplied his department, that of Social Anthropology, with information about my country and its customs. Some men of a different kind became interested in me, and thought that I might give a good novelty act on the vaude-ville stage, doing a native dance, in native costume, and a fire-dance; then making a quick change into a Scotch kilt and singing Scotch songs. I had practised putting fire on my body so much since the time I had been engaged at the dime museum in Philadelphia that I had begun to believe that I was really and truly a fireproof man.

With pleasure I recall meeting a very kindly gentleman. One day he invited me to tell something about my people. While I was with him, I demonstrated how I could withstand injury from flame, by passing a lighted match over my fingers. He was so enthusiastic about this that he wrote a letter to Mr. Gaynor, who was then the Mayor of New York City, and he also tried to interest the New York Fire Department in me. Mayor Gaynor requested my new friend to take me before the Fire Commission and have me demonstrate my fire act before him. The Fire Commissioner, however, did not become enthusiastic, because he discovered that one of his own men also could put a lighted match over his fingers. Still, it is a surprising act.

Because of wide publicity through the New York daily newspapers, I secured many engagements on the vaudeville stage. My picture appeared in a motion-picture weekly and I was heralded far and wide as "The Fireproof Man." A vaudeville circuit gave me bookings through theatres all over the eastern part of the United States, and it seemed as if my star were in the ascendant.

But good things in my life have never had long duration. Even with the experiences that I had had, I was still ignorant of the proper use of money, and I did not know its value. My early life had been a life of no restraint, as well as of savagery, and because of that and other influences that came to bear upon me, and because no one successfully

351

taught me the proper use of things, I ran rampant. I had already suffered for my folly with the money of the black man in London. I was at a loss to understand why someone had not been made to suffer for having taken money from me, not even spending it for my comfort. Perhaps it is part of the Western social system to make the stranger pay for everything that he does, but to do to him anything that one likes.

I had long since become a disciple of modern thought and therefore I never shunned anything that attracted me. I was a savage running wild in civilization. Naturally that led me into a terrible mess. The circumstances are such that I do not wish to mention them, other than to say that I was arrested more than once.

Since I was a small boy, I have never been able to make up a good excuse, especially a lying one. I always admit the truth when I am confronted with an accusation that is really true. Of course, through having had many hard knocks, I am now learning very rapidly to be reluctant in admitting anything. But I was different at that time, and my honesty and my frankness often made me looked upon with derision and suspicion. People called me, not an honest man, but "a suave duck" or "a slick customer." I am still misunderstood today. And yet I am as natural as any man ever created. I could no more help doing the foolish and bad things that I did than a person can help drinking water. How did I know then that I was wrong? People in these Western countries wait until a deed is done before they give instruction, and instruction comes usually as a sort of revenge; that is, it claps the wrong-doer into prison, thereby arousing all the bitterest opposition that the sinner can muster. If, when I first did wrong, I had been taken aside and told that I was wrong, good would have accrued from that. Instead I was put into prison and left to my own thoughts. I sincerely believe that all cases of crime should be treated individually, and not as they are usually treated. The aim should be to eliminate law-violations by striking at the causes and not so much at the individual or the act. If I had been treated in such a manner in the beginning, the authorities would have found out the real cause of my actions and thereby have made me a useful member of any community. It is true, you cannot let a rat live, but I am convinced that if you could tell the rat why he is not permitted to live, you would soon add another domesticated animal to the household. That applies to human beings. We should be able to say of a man who has abdicated his throne of manhood that he is a different man, in need of training, and not a criminal.

For a time no one wanted me. The theatres would not engage me. Finally I settled down in a small town in northern New York. There I found a job in a barber-shop as boot-black. The barber himself was a tolerant man, and he pitied my plight, although he did not understand me. He taught me how to polish shoes and to clean his shop. I made a living and managed to put a little money into the bank.

Chapter XXXVI

A SAVAGE IN THE WORLD WAR

The World War. Enlistment. The Secret Service. Discharged. A British volunteer. Reported dead. Corporal, and Quartermaster Sergeant. With the Royal Fusiliers. In Palestine. An unhappy man. Lance-corporal. In Egypt. Orderly Sergeant. Base-hospital work. Enemies. Sent to England.

America entered the World War and drafted her available citizens. I was duly registered, but was exempted from service because I was a foreigner.

A young barber working in the barber-shop annoyed me by saying that we "foreigners" come over to this country, make a living, and are all "slackers." I did not like to be talked to in that manner. I left the barber-shop and volunteered my services "for the Allied cause," whatever that was. I did not know then. I met many others who did not know. It was my duty not to question why, but to serve; so I joined.

I was sent to Camp Upton, and many of the upstate papers praised my action in volunteering. I was popular with my Captain and with all the men. The officers directed me to give talks to the men. In fact, I talked to the troops at nearly all the camps. I had just been drafted to go overseas and had been sworn in as an American citizen. I had been given a certificate, my first American citizenship paper.

Then I was called in by the Intelligence Department and told that it had been informed that once I had been convicted of a crime, and that I was not a fit person to be in the United States Army, as I was a very bad man.

I was broken-hearted. My Captain was much disappointed. No one could understand when I said that I had had to leave the Army because of a surgeon's certificate of disability. I could not discuss the subject with the men. I entrusted my citizenship papers to my Captain. I was put in the hospital and kept there a week under observation. At least I was not to be disgraced. Then I was discharged.

The daily papers, that had, just prior to that time, been praising me for volunteering, were forced to tell of my discharge. That was one of the biggest bits of mischief that ever was done me, but since I believe devoutly in God, I also believe in a just law of compensation.

I worried much. I did not wish to go back to the barber-shop, and I had nothing to do in New York City. All this happened near the time of the Jewish High Holidays. I had made some Jewish friends, whom I had met in a synagogue where I went to worship. There is no absolute certainty about my Jewish origin, but I clung to the Jewish religion, nevertheless, in spite of my Scotch Calvinistic training.

At that time there was a recruiting service in New York, for the purpose of recruiting British subjects to the British colours. The service also made it part of its program to recruit certain Jews who were exempt from the United States Army for the British army then fighting in Palestine. Here was my chance and I seized it. I became associated with the Zionist organization and served as a talker to recruit Jewish men. I was introduced to the Major who was the head of the service, and he favoured my joining the British Army.

After talking all over New York City, in schools and synagogues and on street-corners, I signed the necessary papers and applied for examination by the doctors, as preliminary to being sent to Canada to embark for England and the Near East. One of the doctors tried his best to show that there was something wrong with me, but four other doctors disputed him. One of the doctors, after examining me thoroughly, said: "There's a man that will go to hell and back, with that body." I was duly passed, and at last I boarded a train at the Grand Central Terminal, amid hand-shaking, tears, promises, and kisses, bound for Windsor, Canada.

On the same train were some West Indies Negroes, who had also enlisted in the British Army for the British West Indies Regiment. One of these Negro recruits was taken off the train, sick with Spanish influenza, before we reached our destination. He died in a hospital, without revealing his identity to the hospital authorities. Somebody said: " That must be LoBagola." When I reached Canada, I saw clippings from New York daily papers, saying: " LoBagola is dead. He died on his way to Canada."

"LoBagola is dead!" It was very terrible, and also very amusing. I did not write a single letter back to anyone informing people differently. I let myself die.

As has always been my good fortune, I made good friends, especially with my officers. The first thing that was done for me was to elevate me from the rank of private to that of corporal. My officer elevated me again from corporal to quartermaster

Serial No. RF 44 Army Form B. 2

NOTE.—The character given on this Certificate is based on holder's conduct throughout his military career.

Character Certificate of No. 79298 Rank Private

Name Lobagola Kanda
Surname, Christian Names in full.

Unit and Regiment or Corps from which discharged } Royal Fusiliers

This is to certify that the ex-soldier named above has served with the

Colours for .... years ....6.8.... months, and his character
To be inserted in words

during this period Has been VERY GOOD

Sober industrious & trustworthy

Signature and Rank

VC INFANTRY RECORD OFFICE,

Officer i/c LONDON

Date of discharge 13/12/20 Place.

To safeguard the holder of this Certificate from impersonation it should be noted that, in the event of any doubt arising as to the *bona fides* of the bearer, reference should be made to the description, when he left the Colours, of the soldier to whom this Certificate was given, which is recorded on his Discharge Certificate (Army Form B. 2079, Serial No. RF 158.57.), and should be in his possession.

*Facsimile of LoBagola's Certificate of Discharge
from the British Army*

sergeant, for the trip over. I had charge of all the supplies for all the troops. Of course there was a good deal of envy and I had to be careful in order to keep the men from rising against me. Though they were all Jewish, they lost sight of the fact that I was taking up their cause even if they did not wish me in their race.

We left Halifax bound for some port in England, we did not know where, nor did we know the name of the transport we were travelling on. We arrived at Avonmouth, near Bristol. I knew the place well.

It was whispered about that I had been discharged from the United States Army, and one of the men said he knew all about it. So news flies.

We were all sent to a camp at Saltash, in Cornwall, after we had landed and had been attached to the Royal Fusiliers Regiment. After nine weeks of rigid training we embarked at Liverpool on a steamer for Port Said, Egypt. We were then separated and put into three battalions on active service in Palestine. I was assigned to the 38th Royal Fusiliers, then stationed at a place called Rafah, and afterwards at Bir Salem, Palestine.

I lost my rank as quartermaster sergeant and reverted to the ranks, as private. That was to be expected, as all ranks made for sailing were taken away upon reaching the battalion, unless made by the battalion commander. I was made very miserable because of this loss of rank, although all the men had known that the rankings were temporary. They taunted me. I was the only black amongst them. They were not willing to accept me as a Jew, because of their prejudice against my colour. All that made me wretched.

My commanding officer favoured me and put me in charge of the battalion library, giving me a protection stripe as lance-corporal. Not long after this the evil seed that had been sown against me took root, and I was soon looked upon as a scamp and a scoundrel. I did not have a friend in the whole three battalions outside of the officers.

I gave lectures, at the request of my commanding officer, who tried to interest G. H. Q. to send me to all the British troops in the East, to lecture to them. My Colonel was fascinated by my talks. He succeeded in sending me before all the Scotch brigades.

The men in my own battalion, my comrades, were furious at my success. A scheme was hatched to undo me; I am sorry to say that I did not scent it until too late. My Colonel stuck to me. His aim was to have me sent back to England, away from the battalion, but when I was sent to the base, awaiting the necessary papers from G. H. Q., I was attached to the combined base depot at Kantara, Egypt.

There again the Colonel of that base elevated me to the rank of orderly sergeant, in charge of all Jewish soldiers coming through the base. I fought being discharged, because I had a clean record, and I won. I served under that Colonel, at the base depot, for several months. All troops coming from England, and all casualties from the hospitals, had to come to the combined base depot at Kantara before reporting to their battalions. I had the job of assigning all Jewish troops. Those that came out of hospitals always stayed in my camp about a week before going back to their units. My orders were to give them, when they did go back, some escort duty going up the line, such as to go with canteen stores. Many of the boys liked to remain at the base at Kantara, in order to escape doing guard duty in their own battalions. Therefore all were especially good to me when they came through, and many offered me bribes or tips to keep them there longer. There is a law of compensation! I had won the day up to that time, anyway.

I visited the base hospital every day and gave the patients papers and periodicals. My Colonel was delighted with my actions and openly praised me. He did for me what is not customary in the British Army: he wrote for me a personal letter of commendation and actually put the base stamp upon it, testifying to my good character while under his command.

There were three Jewish battalions, the 38th, 39th, and 40th. Two of the Colonels were gentiles and one was a Jew from Australia. My original battalion, the 38th, had long since been disbanded, and most of the troops had returned to England or to America. When my demobilization papers came through, my Colonel shook hands with me, and so did his Adjutant. Before being demobilized I should have reported to my own battalion, up the line, but since my own battalion was no more, I was sent to the battalion commanded by the Jewish Colonel.

I wanted to remain in Palestine, but the Jewish Colonel opposed it, saying that I was a man of bad character. Since my record sheet disproved his statement, I fought him by protesting to G. H. Q. That action kept me waiting at the demobilization camp at Kantara a long time. While waiting there I was given duty in the orderly-room of my section. I had the job of assigning troops that were waiting to be sent to England to the ship that would take them. So I was still top dog, even in spite of the Jewish Colonel and other Jews who had wrongfully treated me. But in the end the Jewish Colonel got his wish—temporarily, anyway. (I lived to meet him again much later, in Palestine, where he had so bitterly opposed my staying.) I was sent to England, accordingly, for demobilization.

Chapter XXXVII

A VAGABOND LIFE

I petition to go to Palestine. I win the Derby. A college teacher. A holy friar. I become a Christian. Sent to Cairo. Teaching in a Coptic school. Heavy drinking. Again in my old African home. Not wanted in Africa. Again in Europe. A cattle-boat. In America. A fallen " brother." Hopeless. A lecturer.

The moment I landed, I applied to the War Office to be repatriated to Palestine, a request that was granted immediately. I had to wait quite a while in London, however, before a troop-ship sailed for the Near East, but I waited at the expense of the Army. I was given indefinite leave and therefore did not have to remain at the depot for duty.

It was then that I won my first Derby, in 1920. I backed the horse Spion Kop for five pounds to win, and it came in first, at sixteen to one. I did not have to draw my money from the depot, and all my winnings went to my credit.

HOME OFFICE.

32.196.

To the Aliens Officer,

Liverpool

Permission as given by the Secretary of State for Cpl.

Kindai LOBAGOLA. 30 years. to embark for Egypt en route to Palestine on or before 30th June 1920.

31st August.

W. Haldane Porter

H.M. Inspector under the Aliens Act.

This permit is to be given up to the authorities on arrival and must be visé by the Passport Office, London, and Military Permit Office, London.

Facsimile of LoBagola's Passport

My principal reason for wishing to return to Palestine was that when I had been in Jerusalem on a long leave, I had received an appointment to teach at the Frères College. My teaching method was pleasing to the headmaster of the college, and when the time came for me to leave, he was sorry and said that, if I should ever return to Jerusalem, he would be pleased to appoint me again. So I was eager to return and to teach there.

When I did return, things were not just as I had expected them to be, especially with the Jewish people. The Jewish Colonel had contributed his share to painting me in dismal colours, and that had affected opinions, even in official circles. I returned to the Frères College, however, and taught there for some time. I also taught private pupils in English, and made my living secure.

The way I was treated by the Jews preyed on my mind. I felt lost. I had no one to run to. I had no real friend. When I explained my position to a most lovable holy friar of the Franciscan order, whom I frequently met on my daily walk outside the Golden Gate of Jerusalem, the holy man talked to me like a father and pointed a way out of my sad plight. I felt like kissing his sandalled feet, he was so good to me.

I interviewed the Patriarch of Jerusalem and

requested that I be given instruction, with a view to joining the Roman Catholic Church. At first the Patriarch questioned my sincerity and said that he did not believe that I wished to be a Catholic. I was finally heard, however, for I really was quite serious and fervent. I was instructed by the good sisters of the Order of Marie Réparatrice and by the holy Franciscan friar Father Barnabé Meistermann.

When it became known that LoBagola had become a Christian, many of my enemies said that I had received a thousand pounds to change from the Jewish faith. Of course, that was not so. It would not have been worth it to the Catholics, anyway.

Life was so wretched for me after my change of religion that the Patriarch himself ordered that I be given shelter and protection in the Austrian Hospice, in the old city of Jerusalem.

My instruction covered a long period, because I had to understand everything before I would accept it, but all was made extremely clear to me, and I am proud to say that, in my way, I understand it all. The good sisters of Marie Réparatrice thought that it would be a good thing if I should be sent down to Egypt, to the Catholic missionary fathers of Lyons. They had a mission station on the west coast of Africa. A savage trait in me causes me to despair quickly. I began to think that I should never be received into the bosom of the Holy Church.

His Lordship the Bishop of Cairo, Egypt, where I was sent, received a letter from Jerusalem that was not complimentary, according to what I learned afterwards. That prolonged delay before my baptism. All these matters were explained to me by one of the best friends I have had since I lost my master in Scotland. My new friend was James Kyan. This man was goodness personified. He did me the honour to stand as my godfather when I was baptized, at Tanta, Egypt.

I received an appointment to teach in a Coptic school, while in Egypt. While teaching at Tanta, I mixed freely in the company of Egyptian effendis, or notables, and I acquired many of their habits, good and bad. The other teacher of English in the school was a very kind man, but a heavy drinker. I frequently sat in his company, and naturally I drank with him. In fact, I tried to out-drink him. As a result, drink got the better of me, because I cannot stand much liquor. Since it was a novelty to see a black man teaching English, my every move was more noticeable than the other teacher's was. Native Egyptian teachers merely laughed at me; so I resigned my post and returned to Cairo.

I remained in Cairo a long time. When I saw that I could do no good for myself or anyone else by staying there, I took a steamer and ultimately went back to my own native land.

When I arrived once more in my own country, I honestly hoped that I should die before I could ever leave there again. Now I met new opposition. I could talk excellent English, and I had the appearance of a well-educated European. I had travelled much, and my experiences out of my own country had been as harrowing as they had been at home. I knew white men too well, and that was against me in Africa. I was not going to be a martyr for my people, or for any other people.

Where should I go for peace and comfort? I had no one in Scotland. I did not know where my young master was. I had no training in any special field of labour. My life was a problem, and it still is. Nobody wanted me, not even my own people in Africa. I decided to return to America. Perhaps, since I had become a Roman Catholic, there might be some place for me. I went to London and made myself known to the Reverend Father A. F. Day, S. J. He was exceedingly good to me, and through his kind offices a gentleman contributed fare for

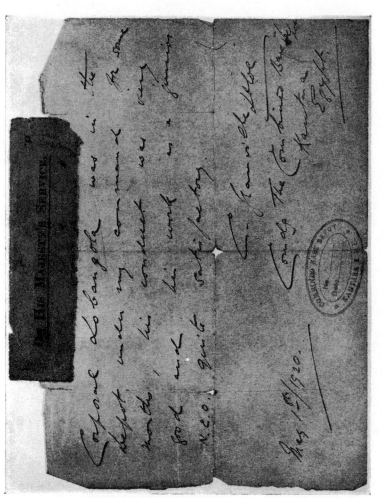

Facsimile of LoBagola's Military Recommendation

me to return to America. In order not to use up all
the money for fare, I took a ship that carried cattle
from the island of Jersey. I helped look after the
cattle.

I arrived in America safely, after a rough voyage of nineteen days, and was again admitted to
this "golden shore." I was lost for a little while,
but I soon found my way to Harlem. I was much
wiser on this trip than before, and therefore no one
robbed me. I gave a few lectures, but had the feeling that I wished to settle down for life in a
cloister. Somehow I interested the fathers of
the Maryknoll Missionary Society and was accepted as a brother. I remained with them only a
month, and then I fell. Enough said. I had to
leave.

I returned to my lodgings in New York, a de-
jected, wretched man. I could not obtain lecture
engagements as I had done before. Through the
kindness of the Right Reverend Monsignor R—,
I secured a job at Fordham University. The Presi-
dent of Fordham University was most kind to me
and gave me a fair opportunity to earn a living.
My pay rose from seventy-five dollars a month to
one hundred and twenty dollars a month within
fourteen months. Then I fell into trouble and lost
the job. The men that I was associating with were

heavy drinkers. I became both a heavy and a loose drinker, just out of smartness. I could not see that I was digging a pit for myself.

One Sunday, after drinking heavily, I fell into trouble on the streets. All my companions deserted me. Not one stopped to say a good word for me. For my offence I was given a workhouse sentence of thirty days. When I came out of the workhouse, no one wished to look at me. I did not have a single friend. The black people rightly said: "When you were on your feet, you ignored us; now that you are in need, you fly to us; we do not wish to have anything to do with you." No white person would befriend me, so I was left to drift. In fact, I was worse off than I had ever been before. I went for days without food. I was put out of my little room because I could not pay the rent. At last, by good luck, I got a small job in a watch concern. After working there as a packer for five months at twenty dollars a week, I was discharged, partly because I asked for an increase in pay.

One day, in despair, I strolled by the door of a public school. The thought came to me to go inside and ask the principal to pay me to give a lecture before the school. I did not expect that he would do so, but I tried; there is no harm in trying. He paid me ten dollars for a talk, and ten dollars to me at that time was like a gold-mine. From that time, I have given many such talks before many kinds of audiences and have aroused much real interest.

Chapter XXXVIII

THE JUNGLE RELIGION

The ju-ju. *The future life. Prayer. Feast-days. The many names of God. The fetish-doctors. Their powers and duties. Body spirits. How fetishes are made. Blessing the* ju-ju. *Vows and sacrifices. The Ogboni society. Secret signs. Degrees. Organization. Jungle ethics illustrated by folk-tales.*

People say to me: " Are the people in your part of the world religious? " I answer: " Yes, they are very religious, even more religious than the people here are; but they are religious in a different way."

My own people, as I have already said, follow the principal practices of Judaism, for they believe themselves descended from Jews who came to Africa many, many centuries ago. They have the Torah — that is, the laws of Moses — and they observe these laws to the letter. They celebrate Pesach, Shebuoth, Rosh Hashanah, Yom Kippur, and Succoth. They practise circumcision and live under the rule of seven rabbis.

We of the *Emo-Yo-Quaim,* or "Strange People," are few in numbers, and we live surrounded

Ibn LoBagola Today

by fetish-worshippers and by Mohammedans. Of course I do not know about fetishism in the complete and detailed way that a scientist knows about his subject, but I do know a great deal about it. I have written down some of the main beliefs of fetishism, which, after all, is not such a bad religion.

1

THE FETISH GODS

The fetish of Bandiagara is called Ju-ju, although there is supposed and understood to be another Spirit higher than Ju-ju. The name of this higher Spirit or God is given according to the events at the birth of a child. For example: When a mother feels sad at the time of delivery, she says with a groan: *"Ekuseka,"* meaning "Death has done much harm." If a woman feels pleased when she is delivering, she claps her hands and shouts: *"U lau-u mi,"* meaning " A valiant man has come "; or she says: *" Aw mondoiy-u ga* (It is a great man all in one) "; or she says: *" Ebun,"* meaning " A gift of God." All these names are given to the one Great Spirit, who rules over all things. No native ever addresses himself to the great God, but only to the ruling spirit of the thing which he invokes — the river, the tree, the bush, the beast, etc. These

373

lesser spirits have supreme control over each element in which they preside.

The thought is that the Great Spirit made or brought all things, even the lesser spirits (it is not quite clear in the native mind just what or how, whether made or otherwise; the native believes firmly in its existence chiefly), and that all are subservient to it. This Great Spirit never interferes with any of the arrangements of the lesser spirits, but merely sits waiting for the end of all things. Where everything finally goes is not quite clear; every native believes that he must work out a certain task in his life in order to attain a higher life, but in what capacity is not known. There surely is, according to the native mind, a higher organization on a higher plane.

Every native man carries with him at all times a little image, or fetish, or *ju-ju,* made of the particular material which he thinks is best to guide his destiny. *Ju-jus* are made from metal, stone, and wood.

The effect of the little *ju-jus,* which are worn about the body, is supposed to be very powerful in protecting the wearers from any danger whatsoever. If it happens, as it frequently does, that evil overtakes a person who is wearing a fetish, it is not the fault of the *ju-ju,* but of the person, because that person has not pleased the *ju-ju* in conduct. For instance, not enough sacrifice was offered, or, if so, then not the right kind of sacrifice; or maybe there was not sufficient charity, or the man did not ask fervently enough for what he wanted. Any of these may be the cause of the fetish's not answering a prayer or granting a request. But no native discards a fetish for any of these reasons; he just perseveres, and finally he attains, or does not attain, his wish, according to the temper of the *ju-ju*. It must be understood that a *ju-ju* does not will a thing. The native believes strongly in the temper or good humour of the *ju-ju*, or the smiling or frowning countenance of a *ju-ju*.

There is always one principal fetish (*ju-ju*) in a community. The material from which that is made is largely determined by the fetish-doctor or witch-doctor, who is the chief priest of the fetish-worshippers. The last appeal for an ordinary layman is the appeal to the principal fetish, which stands in the *ju-ju* house of the community. When that fails, if he can influence or bribe or otherwise move a fetish-doctor, then that fetish-doctor appeals to the great god through the medium of the main *ju-ju*, in your behalf, as he has a greater influence with the *ju-ju* than any ordinary man.

The principal feast-days for fetish-worship

occur three times during a native year, which has about fifteen months, there being about twenty-four days to a native month. The worship is carried on seven days at each feast-time. At these sessions there are elaborate feeding and much dancing, chiefly by the fetish-doctor, because everyone brings presents, gifts, and special offerings to the fetish-man during these festivals. The feasts are fixed by the fetish-doctor, and usually come in the same month each year — namely, in February, which is, in the native tongue, *Osorora,* meaning "budding-time"; at the end of April, called *Iktashitaa,* meaning "welcome of rain"; and in September, called *Xalas il shita,* meaning "the end of rain."

The great fetish has many names, but is commonly addressed as the *Su Kuo-Jen,* meaning "the Fetish-Spirit," the native idea of God. Other names are given to the Great Spirit, such as A Valiant Man, The Life of the Soul, A Worker of Good, A Great Man All in One, One Mighty One, He that must be Feared, The Voice of Waters, The Strength of Trees, The Father of Men, The Ruler of Women, The Trainer of the Young, The Awful, The Visitor, The Stranger, The Friend, The Helper, The Avenger, The Punisher, The Handsome, The Sweet, The Pure, The Beautiful, The Pretty,

The Scenter, The Detector, The Listener, The Quiet, The Noisy, The Settler of All, The Ever and Ever, He that Is, The Father of My Father, The Father of Me, The Lover, The Hater, The Gentle, The Clean, The Just.

2

THE FETISH-DOCTORS

The fetish-doctor is not born to his position; he is made; that is, he is a fetish-doctor from birth, but he does not always hold the same position in a community. If there is a fetish-doctor residing in a place already, then any other fetish-doctor must serve under him, or if he does not wish to do so, he has no power above the ordinary layman. The direct descendant of a fetish-doctor is the successor of the fetish-doctor presiding. Fetish-doctors often move from one community to another in order to get business in charms.

Each fetish-doctor has a number of followers, called *jeu-kadam,* or witch-doctors. Their duties are to collect alms and presents and exact penalties for the fetish-doctor or for the chief of a community.

All punishments are inflicted by the witch-doctors, and they take full advantage of their position. They extort all kinds of things from their

victims, and they have even been known to black-
mail the King. They very often choose any girl of
any family on the pretence of protecting them from
the wrath of the *ju-ju.*

The power of a witch-doctor knows no bounds,
but he never uses his power to any good purpose.
The fetish-doctor never seems to have time for
ordinary dealings, as he himself is always busy
with marriages, finding lost property, blessing
ju-jus, praying, and waiting upon the chief of his
community.

Every community has a fetish-doctor. He is
known by his peculiar devilish-looking costume.
He generally wears a mask, and unmasks himself
only in the presence of his wives. His mask is not
always the same. For religious affairs he wears a
green mask, made by himself, and resembling a
pollywog. Green is the sacred color of the fetish-
religion. The colours of his other masks vary according to his taste; only green has any significance. Many charms and shells are tied on to his
masks. He also wears bones of birds and other
rubbish around him, including a number of
charms, with a short loin-skirt made of wild grass.
He wears no sandals nor shoes, but he has great
gold rings around his ankles, knees, and arms. He
wears rings of solid ivory in his ears, and around

his neck a string of native beads, with leopard teeth on it.

A fetish-doctor inherits his power from his father, but the right generally falls to his bride's child — that is, the child of the latest wife, who is called *ya-wo*. The other boys and girls usually become witch-doctors and witches.

The duties of a fetish-doctor are many; he is responsible for everything that happens in his community. The first duty of the fetish-doctor is the religion itself; he must instruct all of his people in certain forms of prayer. He must always be prepared to appeal to the principal fetish for anyone that wishes it. He must also make the division of time and is responsible for the making of laws and for the administration of the law. If there is a code in the native law that cannot be understood, he must interpret it to the chief of the community. All punishments are given to him to carry out, and the penalties are also set by him. The law, trade, religion, are all subject to the regulation of the fetish-doctor. The ceremonies of marriage and festivals, religious and otherwise, are adjusted and ruled by him.

The witch-doctor desires to keep himself as mysterious as possible; and even the chief dare not break into his disguise unless with his full consent.

You generally see him in the evening walking slowly through the different villages of the community. Everyone gets out of his way when he comes along, but, strange to say, he never receives much homage while he walks about in this manner. When the religious festivals are on, the people actually crave to kiss his hand, but at other times they appear to shun him. His costume looks so devilish that it is hardly reasonable to expect a native to approach him, unless the native has need to do so, because all natives are superstitious and are afraid of spirits, ghosts, and demons.

3

BODY SPIRITS ACCORDING TO FETISHISM

Good spirits or souls reside in the head, the eyes, the ears, the nose, the tongue, the teeth, the throat, the lungs, the breasts of women, the abdomen (upper part). Bad spirits or souls reside in the abdomen (lower part), the liver, the kidneys, the sex organs, the knees, the feet.

These are the names of spirits or souls: in the head, Ras-Sukuo, a spirit that controls the entire head, including the eyes, throat, palate, ears, tongue, nose, and teeth; in the lungs, Daushabat-

Sukuo, a spirit that controls and protects the lungs, the breath, and the voice; in the breasts of women, Chopare-Sukuo-Muse, a spirit that controls and protects the breathing and the giving of milk; in the abdomen (both upper and lower), Butnake-Sukuo, a spirit that controls and protects the breath, and also the food, the bowels, and the entire intestinal region; in the knees, Batte-Sukuo, a spirit that controls and protects the legs; in the feet, Rigilah-Sukuo, a spirit that protects and controls movement.

4

FETISH CHARMS OR JU-JUS

How is a fetish made and blessed? A fetish is made by a fetish-doctor, who chooses the material to his liking, either wood or stone. The fetish-doctor prays seven days to the principal *ju-ju* for inspiration, power, and strength to enable him to carve out his images correctly, as every fetish must be precise, although the design of each one is the choice of the fetish-doctor, resulting from the prayers sent up to the principal fetish or *ju-ju* in the *ju-ju* house.

When the *ju-jus* are made (several at one time) the fetish-doctor proceeds to bless them. The ceremony in blessing a *ju-ju* (each one is blessed

381

separately) is long and elaborate. First the doctor makes a fire, and then he burns in the fire a live female bird, usually a guinea-fowl. When the fowl has burned up, leaving only the bones, the doctor places the two wing-bones and the leg-bones on the ground across each other and makes a sort of exhortation by dancing a weird dance and singing a kind of chant all the time he is dancing.

During this part of the ceremony no one is permitted to be present except the youngest son, who says nothing, but simply looks on. The boy is supposed to learn his father's crafts, and so he is called " a student to the *ju-ju*." What the fetish-doctor says at this time, no one knows but the boy and himself, for no one would dare to interfere with a fetish-doctor when he is going through this ceremony except he be called up by the fetish-doctor. It is considered a great honour to be called on by a fetish-doctor, especially at this part of his ceremony of blessing. It is very rare to see anyone else at these ceremonies.

The wing-bones of the guinea-fowl are next tied to the *ju-ju,* and the fetish-doctor says another prayer and ties the feet of the guinea-fowl to the *ju-ju*. This ceremony lasts three days. Then the *ju-ju* is ready for presentation. The same ceremony is carried on at the blessing of each *ju-ju*.

The wings are to give power to the *ju-ju* to fly from the Great Spirit to the person who is wearing the charm. The feet are supposed to help the *ju-ju* on its journeys to and fro if the wings get tired.

When the presentation is about to take place it is a joyful time. The fetish-doctor receives many presents, and great homage is done to him at these festivals. The presentation is generally on the feast of Osorora, or budding-time, and it lasts three days also. Presentations may, however, occur on any day that the fetish-doctor wishes.

When a native boy reaches the age of thirteen, he is eligible to wear or to carry a *ju-ju*. A girl cannot have one until she is married. Charms for girls are usually made with a special power to give birth to a large family, boys preferably. Before he is thirteen, a boy's father is responsible for his actions, and the boy has recourse to his father's fetish through the medium of his father. The same thing applies to a girl, only she must go to her mother instead of her father.

Fetishes governing parents, as parents, have a peculiar power; that is, the fetish for a mother may be expected to protect in every way the maternal instinct. The father's fetish protects his strength.

There are no special fetishes made for vows. If,

however, one swears by the head or by any member of the body of the *ju-ju* in the *ju-ju* house, he is generally believed; in fact, no one would dare to take a false oath on a *ju-ju,* because it would mean disaster, positively.

The personal fetish plays a great part in the life of a native because he or she attributes everything, good, bad, or indifferent, to the influence of a fetish. If it is good, then the fetish is laughing with them and is pleased with them. They have been faithful in prayers, given much in charity, and saved the life of someone, or killed an enemy of the fetish, such as a snake, or have done some act considered good by the fetish-doctor, which includes giving many presents to him. If, on the other hand, something bad happens, people always blame themselves for the misfortune, and they believe that something good must be done in order to appease the wrath of the *ju-ju.* This they keep up until their luck changes. Then it is believed that they have done the right thing to appease the *ju-ju.* In any event the fetish-doctor receives his share of reward.

The native resorts to his fetish many times during the day; in fact, in every little event he grabs his *ju-ju* and says: "Now look at that," or: "My fetish can never desert me." One prayer to a personal fetish is especially common: " My fetish, I know that you are too noble to be spoken to by such dirt as I, but I beg you to condescend to hear my plea. I have done such evil things that the evil spirit has taken a lease upon my very body, but because you do not love the evil one, and because you are stronger than he, and because I have sought hard on many occasions to kill your greatest enemy, you truly love me and will give me this one last favour." The native continually accuses himself and lauds the virtue of the fetish. The native believes self-accusation to be efficacious.

Many natives sacrifice very frequently to the personal fetish. Even a human sacrifice is considered to be necessary in some instances. A human sacrifice is the killing of a girl baby, or the bleeding of a fallen wife or daughter. The sacrifice is generally made by bleeding the victim to death, but sometimes the victim is burned. There are other forms of sacrifices, and they are all carried on in a very sincere manner, because the native believes thoroughly in his religion and fears greatly the consequences if he fails to offer up some form of sacrifice. Any native at any time he feels disposed may, and does, sacrifice. Once a year everyone is obliged to make an offering of some kind to the principal *ju-ju.*

385

5

THE SECRET SOCIETY OF THE OGBONI

The secret signs used by the Ogboni society are many, and not all are confined to action; many are in sound. For example, such calls and yells as *" Olowowowoi,"* meaning " a place of refuge "; or *" Katinga-ohoooo,"* meaning "We have it "; etc. If, for instance, an Ogboni wishes to speak privately with a certain person, then a call like the first is given, in order that the person wanted, or someone near that person, may go to the place named and speak with whoever may be there to see him.

This system of call-sign is secret and very intricate. Only those governed by the call understand it. Everyone is not controlled by the sign; that is, there are secret signs peculiar to certain people, and others, who may be in the same order, know nothing about them.

All individual signs are given to the Ogboni member during the different degrees or periods of advancement. There are forty stages or degrees to go through in the Ogboni society, and each stage takes a member higher in knowledge of the society and its laws and secrets and gives him more influence in the society. The work is generally very difficult during the first three degrees or stages, but becomes much easier as the member advances.

Signs and other things belonging to the Ogboni are taught by the officers who have attained the twenty-fifth degree. The members from the twelfth stage and upward to the fortieth are compelled to take part in all the activities of the Ogboni society when called upon to do so, but no member may do anything unless instructed by the officers of the society, under pain of death by being burned alive. Unscrupulous natives have been known to use their knowledge of the Ogboni society secrets to obtain favours of girls, and anything they desired from their victims; hence the severity of the penalty.

The degrees or stages of the society are given and examinations are made by a special number of the twenty-fifth degree members. There are signs for greetings, and salutations and signs for sickness, for travelling, for working, for marriages, etc., as well as signs for meetings, special and general, of the Ogboni society.

Dumb signs are used between members in the same degree, and in all the degrees. Every member of the Ogboni society also has a set of personal signs known only to him and to one high official in the society, and these signs are used only for special affairs, such as wishing to consult the main council or to appear to the " O'ba " or chief Ogboni, and for whatever personal business one may care to do. It is a very serious offence to make use of personal signs for any general affair, or for anything other than a personal matter. The penalty is to lose one's stages and revert to the third degree. If the offender is only in the third degree, or under that degree, he loses whatever degrees he has. It is a very serious thing to lose your stage in any degree, because you are always marked by the Ogboni members and abused by everyone, especially women, who become your chief persecutors, even more so than the men; the shame is awful. It has rarely happened that any member has lost his degrees in the lower stages, but in the higher stages I have known members to lose their stages and thereby lose their lives through the great shame. It is needless to say that the man who has thus fallen is poisoned through the medium of the witch-doctors, which is an easy matter.

An Ogboni member in one stage may not be present at the councils or meetings of Ogboni members in another stage, unless there is a general gathering, such as frequently occurs during the year. These general gatherings are held in order to pick certain members for different duties, such as punishments for the governments, burials, and even the death penalty.

The men who are assigned to a particular duty hold place only for a certain period, regardless of whether they have anything to do or not, and then they are succeeded by others, and then others, until such times as they are chosen again for the same duty. When a man is chosen for one duty, he is not necessarily confined to that duty after his time is up; he may be called on for any other duty that may be fixed by the supreme council, which makes all the appointments.

Members of equal rank may always commune together, and they have signs in common. No member is allowed to make a sign by himself, as all signs must come from the principals. Although there are thousands of signs, no one man is called upon to learn them all, for each individual uses and learns only the signs that have to do with himself and his stage. If, however, one becomes a twenty-fifth stage man and knows all the signs up to that degree, he is liable to be called on for work with any stages less than his.

There is such a thing in the Ogboni society as the " open day." This is a day when all signs are given an airing — that is, no sign is secret to any

member of the Ogboni society. This " open day "
is called once in every twelve months by the senior
council, and that body fixes the time. Nothing unusual happens on that day, except that every man
has the right to question another about the particular sign that he may be using then. This, of course,
applies only to signs that are used during that day.
There is very little danger of one man's using the
signs of another man after that day, because they
know the penalty for doing so.

As there are no written records kept about signs
or any other business, and as all depends upon
memory and constant drilling, it appears very difficult for natives in the higher degrees to remember
all the business, but it is not so difficult as it appears. If you could see one of these old officers go
through with his work, you would imagine that he
had been taught only the day before, so fresh is it
all in his memory.

Some of the word signs are as follows: if you
meet one who has given you the sign that he is an
Ogboni, and also given you his particular stage,
you say: " Do you know your master? If you do,
name him. . . . How is it that your family, which
is not worthy, has the shielding arm of a master so
great? . . . When were you first made an Ogboni?
. . . What wind blew? . . . Are you weary? . . .

Perhaps you know how to eat. . . . Do you imitate the monkey ? . . . What is the leopard ? . . . Who made the elephant ? . . . For what purpose ? . . . Are you a man ? . . . Show me ! . . . Why not ? . . . . If so, do you know your duty ? ''

Now if these and a good many more trifling questions are answered satisfactorily, as they usually are, the questioner continues in another vein.

6

OUR ETHICS

The general conduct of people in my country, the distinction between what is good to do and what is wrong to do, and the explanation of what we see about us are all contained in thousands of folktales, several of which I have already told in previous chapters. The following illustrate still further what I mean.

(A) THE PROPER REWARD FOR
TREACHERY—THE MONKEYS
AND THE HUNTER

One day some monkeys planned to go out and have some fun. One of them said: '' Let us look for a man,'' but at first all the rest were opposed to the suggestion, because it is a great shame to the monkey tribe for any monkey to have anything to do with human beings. But finally this monkey succeeded in persuading the others to look for a man just for fun. They agreed to have their fun and then to kill whomsoever they met.

The monkeys ran, laughed, jumped, and gambolled about, first up this tree, then over this vine, and then up other trees. In fact, they were very lively. Suddenly one of the younger monkeys who had just started to jump from a branch of a tall tree got his tail caught in a fork of the tree. Now, as everyone knows, monkeys are always cowards, for they always squeal when in any difficulty, and they never try to get themselves out of it; they depend upon the help of others. So they began to cry and wail. Some were ready to run away and leave their brother, but at the same time they feared what might happen to them if they should return to the herd without their brother. They were truly in a bad case.

One of the monkeys said: " Let us cut off the piece of the tail that got caught." Immediately there were cries of " No! No! " not because of the pain that they might inflict, but because cutting off the tail would make the poor monkey look like a man, and that would be terrible shame, for the whole herd would shun him for ever.

While they were thinking what to do with their brother, they heard the grass crackling, and a moment later out stepped a man. At first they wanted to rush at him and catch him and kill him, but the monkey that was caught said: " No, that will not help to set me free, but perhaps if you are good to the man, he may be able to free me."

Then they sat and waited to see what the bull (the man) would do. After a little while the man came over near them, and they asked him kindly to free their brother.

The hunter, for he was a man setting traps for birds, said to them that if he set their brother free, they would perhaps repay him only by trying to kill him. They all assured him that they would not do such a thing, and they promised never again to raid a village. So the man unhooked the tail of the monkey, who appeared very grateful.

Now, near by was the village of the hunter, and he was tired and hungry; so he went home, first saying good-bye to all the kind monkeys.

The monkeys were bent on mischief, and they followed him a little way off. When he came to his village, they all jumped out and grabbed him. The poor hunter begged them to spare his life, for he had a large family waiting for him, but the monkeys dragged him back into the bush and said that

393

they would give him over to the chief monkey, who would surely have him killed, and they would get the honour of his capture.

When the hunter saw what the monkeys intended to do, he thought of a plan to get away from them. Now, you all know that monkeys are always afraid of anything, so the hunter asked them to take him to his traps, for he had captured a nice goat, and he would share it with them. When they got to the traps, the hunter led the monkeys right into another trap that they did not see. When they found that they could not get out, they began to plead for mercy, but the hunter simply left them there. Later, when the hunter returned, he could find only their bones, for they had all been eaten by vultures. One good turn deserves another.

(B) THE PROPER WAY TO TREAT INFERIORS—THE LION AND THE ZEBRA

Once upon a time, as a lion was roaming through the bush, he came upon a zebra who had got lost there. The lion had never liked the zebra, because he thought the zebra was better looking than he was, so it pleased him to see the poor thing in trouble. The zebra, too, had never liked the lion, because he thought the lion was a bully and a coward.

394

When the lion asked the zebra what was wrong, the zebra said that he had lost his way because he had gone too far on the way to visit some friends. The lion laughed aloud and said: " You are telling a lie because I caught you, and you are afraid of me, as you should be, because you know that I am the king of all the beasts. And now to prove to you that I am your superior, I shall show you how easy it is for me to give you a good beating, as you deserve, for not having asked my permission to wander about in my bush."

At this the zebra began to weep and to wail, but the lion only laughed and, walking over beside the zebra, hit him a blow with his paw. The zebra cried all the more, and the lion said: " You need not cry, because no one will come to assist you, and if anyone did, I should soon show him who is boss. Now I am going to kill you and make an example for the rest of your bold people who go about here without my permission."

Just then up bounded a leopard, and before the lion could jump away, the leopard was on top of him, biting him badly. The lion then appealed to the zebra to intercede for him with the leopard and ask him to spare his life. The zebra only said: " If you are the king of all the beasts, then you will order him to leave and he will surely do so; but if you are not the boss, then take your punishment and die, and be an example to all your kind not to take advantage of your inferiors."

At this the leopard only said: " Well spoken, zebra; let us alone." And the leopard killed the lion.

(c) MERCY AND THE PUNISHMENT OF WRONG-DOING—THE ELEPHANT AND THE BOA CONSTRICTOR

One day a boa constrictor was twisted around a vine, when an elephant came along and was about to break the vine with his mighty trunk. Now, when a snake is twisted around a vine, it is helpless, because then it is easy for anyone to break its back. So the elephant had the snake at his mercy at last.

The snake began to plead and to beg for mercy and even promised to protect the elephant whenever he might call upon him. The snake added that the elephant should remember that the snake had young ones to take care of, and so it would be a shame for him, and for his whole tribe, to deprive those dear young things of a father.

The elephant told the snake that he had never merited any pity and asked the snake if he had ever thought of dear young things when he caught anything in his tail. " You have not even given anyone a chance to plead for mercy, as I am giving the chance to you, let alone showing any; so how do you deserve pity? "

Nevertheless, the elephant added: " I will give you this one chance more: if you can untwist yourself and drop quicker than I can raise my trunk and bring it down on you and crush you, then you may go free."

Now, while the elephant was saying this, the snake dropped suddenly to the ground and caught hold of the elephant's leg, and then began to laugh, saying: " Now, Mr. Elephant, I have you at my mercy, and since I have no mercy, you must die." At this the snake started to bite the elephant in the stomach, but the elephant was cool enough quietly to lift a foot and bring it down with all his force upon the back of the snake. The snake yelled and let go of the elephant's leg and began to plead again, but the elephant simply put another foot on the snake's head and crushed the life out of the snake, saying at the same time: " To him that has no mercy, show none."

(D) TELLING THE TRUTH—A RACE BETWEEN A SNAKE AND A LEOPARD

One wet day just after the rainy season a leopard ran into a nest of horned vipers. The snakes laughed and shouted for joy at seeing the brave leopard in such awkward embarrassment.

One of the snakes said: " Now, Mr. Proud Leopard, how do you find it in such strange company ? "

The leopard, who is never a coward, although in this instance the odds were against him, said: " As I find myself, so it was surely ordained. As you all know, I do not like company of any kind. You cannot say that I am as unpleasant company as the lion or the monkey. I have always been a good sport."

At this there was much dissension as to what to do with him, whether to let him go or to kill him. One old snake spoke up in favour of the leopard and said: " We should at least give the brave *Thaw* a chance to win his life, since it was not by his choice that he fell into danger."

It was thereupon agreed that one of the younger snakes should run a race with the leopard. If the leopard should lose, he should return and give himself up; but if he should win, he could not only go free, but also eat the snake that lost the race.

The race began, with odds a hundred to one in favour of the leopard. But the leopard, seeing that he had such an advantage over the young snake, became careless and took the most difficult way. It happened that in his going he came across a zebra. He wanted very much to eat this beast, because he was very hungry, having been kept at the court of the snakes a long time without food. So he rushed off to catch the poor zebra, and he ran a long distance before overtaking it.

In the mean time the young snake was travelling fast in leaps and bounds, in order to win the race. The leopard feasted well and long and even slept after eating the zebra. When at last he got to the end of his journey, he waited, thinking that he had won the race and thereby would have a tasty morsel in the form of a good young snake.

To the leopard's surprise, the snake, who had been hiding in the trees, suddenly dropped down in front of him and frightened him so badly that he ran away and never returned as he had promised.

When the old snake heard what had happened, he said: " Old *Thaw,* the leopard, says that he is no coward, and that he is a good sport, but I cannot see this; he surely is a liar, which is the same thing as a coward, for he is afraid to admit the truth."

(E) THE FOLLY OF ATTEMPTING TOO MUCH—HOW A GAZELLE FOOLED A LEOPARD

One day, while a leopard was drinking at a water-hole, a gazelle came up to drink also. Now, as every-one knows, a leopard never likes to drink with any-one, nor does he like to have the company of any other beast. So the leopard could not finish his drinking, for thinking of the boldness of this frail creature in daring to stand before a brave leopard.

The poor gazelle was very thirsty, and truly she did not think of the danger she was in until the leopard spoke to her. When she heard the voice of the leopard, she started to run away, but the leopard called after her to stop, for, he said, he was not going to hurt her. He said that he was about to give a big feast in honour of his wife; she had given birth to babies, and all the babies were boys. He said that his wife was very eager to have the gazelle come to the feast. Of course all this was a lie, told in order to induce the gazelle to follow the leopard to his home; there he intended to invite her in to see his sick wife, and then to pounce upon her and eat her up. The leopard really liked gazelle meat better than he liked monkey meat, although monkey meat is very sweet and is supposed to be best of all.

400

The gazelle said that she was very sorry to hear the sad news that Madame Leopard was still sick, but she added that she was pleased to hear that Madame Leopard had given birth to such a fine set of boys. She concluded by saying that she intended to come to the feast, and she asked when it would take place.

The leopard was so pleased to hear this that he nearly died from his joyous anticipation. He set the time of the feast for the next day, after drinking-time. Then he bounded off in leaps, forgetting that he had wanted to eat the gazelle then and there; he said: " I shall enjoy her all the more when I wait a little longer."

All the time, the gazelle knew that the leopard was trying to fool her, and she tried to devise some plan whereby she could fool this stupid leopard, who was so greedy that he even licked his paws after eating. Then she thought that if she went to his house first, before he got there, she could surely find out if he were telling the truth about the feast. Finally she decided to go on the morrow, but to go disguised as a monkey. So she got a monkey skin and dressed up in it and started out.

The leopard was at home, and he had some nice dishes to offer the gazelle, for, as he said, you should be kind to anyone who is going to die. When he

401

looked up and saw only a monkey, he was angry, for he had looked ahead to having a gazelle, his favourite dish. When the supposed monkey came, the leopard would not eat it. He simply asked what the monkey wanted.

The supposed monkey said: " I just met the gazelle, and she told me of your sadness and of your joy, and I have come both to mourn with you and to rejoice with you."

The leopard then put dishes of good things before the monkey, and the monkey ate heartily. Before the monkey had finished eating, the leopard had slipped away to meet the gazelle and eat her, planning to return and eat the monkey also.

But the leopard could not find the gazelle, and when he returned, he could not find the monkey, and all his precious food was gone. He was furious.

So when the leopard went to drink again, he happened to see the gazelle and asked her why she had not come to his feast. Thereupon the gazelle told him everything and said that she had feasted well and then had left. And the gazelle added: " Now, Mr. Leopard, when you wish to fool somebody, try not to be the fool yourself."